Nigel Dempster entered Fleet [...] Daily Express and then moving [...] American correspondent befor [...] Diary in 1973. He became di [...] 1986 and broadcasts regularly for BSkyB, ABC-TV (in the US) and for Canadian and Australian television stations. He is the author of *HRH The Princess Margaret – A Life Unfulfilled; Heiress: The Story of Christina Onassis; Nigel Dempster's Address Book;* and, with Peter Evans, *Behind Palace Doors.*

working for the
Daily Mail, where he was
beginning his well-documented
Thanks for the Mail in Stowey in
and broadcast widely

Dempster's People

Inside the World of the Gossip's Gossip

NIGEL DEMPSTER

HarperCollins*Publishers*

HarperCollins*Publishers*
77–85 Fulham Palace Road,
Hammersmith, London W6 8JB

This paperback edition 1999

1 3 5 7 9 8 6 4 2

First published in Great Britain by
HarperCollins*Publishers* 1998

ISBN 0 00 653089 3

Set in Berling

Printed in Great Britain by
Caledonian International Book Manufacturing, Glasgow

For Lord R and David English, without whom none of this would have been possible.

Contents

vii

INTRODUCTION

A Diary Day

Half a dozen years ago, Phil Scheffler, an American friend of mine with CBS and who is executive editor of the leading American investigative television programme, 60 Minutes, was over in London and asked me to lunch, saying he was bringing along one of his show's directors. We met at Green's in St James's (run by Simon Parker Bowles, then brother-in-law of Prince Charles's love, Camilla) and the director told me he was extremely keen to feature me and the Diary in a segment of the show. It would necessitate following me with a camera to such telegenic events as The Derby, Royal Ascot, Wimbledon, Henley, Glorious Goodwood, Cowes and (wait for it) a Buckingham Palace Garden Party, and I was asked if this was possible.

Sadly my reply did not meet with their rapturous approval. I told them that 99 per cent of Diary work was done on the telephone in the relatively unglamorous setting of an office and, while I did go to The Derby at Epsom and the four-day Royal Ascot meeting, cameras were banned at the latter venue and my participation for 60 Minutes would only be an act. And in any case, who would want to be seen colluding with a Diary column, which is what the show, founded in September 1968, demanded. I pointed out it was against one of the principle codes of conduct for members of the National Union of Journalists to identify contacts, in whatever manner.

'That's very disappointing,' said Scheffler who anticipated filming a colourful programme behind the British social scene at a minimal cost – there was no mention even of any facility fee! In fact nearly all Diary work does take place in the office on telephones although a fair amount of invitations – especially during the summer – are accepted automatically by the Diary PA, Merryl La Trobe, and suitable events attended by either me, my deputy, Adam Helliker, or one of our two assistants, Janet King and Ulla Kloster. The most popular summer invite is to polo but that has its own problems as the matches are invariably played on Sundays – the Alfred Dunhill Queen's Cup, the Veuve Clicquot Gold Cup and the Cartier in particular – and columns are produced from our office desks not Smith's Lawn, Windsor or Cowdray Park. This is where our resident photographer, Alan Davidson, comes in so handy as he not only enjoys a day out, sometimes with his wife Sandra, but has a camera which automatically wires photographs back to the Picture Desk at Northcliffe House, our Kensington High Street base.

My own day, Sunday through Friday, starts around 7am when I have a quick breakfast – half a pink grapefruit and weak Earl Grey china tea – reading two or three newspapers at my South Kensington home prior to taking our five Pekingese for their early morning walk in Hyde Park beside the Serpentine, following which they demand their own breakfast, usually provided by Sainsbury's or Marks and Spencer. On Mondays, Tuesdays and Wednesdays, I play squash in the mornings with the professional, Greg Pearman, at my club, the Royal Automobile in Pall Mall, and on Thursday and Friday mornings with one of several fellow members. When I joined the RAC in 1974 on my return from America (where the New York Athletic Club fulfilled many of the same functions) it was primarily for the Turkish Bath and the four squash courts, but there is also a heated swimming-pool surrounded by Sicilian marble columns, two bars, a billiards room with five tables, two restaurants and seventy-odd en suite bedrooms for those wanting a place to stay in central London at none too exorbitant rates. (The 11,500 or so members (not to be confused with Associate Members who subscribe to the breakdown services) of the Pall Mall clubhouse and Woodcote Park, the Epsom country club which has two 18-hole golf courses, were rather stunned to discover that they were due a windfall payment of around £35,000 each in 1998 following the sale of the RAC Motoring Services division (The Knights of the Road) to the American conglomerate Cendant, which owns National Car Parks and its Green Flag recovery arm.)

By 11.30am I am in my office, having fully read half a dozen newspapers from *The Times*, *Daily Telegraph* and *Independent* to the *Sun* and *Mirror* (but not the *Star*) and start the daily process of putting a column together. The secret has always been to lead on the best story available but in the quarter century since the Dempster Diary started I have found that fitting in items is the greatest challenge; with several photographs, the page carries an average of just five stories a day and there is always the same number held over vying to be printed. There has to be a mix; for instance, if the main item is about people of a certain age, the top right picture has to be about younger subjects and all items should avoid a clash with the ads which are known to the Diary sub-editor, Willie Bloch, by the mid-afternoon: in other words, writing about a member of the Ford car dynasty should not clash with an ad on the same page for a Ford car but it is uncanny how often that happens. The solution is to hold out the item for a day or so which, given the lack of competition now in Fleet Street, is easy enough to achieve.

Lunch is a prime time to entertain friends and trawl for information and at least four times a week I take out someone who is particularly helpful to the column, usually locally to Launceston Place or its sister establishment, Kensington Place, or further afield to Harry's Bar in South Audley Street, Langan's off Piccadilly, or The Ritz Hotel and Le Caprice opposite.

Certain regulars prefer their own venues (the photographer Patrick Lichfield, for instance, likes The Connaught Restaurant while his counterpart, the Earl of Snowdon, does not move far from Launceston Place which is around the corner from his Kensington studio-house), but The Savoy, which used to be so handy when newspapers were down the road in Fleet Street, and The Ivy in nearby Covent Garden are beyond the pale because of location and the traffic jams that build up in their vicinity between 1pm and 2.30pm.

But while information comes mainly over the telephone (and from as far afield as Australia, Canada and the USA) as well as at lunch, it needs to be thoroughly researched, or in journalistic parlance, 'stood up'. Any error, naturally, is pounced on by lawyers with writs for libel or demands for corrections. The worst in my memory was when my then deputy wrote that a duchess, long divorced by her former husband and living in the Home Counties, had enrolled with the local escort agency. It was totally untrue and her lawyer informed us that the error was compounded when she had gone into the local fishmongers and the man behind the counter had 'winked at her'. I had apologized the very next day and we eventually paid up £10,000. Honour was done.

We receive lawyers' letters on a fairly regular basis and, perhaps once every eighteen months, a writ. While Oscar Wilde once said: 'It is better to be looked over than over-looked', I could do without the attention of lawyers and their uncanny ability to read into an item a nuance that was never intended. However, all complaints of a legal nature are dealt with, in the first instance, by the company's legal department which employs a full-time staff of around half a dozen. But as someone once said: we would be failing if we did not attract legal missives; it demonstrates that we are doing something right and hitting the odd nerve. In any case the people we write about have recourse to the best legal opinions and cannot hide behind the defence of impecunity.

For many years the middle-market, mass circulation *Daily Mail* (owned by the last Fleet Street Press baron and with Sir David English as editor-in-chief) and, *inter alia*, the Diary, has been perceived as the best market-place for stories needing to be aired, which explains why the Princess of Wales had such a close relationship with our Royal reporter Richard Kay and the reason for the co-operation with the *Mail* of many other members of the Royal Family as well as members of the great and the good. It is no secret that Princess Margaret, apart from regarding the *Mail* as required breakfast reading, has been happy to have items about herself in the column and that her cousin-by-marriage, Princess Michael of Kent, is equally content to have her office help with any inquiries.

But only once did the Prince of Wales break cover when a close friend of his, an unnamed woman, telephoned me on Monday 1 July 1991, his wife's thirtieth birthday. Diana had made it known generally that she would be spending the milestone day alone, apart from taking and fetching Prince Harry from school locally, and that Charles had made no plans to entertain her.

This was mentioned in nearly every national newspaper and the general impression that Diana achieved was that her husband was an uncaring soul who did not love her. In the face of the myriad criticisms of his actions, I received the call. It was to inform me that, far from ignoring his wife's birthday, Charles had pressed her to allow him to organize a party. I was informed: 'He told her he would do anything she wanted, but she was adamant. She knew that it would look bad for the Prince.' When I asked what the current feelings were between the Prince and Diana, his confidante told me: 'Hatred. Utter hatred on both sides.'

In the event Charles stayed at Highgrove where he held a fund-raising drinks party in aid of the Tetbury Church Restoration Fund and then took the Royal Train overnight to Edinburgh where, on 2 July, he attended the installation of the Knights of the Thistle at St Giles Cathedral. For her part, Diana lunched at The Savoy on her birthday with 380 guests who paid between £400 and £1,000 each to join her in aid of Rainbow House, a children's hospice in Walsall; Phil Collins serenaded the gathering, but did not sing Happy Birthday, after Diana blew out thirty candles on a cake presented by twelve-year-old Sharon Carter. That day, she did the school run to Notting Hill twice and in the evening entertained her sister, Jane, and her brother-in-law, Sir Robert Fellowes, who had been knighted the month before in the Queen's Birthday Honours List (he was HM's Private Secretary).

Following the call from the innermost sanctum of Prince Charles, I went to see my then editor, Sir David English, and explained what I had been told. He decided to splash the story on the front page of the *Daily Mail* under the banner headline: 'Charles and Diana: Cause for Concern', with nineteen paragraphs on pages one and three explaining the situation. It was to be the first confirmation of the loveless marriage of Charles and Diana and the story was to have far-reaching consequences. No longer feeling that she had the total support of the newspaper of her choice, the Princess decided to tell her side of the story and set in motion events which led a year later to the publication of a blatantly biased book, *Diana: Her True Story*, by former Fleet Street 'Royal Reporter' Andrew Morton with (as we all discovered later) her co-operation.

By four o'clock the general composition of the column is clear with the stories to be published chosen and ready for writing while Willie Bloch has gathered a full complement of photographs from our own sources and the Picture Library to illustrate the items. Very occasionally there is a late-breaking story which will clearly not hold over for a day and alterations have to be made quickly to include it, but this does not happen too often. Events covered in the evenings (such as openings, first nights and premieres) are discussed the following day for interest and if, there happens to be a story and a picture that takes the fancy, it is submitted for inclusion in the next edition.

There was a time in the Sixties when Diary columns changed up during the night, to include events and photographs a few hours old which came hot off the press from the evening's happenings. Those days have long gone, but newspapers still like to have a first night review in their later editions for the morning after, which requires theatre critics to work extremely fast after the final curtain and precludes them from the parties afterwards.

Sometime before 7pm, Willy Bloch provides proofs of the page which are pored over for errors, grammatical mistakes and the like and then the page is finally ready for transmission to become part of the first edition of the *Daily Mail*, copies of which are in the office around 11.30pm for general perusal.

After a long day, including a lot of exercise, it takes a particularly appealing function to drag me out for the evening – I cannot remember when I last went to a dinner party – but Diary personnel and photographers, including a core group of freelances, cover all events, hoping to find interesting items, and bring in their wares the morning after for consideration.

The Dempster Diary has evolved into a set pattern, rather like the annual peregrination of the Royal Family started by Queen Victoria and still strictly adhered to by the Queen and her relations who always spend Christmas at Windsor, see in the New Year at Sandringham where they stay until February, move to Buckingham Palace before going to Windsor Castle for Easter and then journey to Balmoral at the beginning of August for two months of country pursuits such as grouse-shooting, salmon fishing and stalking.

Following the Annual Christmas Quiz, an alternative Honours Column on Boxing Day and a page devoted to New Year's Resolutions solicited from Diary regulars, the column comes in February from Cape Town where, fortuitously, Earl Spencer and his family live and now home to Mark Thatcher, his Texan wife, Diane, and their two children. At the end of March there are pages from the United Arab Emirate of Dubai where keen Anglophile Sheik Mohammed has mounted the world's richest horse race with $4 million prize money. During the spring and summer the page reflects the traditional English 'Season' which stretches from the annual Royal Academy Summer Exhibition and the Chelsea Flower Show through The Derby at Epsom, Royal Ascot, Wimbledon, Henley and Glorious Goodwood to end with Cowes Week at the beginning of August.

Other events which are covered include the various races in the Formula One Grand Prix calendar, the finals of the Stella Artois Championships at Queen's Club in June, Deauville races, polo and horse sales in August, a late summer report from Gstaad in the Swiss Alps, home from home of Mohamed Al Fayed, Bernie Ecclestone and lesser mortals, and the Melbourne Cup on the first Tuesday in November, a day's holiday for all Australia and the greatest social jamboree Down Under. During the year there are additional columns from places like New York and Los Angeles and just about anywhere I find myself with interesting tales to tell – the finals of the World Cup in Paris in July 1998, for example, spent with Oscar-winner Jack Nicholson.

Apart from my colleagues, fellow journalists tend to involve themselves in the Diary, calling in with possible stories or photographs and all are paid for their endeavours, as is just when professional people ply their wares. One of the time-honoured charges against Diary journalism is that payments are made, as if this is something shameful. Of course money changes hands, as it does in all other areas of newspapers when information is offered. Workmen are worthy of their hire and, while I do not deal financially with publicists, they have become a necessary adjunct of downmarket Sunday journalism, brokering stories which might otherwise not be handled too sympathetically (but try telling that to David Mellor!).

When I began the *Mail* Diary, gossip columns were at a low ebb, some would say virtually moribund. But by making a Diary page interesting, challenging and controversial, the genre has been revived and now gossip permeates newspapers from the front cover to the back. There are columns these days for The City, Real Estate and property, Show-business, Music Business, Political, Health, Style, Sport, all of which add to the burgeoning good health of Britain's publications.

If anyone had asked me when I started if there would be such a thing as a newspaper in 1998, given the forecasts two and a half decades ago for the electronic information industry, I would have replied that I doubted it. How wrong, thankfully, I was! Here's to the next quarter century . . .

Prince Enigma

PRINCE PHILIP

The personal life of Prince Philip has always been an enigma and he makes sure it remains that way. When waspish American biographer Kitty Kelley arrived in Britain in the early Nineties to research her tome on the Royal Family – originally intending to home in on Prince Philip and his circle of female friends – he fired a warning shot in May 1994 stating that he would sue for libel, adding: 'I will protect my good name.' 'Catty' Kitty quickly responded by broadening her canvas to write a book entitled *The House of Windsor*. The advance was estimated at $3 million but, because of the stringent British libel laws, the finished work (published in the United States in 1997) never appeared in British bookshops.

Among Kelley's bolder initiatives was to telephone me and ask how she could arrange interviews with the Duchess of Abercorn, Jane, Countess of Westmorland, Lady Susan Hussey and Hélène Cordet. I informed her that these ladies had spent a lifetime refusing to utter a word and were hardly likely to break their silence on the matter of their friendship with Philip, spanning four generations, to a complete stranger. Kelley took the hint and foraged elsewhere for so-called 'nuggets' about the Queen's husband.

In fact, the Duchess of Abercorn did break cover when she telephoned me at the *Mail* on 13 November 1992 after I had printed a story about her and Prince Philip. The gist of it was that the duchess – formerly Alexandra Anastasia Phillips, whose younger brother Nicholas was the Prince's godson – had danced the night away with Philip under the approving eye of her husband Jamie who, as the Marquess of Hamilton, had been the Ulster Unionist MP for Fermanagh and South Armagh from 1964 to 1910. So approving, in fact, that Jamie called his wife, known as Sacha, 'Regina'.

Her closeness to Prince Philip went back to childhood. With the future Queen, he had spent part of his honeymoon in November 1947 at Luton Hoo, the historic Bedfordshire home of Sacha's grandparents, South African minerals millionaire Sir Harold Wernher and his Russian-born wife Lady Zia, herself the daughter of Grand Duke Michael of Russia and therefore related to Philip. The couple made a habit of returning every year to spend their anniversary at Luton Hoo and, when Lady Zia died in December 1977, the house, its priceless collection of Fabergé and the 1,500 acre estate passed to Sacha's brother Nicholas: the Wernhers had lost their only son, George, in the Second World War when he was killed in action in December 1942 and Nicky (who died, beset by financial problems, in his fume-filled BMW in a stableblock on the estate in 1991) was the only son of their elder daughter.

Sir Harold and Lady Zia had been noted racehorse owners

– among their successes was the 1966 Epsom Derby winner Charlottown – and avidly courted the Press. Lady Zia and I had become good friends over the years and through her I knew her granddaughter Sacha. She invited me that evening in November 1992 to her house off Belgrave Square to 'discuss her friendship' with Philip. The first inkling of their closeness had come in 1987 when a Sunday newspaper published a photograph of Philip, naked from the waist up and wearing a towel, flanked by the Abercorns. The snap had been taken by the pool at Hamilton House, their Bahamian retreat at the Windermere Club in Eleuthera, where Philip had holidayed for eight years, and Jamie Abercorn's inclusion was significant.

When I went to see her, I was greeted by the statuesque Sacha who was wearing jeans; and, shades of her Russian background, she had put a bottle of Stolichnaya vodka on ice in a bucket. After bidding me sit down, she poured a glass for herself (I declined) and said that there was 'absolutely nothing' between her and Prince Philip, that he was a quite brilliant man who listened to her suggestions and occasionally acted on them. When I told her that the rumours were hardly going to abate, she sighed and said: 'I suppose they'll start up again in February. We're all on *Britannia* to the Galapagos Islands.'

Sacha, born in February 1946, had previously enjoyed a close friendship with J. G. 'Algy' Cluff in the Seventies. He had made a fortune after going into the oil exploration business in 1971 (backed by aristocrats including the Duke of Marlborough and the Earl of Lichfield) and, during his two years escorting Sacha, had occasionally jousted with her husband Jamie. Algy once told me: 'We would be in my flat in Eaton Square and Jamie would ring up and ask me to bring his wife back. I used to tell him to bugger off!'

The first reports of Prince Philip and female company were in the Thirties when he was best man at the first, short-lived wedding of Hélène Founounis (later Cordet) to Neal Kirby. He became godfather to her children, Max and Louise Boisot, whose father, Marcel, was a Free French air force officer. Philip was a seventeen-year-old Gordonstoun schoolboy when Hélène married Kirby and tongues wagged when he arranged for Max to be sent to his old school and helped with the fees. In 1988 Max, by then forty-five and a Professor of Economics at a Euro-Chinese business centre outside Peking, finally made a statement about the Prince: 'I have heard these rumours that he is my father all my life and they are ridiculous. My father – my real father – lives in Paris and it is ridiculous to suggest otherwise. My mother and her family were Greek exiles and were very close to the Prince's family. They were simply close family friends.'

And Hélène, who achieved celebrity in the early Sixties with her club, the Saddle Room, in Hamilton Place, Park Lane (London's first discotheque and home of the Twist) said three months before her death in Lausanne in April 1996 at the age of seventy-eight: 'Prince Philip was beautiful and blond as a boy, of course. But he was never my type. I was attracted to tall, dark, handsome men like my second husband, Marcel.'

There was also talk of a relationship with actress Pat Kirkwood, which she denied strenuously, as well as closeness to Lady Susan Hussey (sister of former Tory Minister William Waldegrave and wife of the one-time BBC chairman Marmaduke (now Lord) Hussey, she has been a lady-in-waiting to the Queen since 1960). Jane Westmorland, a noted beauty and Pekingese owner, is the widow of the 15th earl who was Master of the Queen's Horse and a Buckingham Palace insider from 1978 until his death five years ago.

Before I left Sacha, I asked her exactly what Prince Philip thought of the disasters that had befallen the younger royals and had brought the Royal Family into disrepute – citing Diana's separation from Charles and Andrew's impending divorce from Sarah Ferguson – and she replied: 'He says that everything he has worked for for forty years has been in vain.'

There is little doubt that Prince Philip of Greece has been the only man for the Queen since, as Princess Elizabeth and heir apparent to the throne, she had met her future husband at the Royal Naval College, Dartmouth, on 22 July 1939 when visiting with her parents. A second cousin of the King and nephew of Lord Louis Mountbatten, Dartmouth cadet Philip had not a drop of Greek blood in his veins and was compared to a Viking because of his ash-blond hair and sculpted features. In fact, he was essentially a Dane of the Royal house which had been invited to take over the Greek throne in 1863. He was five years older than Elizabeth who, according to a first-hand report of the meeting, never took her eyes off him for the whole of that first encounter. His manner to her was offhand and, although he knelt beside Elizabeth as she played with a clockwork train set in the house of the officer-in-charge, Admiral Sir Frederick Dalrymple-Hamilton, he soon became bored of that. The girls – Princess Margaret was also on the visit – were joined by Philip for ginger crackers and lemonade and then he suggested they adjourn to the tennis courts 'and have some real fun jumping the nets'. Lilibet squealed to her Scottish Governess Marion Crawford, known as 'Crawfie': 'How good he is! How high he can jump!'

The war ended as it had begun, with Elizabeth hopelessly in love with Philip. On 10 July 1947 her engagement to 'Lieutenant Philip Mountbatten' was announced and he became a British citizen, giving up his title of Prince. He changed his name from Schleswig-Holstein-Sonderburg-Glucksberg to the anglicization of his mother's name, Battenberg. The marriage took place on 20 November 1947 and a year later their first child, Prince Charles, was born, followed in August 1950 by a daughter, Princess Anne. There followed a lengthy hiatus and Earl Mountbatten said: 'Philip was anxious to secure his place in posterity and urged the Queen to formally change the family name of Windsor to Mountbatten-Windsor. The Queen would have none of it so Philip retaliated by moving out of her bed for nine years.'

Matters had clearly been patched up by the spring of 1959. When Philip returned to Britain on Thursday 30 April from a six-week world tour of India, Pakistan, Burma, Singapore, Sarawak, Brunei, North Borneo, Hong Kong, the Solomon Islands, the Gilbert and Ellice Islands, Christmas Island, the Bahamas and Bermuda, the Queen was at London airport to welcome him home. During the next month, when the future Prince Andrew was conceived, they went to Wembley to watch Nottingham Forest beat Luton Town 2–1 in the FA Cup Final, hosted a four-day state visit by the Shah of Persia, attended a dinner at the Guildhall to celebrate the Tenth Anniversary of NATO, went to Lords to see the MCC beat India by 147 runs, attended the Chelsea Flower Show and welcomed the King of Norway to Windsor Castle.

Apart from Prince Philip being on his own for thirty hours in Northern Ireland on 20 and 21 May, the couple were a picture of togetherness. Prince Andrew Albert Christian Edward Windsor was born on 19 February 1960 at Buckingham Palace, weighing 7 pounds 3 ounces and such was the delight of the Queen, that in Royal circles the baby was referred to as 'the love child'. His cousin, the photographer

16

Earl of Lichfield, told me: 'Andrew was the favourite and in the Queen's eyes, could do no wrong.' Four years later Prince Edward was born and those at Court felt that another baby had only been wanted 'to round off the numbers and give Andrew a companion'. While there has long been conjecture about Philip and women friends, little has ever been heard of the Queen. The Earl of Carnarvon, known as Henry or Porchie (he used to be Lord Porchester), has been close since childhood and became her racing manager in 1969. But James Tennant, the late brother of Lord Glenconner who is Princess Margaret's best friend, told me that she had a twinkle in her eye for tall, blond men. In the Eighties, he named the bachelor Lord Plunket, who had been HM's Deputy Master of the Household from 1954 until his death from cancer in 1975 (and Equerry to both the late King George VI and the Queen) and added, mischievously: 'She's particularly taken by Michael Heseltine. He's just her type.'

Hello and Welcome

DAVID FROST

It was the week before the wedding of the Prince of Wales and Lady Diana Spencer and Harry's Bar, the Mayfair club-restaurant co-owned by Mark Birley and James Sherwood, was packed. I had arranged to meet a producer from ABC, the leading American network, for lunch to discuss my participation in their broadcast of the ceremony from London on Friday 31 July 1981.

I arrived early at Harry's Bar and found ABC doyenne Barbara Walters seated alone at a table for two. She beckoned me over and then tore me off a strip concerning the *Mail* Diary lead that she had made demands upon Buckingham Palace for an interview with the Royal couple. 'Totally untrue,' she screeched before calming down and becoming friendly again. It was at this point that David Frost arrived at the restaurant and, passing the table where I was temporarily seated with Barbara, he hissed: 'I ought to punch you on the nose for what you wrote about Lynne today.'

Before I could tell Frostie that every word was true, he had marched on to his table leaving Barbara to observe wryly to me: 'I guess it just isn't your day.'

Frostie's threat was a chivalrous but futile one. On 17 July I had written that casting director's daughter Lynne Frederick, whom he had married in a surprise ceremony in the tiny Suffolk village of Theberton in January, had inherited an estimated £5 million fortune on the death of her previous husband, Peter Sellers, from whom she was estranged, and had rejected an 'impassioned plea' from Spike Milligan to settle some of her windfall fortune on Peter's three children.

But sometime-actress Lynne, then twenty-six, told Spike she had read a pre-publication copy of *PS I Love You*, by Michael, Sarah and Victoria Sellers and did not intend to part with a penny. The book frankly revealed that Sellers was on the point of disinheriting and divorcing Lynne at the time of his fatal heart attack at The Dorchester in July 1980; she was in Los Angeles and had flown to his bedside but he never recovered consciousness. Sellers had instigated the proceedings when he discovered that Lynne had been canoodling with Los Angeles-based journalist, Roddy Mann, and claimed to have a tape of their love-making.

It was all too much for the lovelorn Frostie who was totally smitten by Lynne after twice being left at the altar. In February 1973 I had reported that Frostie, after being given a bachelor party by New York magazine owner Clay Felker and David Niven Jnr, had called off the marriage to coloured actress Diahann Carroll after two years together. And then in March 1974 his fiancée, model Karen Graham, married her former boyfriend, mysterious Las Vegas businessman Del Coleman, the day before she was due to step up to the altar with David, who had again been given a futile bachelor bash by Felker and Niven.

Given these rebuffs and two fruitless long-term romances with actress Carol Lynley and former British debutante Caroline Graham, it was perhaps natural that Frostie should be protective of his new wife. They had started romancing just five months after Sellers' death and by Christmas in Gstaad they were an item. But he obviously knew little about her. Before her marriage (when she was twenty-two) to the comedy genius in Paris in February 1977, she had spent four years with Julian Posner, a man three decades her senior, who had run the Curzon House Club casino in Mayfair before moving half a mile to be a director of the Casanova Club.

That Lynne was avaricious and cunning was beyond dispute but Frostie was not about to listen to any criticism of his wife whose inheritance from Sellers had included a Gstaad chalet valued in excess of £1 million. When she became pregnant his joy knew no bounds. In my lead Diary item of 3 March 1981 I had quoted her as saying: 'David wants children and I could not be more thrilled,' while he added: 'I have always wanted children and I know Lynne would be a perfect mother. She wants very much to have a baby.' However, he was devastated when she reportedly miscarried in March 1982 (there were rumours that Lynne had an abortion) and within three months the couple were planning to end their brief union. Said Lynne: 'I cannot say that I recommend divorce. No one who has been through it wants it to happen and that applies to me as to anyone else.

'It's very upsetting. I'm upset now and that's why I appear to be flippant and jokey. You cover up one emotion with another. We had our own reasons, very private reasons, for splitting up. But we made an agreement not to air them in public. People look at David and me and think of our houses and chalets and constant travelling, and our cars. David has a Bentley and I have a Porsche which was Peter Sellers' last present to me. But it's not that that really counts. It's what is in the heart that really counts. David and I had planned to have children after my miscarriage earlier this year, but for medical reasons you have to wait quite a time before trying again. Before that point was reached, the divorce had been arranged.'

By October 1994 when Lynne (brought up in modest circumstances in Southall and Golders Green) had remarried and died, tragically, in Beverly Hills, she had got through the Sellers inheritance. She had been married to Los Angeles heart surgeon Barry Unger, had a daughter, and had been drinking heavily before collapsing. She had spent years struggling with alcoholism, drug abuse and depression and her estate in England totalled a puny £27,816.

Frostie, however, had become the great survivor (and today is the only Sixties television star to remain in the public eye in the present decade) and, following his divorce, became involved with Lady Carina Fitzalan-Howard, middle daughter of the Duke of Norfolk who is regarded as leader of Britain's lay Roman Catholics. Known as 'Keeks', Lady Carina had taken over the job at the New England Kindergarten in Pimlico vacated by Diana Spencer on her engagement to Prince Charles. For two years before that she had enjoyed an idyllic affair in the West Indies with dusky Noel Charles, a nightclub owner in Barbados but of Trinidadian origin. He had a Swedish beauty queen wife, Alexandra, and when the duke, whose title goes back to 1483, visited his daughter in Barbados to remonstrate, he pointed out that the family was not disappointed because of Noel's colour, but because he was married. Keeks duly returned, alone, to Britain and accused me of 'ruining' her life.

In May 1982 she became engaged to Knightsbridge property man Charles Delevingne, who was thirty-three, but by Royal Ascot the following month he was to be found escorting Derek Nimmo's daughter, Amanda, and the nuptials were cancelled. He told me at the races: 'It's all off. Better now than later.'

Keeks did not pine for long and was soon to be found with Frostie. She even went to stay in Beccles with his widowed mother and was with him on New Year's Eve 1982 when he was breathalysed after police stopped his Bentley on Chelsea Bridge and arrested him for drink-driving. On his TV-am show the next day, when asked what his resolutions for the New Year were, he quipped: 'To keep breathing, but not into one of those machines!'

In March 1983 Keeks and Frostie wed at Chelsea Register Office and among the guests were the Duke and Duchess of Norfolk, Peter Jay and Roddy Llewellyn and his wife, Tania. The couple now have three strapping sons and live between a Chelsea mansion valued at £2.5 million and a country estate near Romsey in Hampshire.

In May 1995, a memorial service was held for Peter Cook, who had died in January. Of those who paid tribute to Cook, Stephen Fry recalled an occasion when Frostie rang Peter Cook to invite him to dinner with Prince Andrew and his then fiancée, Sarah Ferguson: 'Big fans . . . Be super if you could make it: Wednesday the twelfth.' 'Hang on, I'll check my diary,' said Cook, and riffled through the pages. 'Oh dear, I find I'm watching television that night.'

Mellor Keeps his Kit on

DAVID MELLOR, MONA BAUWENS AND ANTONIA DE SANCHA

T he man pouring the drinks in the chairman's dining-room at Stamford Bridge before the December 1989 Chelsea vs Liverpool match was David Mellor. He was without his wife Judith (they had been married for sixteen years) and their two sons. And he had a secret.

That Saturday he appeared to be totally subservient to rough diamond Chelsea chairman Ken Bates and it was a slight mystery why Mellor, MP for neighbouring Putney and lately dubbed the Minister for Fun, should be so prominent at Stamford Bridge. On being asked of his relationship with the MP, Bates, who was facing eviction from the 11.5 acre site, told me ingenuously: 'David has nothing to do officially with the club, but he's a great supporter of football in this area and, like other fans, wants us to stay here.'

Mellor, a QC who had attended Swanage Grammar School and taken an honours degree at Christ's College, Cambridge, had, I was reliably informed, evinced a passion for Mona Bauwens, a peroxide blonde Palestinian who claimed to have been born in 1961. She lived in a Mayfair apartment away from her Belgian husband, Arnold, by whom she had a daughter, Soraya, born in November 1987. Her curriculum vitae stated she was a film producer of independent means: her father, Jaweed Al-Ghussein, had a £3 million or so house in the Bishop's Avenue (the north London road known as Millionaires Row) but was based in Abu Dhabi. Since 1984, he had been chairman of the Palestinian National Fund, which he likened to the 'department of finance in any other government'.

In August 1990 Mona, who was then still with Arnold but heading for a final separation, took a villa for the month in Marbella and among her guests were Mellor and Judith with sons Anthony and Frederick (then ten and six). A Sunday newspaper made a meal of the holiday, which started the day before the Iraqi invasion of Kuwait, and their article bore the headline: 'Top Tory and the PLO Paymaster.' Mona duly felt constrained to sue the publication for libel, after fully consulting the Mellors, as she felt she had been labelled unfit to be hostess to a Government Minister and was therefore deemed a 'social leper'. The case was set down to be heard in the High Court in the Strand in September 1992.

In the meantime, I had been told that Mellor had taken such a shine to Mona that he telephoned her many times a day. And she told friends: 'He calls on his way to media interviews, after them and then asks me if I heard him on the radio or TV. He comes round for tea and rings up to a dozen times a day.'

It was no secret that Mellor's marriage to former Parliamentary researcher Judith Hall was disintegrating. Much later, in the *Mail* Diary of 20 July 1992, I wrote: 'Among friends it is well-known that Chelsea football fan Mellor's 1974 marriage . . . has been one of convenience for at least five years and the couple have stayed together because of their young children.'

Mona's position was simple: she was not about to become involved with a married man (they had met through her cousin, Zaki Nusseibeh, who worked for Sheik Zayed, the Ruler of Abu Dhabi) and a friend told me: 'He has promised to move out of his marital home and find a flat on his own and until he does she doesn't want to have anything to do with him. If he becomes free, that's another matter.'

In the meantime Mona remained friendly with Mellor's wife Judith and, when her musically gifted son Anthony was cast as Oliver in the Lionel Bart classic for the Christmas season at the Wimbledon Theatre, she was at the November first night in the Cabinet Minister's box. Judith remained backstage and told me for a *Mail* Diary lead when Mona finally separated from Arnold on 5 February 1991: 'Mona is a very generous girl, we both know her and her husband very well and go to each other's dinner parties. I couldn't comment on their splitting up.'

When John Major succeeded Margaret Thatcher as Leader of the Conservative Party and Prime Minister in November 1990, among his greatest supporters were Jeffrey Archer and David Mellor, by coincidence a former aide to the multi-millionaire novelist. Jeffrey, ever keen to help the new PM, telephoned me for my assistance. In the course of the conversation, he said: 'He's a remarkable man – I've just left him after sitting on his loo while he was shaving! He wants to know if there are any scandals on the horizon which could affect the Government. John feels that if he heads them off at the pass that will limit any damage. Do you know anything?'

I immediately thought of David Mellor and, on mentioning his name, Archer told me: 'Ah yes, he likes money and women and by the way, I know all about him – he used to work for me as my personal assistant.'

So I told Jeffrey about Mellor and the intriguing nonrelationship with Mona Bauwens and also filled him in with a brief resume of her life as he had never heard of her. I told him that I felt it was a time-bomb that could explode at any moment. If Mellor, then Chief Secretary to the Treasury and in the Cabinet, did leave Judith and take up with Mona, the subsequent publicity would envelope the Major administration. Archer thought for a moment or two and told me: 'I will pass this on to John. He will be very grateful to you.'

There the matter rested. Mellor did not leave the Putney marital home but continued his platonic pursuit of Mona who was soon to find romance elsewhere. When Mellor heard that she planned to marry Egyptian-born financier Mohammed Shourjabi after they met at a 1992 St Valentine's Day party, he telephoned her 'in a state', warning her of the consequences. In fact love – or rather lust – beckoned for Mellor in the shape of sometime-actress Antonia de Sancha whose mother, Elizabeth, had been married from 1980 until her death six years later to Shaun Plunket, heir to his brother the 8th Lord Plunket.

Mona still believes that the ludicrous affair with Antonia, which was to cost Mellor his Government job, was a reaction to her rejection of the gap-toothed MP. In July 1992 the *People*, the same Sunday which Mona was suing over the Marbella holiday, splashed with a lurid story of the relationship. There followed further humiliation the next day with a front page picture of a squalid bedroom in a borrowed Fulham flat where David and de Sancha made love as a neighbour downstairs taped their telephone calls.

Mellor, then forty-three, admitted that he and his wife Judith had 'difficulties' and the exposé could not have come at a more poignant time: it was the Mellors' eighteenth wedding anniversary and he was soon to feel the approbrium of the masses, with calls for his resignation as Heritage Minister. To capitalize on her story, Antonia employed publicist Max Clifford who invented the fable that the Minister wore Chelsea football kit for his sex romps, a fabrication which Clifford had tried before, when he was promoting Jack the Lad Liverpool councillor Derek 'Degsy' Hatton and claimed he wore football kit in his sex romps with a banking heiress. As Mellor said to me at the time: 'Can you imagine . . .'

In September, shortly after her marriage to Mohammed Shourjabi, Mona went to the High Court for her action against the *People* and was flanked by her husband – and Mrs Judith Mellor. It was a bruising battle with formidable QC George Carman appearing for the defendants while Mona retained Richard Hartley QC. The case ended with the jury evenly divided and Mona facing costs of around £150,000. Her friends looked on the bright side and told me: 'She sees it as a moral victory.'

Packing for a delayed three-week honeymoon with Mohammed in his native Egypt, Mona called me with the news that she intended to seek a re-trial. But wiser counsels eventually prevailed. In March 1973 she settled her action without receiving a penny towards her costs and the *People* stated: 'At the trial of the action, the defendants made it clear that at no time was their intention to criticize the plaintiff personally and the court has heard from an expert in Middle Eastern affairs called to give evidence on behalf of the defendants that the plaintiff's father is widely respected as a leading moderate who advocates a peaceful resolution to the Palestinian issue. The defendants have agreed to appear here today and reiterate that no criticism of the plaintiff was intended and it has therefore proved possible for the parties to come to terms.'

Put more simply, Mona no longer had any stomach for the fight and had decided to resolve her differences with the newspaper on the best possible terms. She said after the end: 'I am glad it is all over. That is all I can say. It is a relief. A big relief.'

Sadly, her marriage to Mohammed was not to endure: in December 1993 a divorce between the couple became final. They had been effectively married for just nine months and the union ended after a weekend in France, with Mona telling me in July 1993: 'We made love in Paris and what happened then was so unexpected and without sense or reason. I thought we were happy. We were looking forward to having a family and I had a miscarriage in January.'

While Mona, whose former husband Arnold died in 1996, has not remarried and has been busy completing a book entitled *Bitter Honey* – 'a collection of fictional short stories about women and the conflicts they encounter in the modern world of East versus West' – Mellor has gone from strength to strength.

Freed of Government duty and voted out as MP for Putney in the 1 May 1997 General Election after eighteen years in the seat, his annual income from all sources, mainly media, has been put in excess of £500,000, certainly enough for him to buy a magnificent five-storey, nine-bedroom property near Tower Bridge which had been on the market for £1.25 million, and move in with his mistress, farmer's daughter Viscountess Cobham, the former Penny Cooper. The Putney marital home was put on the market in February 1995 for £245,000 while Judith, who, it was revealed, was losing her eyesight, moved to a £360,000 property in nearby East Sheen with the two boys.

In September 1995 Mellor was named as 'the other man' in Viscount Cobham's divorce case against his estranged wife after Judith was awarded a decree nisi in March that year. Last August I revealed that roly-poly Cobham had remarried. His second wife was yachtswoman Lisa Clayton, thirty-eight, who worked for him at his stately home, but Mellor sees no urgency is making the other Lady Cobham, nicknamed the 'Quango Queen' for her involvement on more than twenty committees, his second wife. As one wit put it: 'If you look after Penny, the pounds will take care of themselves.'

A Lamontable Tale

OLGA POLIZZI AND NORMAN LAMONT

Neighbours are always a great source of information and when Norman Lamont, the future Conservative Chancellor of the Exchequer, decided to accompany the hotelier Lord Forte's ambitious and attractive widowed daughter, Olga Polizzi, to her £350,000 Bayswater mews house in Clarendon Close for a late night tête-à-tête, little did the badger-haired politician realize where it would lead him.

The incident about to be described took place on Wednesday 3 July 1985, the eve of Independence Day, and followed a convivial dinner-party where Olga, the eldest of Forte's five daughters and then thirty-eight, was escorted by West End art dealer Richard Connolly. They had been an item for six years and, according to the balding Richard, had discussed marriage. They had met when she moved into the house next door (where the trouble flared) and he had later sold his property to Olga's sister, Mary Louise, wife of Mayfair restaurateur Robert Burness.

I was telephoned by the owner of another property in the mews who had witnessed the shenanigans. Since Lamont, who had been married to Rosemary for fourteen years and had two children, was a Government Minister, he felt the fisticuffs deserved a wider audience. The neighbour had been alerted by a man noisily putting his shoulder to Olga's door; there followed the exit of Lamont who was then attacked by the man while attempting to defend himself with his Ministerial red box.

By chance I had met Olga and Richard when I had dined with them the previous year at her father's flagship Grosvenor House Hotel restaurant. On telephoning Connolly for corroboration, this is what he told me: 'I had been with Olga last Wednesday evening at a dinner party, but had stayed on after she left. She may have arranged to see Lamont later because she has seen him several times before. She didn't expect to see me and was very upset about what happened. I was very angry with this man, who is a member of the Government. I was so angry with him that I chased him down the street and caught up with him in the next street, near the Bayswater Road. I won't tell you exactly what I did to him – but he would have difficulty passing it off as an accident with a filing-cabinet.'

According to Richard, he looked through a window when he made his unexpected call and on seeing Lamont, MP for Kingston-upon-Thames and whose family house was a mile and a half away in Notting Hill, demanded to be let in, at first without success. A neighbour – not the one who contacted me – in the exclusive street of five houses was James Hadley, director of the Franco-British Council, and he told the *Mail* Diary: 'My daughter heard this frightful disturbance outside the house.'

In fact, Connolly did manage to land a few blows when

he collared the fleeing Lamont; the politician appeared in the House of Commons sporting a black eye and wore dark glasses when he appeared on the Friday 5 July edition of Any Questions. When I telephoned Lamont at the House – he was then Minister of State for Trade and Industry – he answered that the black eye was the result of 'walking into a door left open by my American research assistant'. But while Mrs Lamont remained diplomatic and opined 'It's all extremely trivial', the Minister's Tory colleagues were making fun of him. Tubby Geoffrey Dickins quipped that Lamont might need a Parliamentary Private Secretary with a record in the boxing ring and said: 'My colleagues are already nominating me for the job. Instead of carrying his bag, I shall be carrying his towel.'

My first item bore the headline: 'Manslaughter in Bayswater' and the next day's follow-up 'The Lady in the Black Eye Saga'. Both were widely followed in all the other newspapers as was the word 'Lamontable', which I coined.

Attempting to forestall any further interest in his misfortune, Lamont told one journalist: 'I don't want to say a bloody thing. There is nothing I can say about such a teeny-weeny ludicrous matter. The whole thing is ridiculous. An incident occurred but it was so trivial it really does not deserve further comment. I have nothing more to say about it.'

Olga was covered in embarrassment by the events of 3 July. She had two daughters but was separated from her aristocratic Italian husband, Marchese Alessandro Polizzi di Sorrentino, when he was killed in a car crash eighteen years earlier. Their wedding in September 1966 at St Mary's Roman Catholic Church, Hampstead, had been followed by a reception at the Royal Festival Hall which took 100 chefs four working days to prepare: on offer were 2,000 oysters,

20 pounds of caviar, 20 large fresh salmon, plus grouse, turkey, hams, lobster, prawns and foie gras. Father Forte also provided 300 bottles and 48 magnums of champagne for the 500 guests, among whom was ex-King Umberto of Italy.

Irishman Richard Connolly was himself divorced with two young daughters, Oonagh and Kitty. Then forty-three and living in a Belgravia hotel, he had known Olga for four years before they became romantically involved. They apparently shared a mutual love of art and Olga used to put on regular art shows at the Café Royal in Regent Street, part of the Trust House Forte empire (which was taken over by Granada in January 1996 following a hostile bid of £3.8 billion). There was a measure of contrition following the incident, when Richard declared 'I overreacted and very much regret the incident.'

While the couple sued the *Daily Star* over allegations that Olga and Connolly shared her house and that his livelihood depended on business dealings with the Trust House Forte group, the fracas led to the temporary ending of their relationship. But just before Christmas 1986 they were back together again, dining at Langan's Bar and Grill off Piccadilly. By the end of the decade, however, Connolly was out of Olga's life and she became involved with the writer Willie Shawcross, highbrow son of the former Attorney General, Lord Shawcross. They finally wed in October 1993 at Marylebone Register Office (it was his third marriage) followed by a party at The Waldorf in Aldwych – the first hotel Charles Forte ever bought – with cocktails, canapes and dancing for 250.

There was also happiness for the former Mrs Connolly that year. The onetime Irish model Catherine Keelahan, she married London property dealer Richard Jacobs and produced a daughter, Alice Victoria, at the advanced age of forty-eight, at St Thomas's Hospital, London, just across the Thames from the Houses of Parliament.

As for Norman Lamont, while the Olga Polizzi business did not damage his chances for promotion (he finally became Chancellor in 1990), there were constant rumours that all was not well between him and his wife, Rosemary. His only son, Hilaire, educated at The Hall prep school in Hampstead and King's School, Canterbury, decided he preferred to be known as James and, after failing to get into Oxford, eventually landed up at Newcastle University. Boundary changes then bounced Lamont out of his Kingston seat, which he had represented since 1972, at the last General Election. Instead he was selected as the Conservative Party candidate for the seemingly safe seat of Harrogate and Knaresborough, inheriting a 12,589 majority, but lost it to the Lib Dems on 1 May 1997 when Philip Willis won by 6,236 votes. But all life's glittering prizes were not to be denied Norman: he was put forward for a Life Peerage by Tory leader William Hague in the Queen's Birthday Honours List in June 1998.

By chance I was introduced to Lamont at a Christmas party at Claridge's in December 1985 by a mischievous middleman. On shaking my hand, a confused looking Norman uttered the immortal words: 'I didn't believe you really existed.'

Burton, Taylor and the Sanctity of Marriage

RICHARD BURTON AND ELIZABETH TAYLOR

C ast as Cleopatra and Mark Antony in the ill-fated 1961 epic which nearly bust producers Twentieth Century Fox, Elizabeth Taylor and Richard Burton scandalized the world by having an affair during filming on location in Rome which led the Vatican newspaper to excoriate Liz for 'erotic vagrancy'. She had been married four times, widowed once and had infuriated Middle America by running off with (and then marrying) Eddie Fisher, thirty, the crooner husband of US sweetheart Debbie Reynolds, by whom he had two children.

While Liz secured a $1 million deal against 10 per cent of the gross, Burton, then thirty-six and perceived as a great stage actor, was performing *Camelot* in New York on Broadway. *Cleopatra* producer Spyros Skouras bought out his contract for $50,000, signed him to play in *Cleopatra* for $250,000 and, for good measure, secured Rex Harrison to be Caesar for $200,000. The stage was set for one of the great movie disasters of all time, a romance which was to see Liz and Richard marry and divorce each other twice and gave rise to Burton's famous quote about the affair: 'It's like fucking Kruschev! I've had affairs before – how did I know the woman was so fucking famous?'

Burton had been married to Sybil Williams since 1949; she was described as a perky actress who had performed alongside him at Stratford and received rather better reviews. Following the marriage, she gave up her career and produced two daughters, Kate and Jessica, and largely disregarded his drinking and womanizing – until Elizabeth came along.

On 27 February 1962 Fisher threw a thirtieth birthday party in Rome for his wife and presented her with a $10,000 diamond ring and Bulgari mirror, while Burton told the world he had no intention of divorcing Sybil. Three weeks later Fisher left Rome for good and the romance prospered although Elizabeth said: 'We didn't want to do anything to hurt Sybil. She was – is – such a lovely lady.' *Cleopatra* opened in June 1963 at the Rivoli Theatre in New York to mixed reviews and never recovered its cost, $300 million in today's terms.

On 5 March 1964 Fisher was divorced by Elizabeth in Mexico and ten days later she and Burton, who was playing *Hamlet* in Toronto, married in Montreal. After taking a curtain call the following night, Burton, who had shed Sybil in 1963, presented his new wife to the audience and declaimed to their obvious delight: 'I would like just to quote from the play – Act II, Scene I: "We will have no more marriages." '

When Liz and Burton divorced for the first time, it was said that they had gone through ten years of marriage, eleven movies and $30 million. In May 1973 I had been transferred to the New York office of the *Daily Mail* for an open-ended period. Much of the work was done from our suite of rooms in the *Daily News* building on 42nd Street – among the sagas covered was the Watergate Senate Hearings – and so it was with some relief that I was sent to interview Richard Burton in Long Island. There had been a snippet in a New York newspaper suggesting that all was not well between him and Elizabeth and the New York Bureau Chief, Dermot Purgavie, felt I should interview the great man, especially after Liz's publicist announced a separation. This is what transpired.

On 12 June 1973, Richard Burton and Elizabeth Taylor – widely billed as 'the last of the really great Hollywood marriages' – arrived in the Long Island hamlet of Quogue in search of peace and privacy. Quogue is just over seventy miles from New York beside the Atlantic Ocean. They were staying in the guest cottage belonging to Aaron Frosch, their lawyer and friend for twenty years. Here they intended to spend three idyllic weeks, to take the sun and the waters and to read their scripts for films scheduled to be shot in Italy during August.

For the next fortnight, however, the weather was un-expectedly bad. The Burtons were displeased but held their peace. They saw few people; they read their scripts; the Press did not bother them; occasionally Mrs Burton would be driven to Manhattan to shop for a dress, a scarf or an elegant bauble or two at Cartier.

Despite the fact that Aaron Frosch's cottage stood only 30 yards down the drive (beside a 25 foot heated pool), he saw little of the guests on whose behalf he had acted in their respective divorces a decade earlier. 'They kept themselves to themselves,' he told me later. 'The guest cottage has three bedrooms. And downstairs there is a living-room and kitchen where Elizabeth cooked for Richard. Occasionally we'd wave to each other and, if they wanted to come up and see us, they did. They've stayed there so often we call it the Jenkins house.' (Burton was born Richard Jenkins, twelfth in a family of thirteen of a Welsh miner and had assumed the surname of his drama coach.)

Towards the end of the month, Mrs Burton received the news that her widowed mother, Mrs Sarah Taylor, who had suffered a stroke, was not responding satisfactorily to treatment after release from an Arizona clinic. She immediately decided to fly to Beverly Hills to visit her. Mr Burton decided to stay. He was expecting Maria, Elizabeth's adopted daughter, and wanted to be there when she arrived. No one was bothering him and the sun, he believed, was about to shine. Besides, he hated Los Angeles, a false environment he considered as far removed from the Thespian ethos as it could possibly be. Thus, on 25 June, Mrs Burton flew to California and Mr Burton remained alone in Quogue.

In a profession noted for its excesses, Richard Burton had a reputation for being a serious drinker. He was not an alcoholic, but actors are often faced with periods of interminable ennui and tend to resort to that diversion. Since the death of his favourite elder brother, Ivor Jenkins, in a bizarre accident four months prior to his arrival in Quogue, Mr Burton had been drinking a great deal. Only the year before, to appease his wife, he had renounced alcohol completely but, following his bereavement, he had fallen off the wagon. Or, as a slightly worried Aaron Frosch put it: 'This drinking is a problem. But Richard has given it up before, and I anticipate that he will be able to give it up again.'

Alone in Quogue, and still kept close to the house by the unseasonable weather, Mr Burton brooded. His mood darkened when reports that his wife had been seen enjoying herself at parties with such actors as Sammy Davis Jnr and Laurence Harvey drifted back to him. On two consecutive nights she had been photographed in the company of Peter Lawford, an actor whose second wife had recently left him.

And so that weekend, Mr Burton put through a call to his wife who was staying in a bungalow of the Beverly Hills Hotel in the company of Bob Wilson, her muscular black bodyguard, who was also Mr Burton's executive assistant. He wanted his wife to come home, but Mrs Burton, when she came to the telephone, seemed not to comprehend the urgency of his request until he said: 'Get your ass back here or you won't have an ass to sit on.' Mrs Burton mulled it over and decided to return to Quogue.

Mrs Burton also liked her drink, but perhaps worried at the marked change in her once trim figure, she had stopped competing with her husband. The days when Burton could brag that his head had a common circumference with his wife's waist – proved by drawing a belt round each – were long past. Not that he minded her corpulence. She might be a grandmother of forty-one with a double chin, but above all Mr Burton loved Rubensesque figures. He particularly loved hers and did not encourage her to diet. 'Elizabeth isn't particularly attractive physically. She has the shape of a Welsh village girl. Her legs are quite stumpy really. Her chest isn't anything extraordinary,' as he always described her.

Giving up drink had been her idea. It had not always been that way, however. When the Burtons were at their villa in Puerto Vallarta, Mexico in 1963 (where he was filming *The Night of the Iguana*), one of their guests described a typical morning's drinking. 'We started with a couple of chilled bottles of Dom Perignon at about 10am. We soon finished those and, because there wasn't any more iced, we went on to wine. Apart from Richard, Elizabeth and myself there was one other person, a British journalist. I suppose we had three or four bottles of cold wine before that ran out. Then we found some tequila. After that we went onto some rotgut that was produced from the kitchen. When that was finished we scavenged for ourselves. By lunchtime, none of us could move and all thoughts of eating, which we had arranged, were out.' But that was in the past. Elizabeth had more or less given up drinking now and wanted her husband to do the same.

It was proving, however, altogether more difficult for Burton who had once boasted of quaffing 21 litres of wine at a sitting and drinking a bottle of brandy a night while playing *Hamlet* in 1964 on a twenty-two-week engagement on Broadway, in Boston and Toronto.

Burton himself explained his prodigious consumption. 'I am one of the few people I know who drinks only when he works.' Actress Carrie Nye, wife of Dick Cavett, discovered this at first hand when she was summoned to Munich in 1972 to appear in the television film *Divorce His – Divorce Hers* which is the last film the Burtons appeared in together. On her first day on the set, she reported, Burton arrived high. The same thing happened on the second, third and fourth days. When work did commence with Richard in a more sober frame of mind, it tended to finish for the day with lunch.

Convalescing after her experience, Miss Nye wrote: 'What was actually eaten, if anything, at these cosy impromptus for up to twelve is lost to memory. What was imbibed will be permanently inscribed on my liver for the rest of my days. There was a goodly amount of joshing about who drank the most Jack Daniels or tequila, or Jack Daniels with tequila, or vodka and champagne, or sterno and scotch and in just which European capital, South American port, or Balkan satellite these epic cases of alcohol poisoning took place. It became apparent that Mr Burton did not do an awful lot of work after lunch.'

It was perhaps with that in mind that Mrs Burton returned to Quogue. Within a short time of her return Mr and Mrs Burton had had a row. He had met her at the airport in a particularly quarrelsome frame of mind and, after driving back to the Frosch household, Elizabeth dropped Richard off and drove back into the city. There, under the name of Mrs Richards, she checked into a suite on the fourteenth floor of the Regency Hotel on Madison Avenue and summoned John Springer, her trusty publicist. Between them they wrote an open letter to the Press in which Mrs Burton, in her own schoolgirlish and slipshod hand, announced that she and her husband were to have a trial separation. She implied that they had been in each other's company too much, that they had loved each other too much. She went on to say: 'I am convinced it would be a good and constructive idea if Richard and I are separated for a while. I hope with all my heart that the separation will ultimately bring us back to where we should be – and that is together. Pray for us.'

Pray for us. The devoted Queen was abdicating, relinquishing the King for his own sake. What magnanimity. But would her people care? When the letter was released by the efficient Springer to the AP and UPI wire services, it elicited the sort of response more normally accorded by the Press to a Royal assassination or the discovery of the Abominable Snowman. The Manhattan offices of the courtly Springer were deluged with calls from journalists representing the Press in just about every part of the world where Burton and Taylor were known – and that's just about everywhere. Doubtless those rabid fans remembered not only that they were 'the last of the really great Hollywood marriages' but they had been the first film stars to be given a million dollars each to appear in the same film *The VIPs*, that she had once been the world's most beautiful woman and he had been Olivier's successor. The world at their feet, the brightest stars in the firmament. It hadn't mattered that they hadn't done a decent film in years. And that, with the benefit of hindsight, was the root cause of their troubles.

They were celebrities and, as someone once said, a celebrity is a person who is known for his well-knownness. They had made eight films together, amassing a shared fortune in excess of $25 million. But all, with the exception of *Who's Afraid of Virginia Woolf*, had been failures. Their friends, professional and personal, had been uttering dark warnings for years. And with the abysmal *Divorce His – Divorce Hers*, which was universally panned, the message had begun to sink in. The ship of state which had been launched with *Cleopatra* had sailed serenely through *The VIPs*, *The Sandpiper*, had been battered by *Boom*, *Dr Faustus* and *Under Milk Wood* before finally being sunk by the twin torpedoes of *Hammersmith is Out* and *Divorce*.

Before they had met on the set of *Cleopatra* in 1962, it had all been different. Burton had become the most admired Shakespearean actor of his time in Britain. He had displayed his formidable talents in a series of subtle and artistically devastating performances in *Coriolanus* at the Old Vic, and as Prince Hal and Iago, which prompted theatre critic Kenneth Tynan to look back in sorrow some frittered years later: 'We all thought he was the natural successor to Olivier. We thought he could be another Edmund Kean, that he was going to be the greatest classical actor living.'

Only four actors in history have played *Hamlet* more than 100 times in a single production: Sir Henry Irving, Sir Herbert Beerbohm Tree, Sir John Gielgud and Mr Richard

Burton, who was, arguably, their peer. In melancholy moments, when he had settled into his relationship with Elizabeth, Burton could be heard to declaim, borrowing from Keats' epitaph: 'My name is written in water.'

But Antony's meeting with Cleopatra had changed all that. From being a happily married actor with two young children and modest financial needs, he burgeoned into a paymaster for Mammon. A yacht, a private jet, three houses, four dogs, six children. Burton was forced to set out to make the necessary income the only way possible – up there on the wide, silver screen. It was a decision, in all its inevitability, much mourned. Gielgud commented knowingly: 'When the movie career is finished, he will have lost his romantic years, his vigorous years,' he said. Olivier himself counselled: 'Do you want to be a household word or an actor? Make up your mind.' And Paul Scofield, the young Burton's hero, added: 'Richard, professionally, is the most interesting actor to have emerged since the war. I think his qualities of heroic presence are not seen to their full advantage in movies. He appears not to be attracted by the best that there is in the cinema. As for his future, he should return quietly to the theatre.'

After the announcement by Mrs Burton on the afternoon of 3 July, Burton, in Quogue, was besieged by calls and turned on the answering machine. At The Regency, the switchboard denied any knowledge of Miss Taylor's presence, despite the statement issued on their writing paper, and refused to put any calls through. But those who knew asked for Mrs Richards and until an enterprising chambermaid blew the gaffe on that pseudonym to the Press a day later, calls were connected to the fourteenth floor.

G. K. Chesterton once said that journalism consists largely in saying 'Lord Jones is dead' to people who never knew that Lord Jones was alive. But the principle did not apply here and the estranged couple made the front pages of just about every newspaper in the western world. Editors, at first suspecting a publicity stunt on account of the couple's waning popularity, decided that it was good copy, a human story, and orders were given to their reporters to ferret Burton and Taylor from their respective lairs. By the evening of 3 July, dozens of reporters milled around in the lobby of The Regency. But the drive leading up to Aaron Frosch's house was deserted when I arrived there shortly before dusk.

I had been asked to drive to Quogue and interview Burton after an initial conversation with Brian Freemantle, my foreign editor in London. A colleague would stake out The Regency and cover the Taylor angle. The Frosch house, clad with grey and green shingles, was easy to find. There was a pine wood nameplate on the grass verge outside, and a police car neatly parked to one side.

When I rang the bell in search of Mr Burton, the door was opened by the rangy, uniformed figure of Lt Doug Edwards of the Quogue police. He seemed embarrassed, somewhat off balance at having to deal with a member of the Fourth Estate.

'Mr Burton is not here. He's gone into the city with Mr Frosch,' Edwards replied to my query. 'What am I doing here? Well, gee, I'm an old friend of Mr and Mrs Frosch and they invited me up here to supper sometime ago.' With that, the door was closed, neatly, in my face. Down the drive the darkened guest cottage showed no lights. No point, I thought, in trespassing, with the watchful Edwards so close at hand.

By 9.30am the following morning – Independence Day – Frosch's drive (the telltale sign had gone but three pet goats grazed the lawn) was filled with twenty or thirty journalists.

Three of them, attached like limpets to television equipment, aimlessly panned the front of the Frosch home, ignoring the cottage at the back which concealed Mr Burton. Finally, one unshaven man dressed in dirty white jeans and scuffed sneakers approached the house and rang the bell. 'I'm from UPI,' the young man said: 'Where is he?' The maid who had opened the door slightly closed it without answering. UPI retired. More cameras and reporters arrived. The crowd, now swollen to about forty, began to edge up the drive. Their advance, massed and menacing, was halted by the sudden arrival of the faithful Lt Edwards who, with siren flashing, drove his car into the crowd and parked it sideways across the drive. He announced that he was there to restore order. The newshounds fell back.

I had spoken to Edwards on the telephone at 8am. Yes, he apologized, Burton had been there all night and he was sorry for misleading me on that fact. But he was sure that I understood. Anyway, Burton was still there, probably asleep. He'd had a heavy night by all accounts. Lt. Edwards sounded contrite and seemed to want to make up for this subterfuge.

I arrived back shortly after 9.30am to find the hordes gathering. Clearly an exclusive interview, our journalistic stock in trade, was out unless there was a way of bearding the brooding Burton alone, so I backed off and drove around the block. There I found a side road which, I estimated, should lead me to the back of Burton's cottage, through the Quogue Golf Club. It did exactly that and I parked outside a frail latch gate, 4 feet from Burton's abode. As I walked around it in search of the door, I could see the commotion at the top of the drive. Nobody saw me as I knocked on the large downstairs window which also served as a door.

'Come in,' boomed Burton in his best theatrical tone. He had been expecting the Mexican maid. 'I'm Nigel Dempster of the London *Daily Mail*,' I said, identifying myself to Burton who sat on a corner sofa in a red and blue silk dressing-gown, shaving with an electric razor. 'Is there any other *Daily Mail*,' asked Burton, apparently unsurprised to be confronted. 'I write for the *Daily Mail*, too, you know. Sit down, while I go and change.' Burton *had* written for the *Daily Mail*, an article which had appeared in May entitled 'When Elizabeth Taylor Caught Measles'. I had forgotten the content. So, apparently, had he. Turning as he went up the stairs he added: 'Can't for the life of me remember what I wrote about, though.'

Burton had dined alone the night before, drinking his usual amount of vodka. The room which occupies the whole ground floor of the Frosch guest cottage looked tidy. A script for 'Under The Volcano' lay half open on a long, low table. Beside it were three pairs of unsheathed reading-glasses. On a table nearby, a portable typewriter.

Burton seemed somewhat elated to be able to talk to the *Daily Mail*, he returned, smiling, within two minutes, dressed in a maroon polo neck sweater, dark trousers and black loafers, looking like a man ready to go six chukkas of high goal polo. His skin was clear, his hair soft and, under the clinging sweater, there was no sign of a paunch. An elderly snuffling Pekingese lolled beside an armchair and looked up at him as he passed to an open bar area. I was offered a drink. 'There's vodka, whisky, gin . . . beer?' I settled for the latter. Burton went to the kitchen, fetched a chilled bottle of Heineken and poured a large vodka for himself, adding orange juice and two ice cubes. He sat down. It was five minutes before 10am.

'Well. What can I do for you?' he asked. I explained that I was interested in hearing, as were the readers of the *Daily Mail*, his side of the separation which had been announced the previous afternoon by Mrs Burton. At that, the air of cheerfulness and self-assurance with which he had re-entered the room seemed to evaporate. He grimaced at my question, which he seemed to think in dubious taste. He looked, as Wodehouse said on another occasion, like a man who, chasing rainbows, had one of them suddenly turn and bite him on the leg.

'Well, I don't know, sweetheart. I don't understand what she is talking about. As far as I know there isn't a separation. But it only takes one to make one. It's a very surprising statement. Women are funny people. I don't know what's going on. We've had no arguments. I thought she was in New York buying clothes. When she left here yesterday, she said "See you soon." You never know what's going on in a woman's mind, though.'

I asked if Mrs Burton had left for another man. Peter Lawford, perhaps? 'Peter Lawford?' Burton's lip curled. 'I don't think I know the fellow. Perhaps I've met him once. I thought she was with Laurence Harvey and Sammy Davis. Laurence Harvey is a very old friend of mine,' he added, somewhat tangentially. He kicked a leather Gladstone bag which was beside his armchair. 'Anyway, Elizabeth can't go anywhere, you know. Her passport is in her bag,' he said. Then he glanced mischievously at me. 'Shall I call her up at The Regency? You can talk to her.' He made as if to reach for the telephone which was beside me but drew back as he inspected his wristwatch. 'It's too early. Elizabeth never gets up before 11 o'clock,' he divulged. He helped himself, instead, to another vodka, nearly draining the bottle, added orange and ice again, and fetched me another cold beer.

'Why has Elizabeth made this remarkable statement? I've no idea what's going on. I have an inkling why she may be annoyed with me, but nothing which points to this sort of behaviour. Her mother is very sick and she is worried about her granddaughter. Perhaps my indifference to her problems has created a faint sort of storm. But I've no idea.'

The Pekingese advanced, hoping for a pat. Burton obliged. I asked the animal's name. 'Do you know *Hamlet?*' I shook my head, remembering that Burton had a photographic memory of Shakespeare's every word. 'Well, there's a part in *Hamlet*, when I stand with the skull in my hand . . .' Burton stood up and assumed a theatrical position close to the wall. He performed a few lines, his hand empty but cupped as if holding a skull. His performance ended with the word 'Eenso'. I applauded. He appeared gratified.

'That's why we call him Eenso. Chinaman you see. Gielgud pointed it out to me first.' He helped himself to the rest of the vodka and brought me a third beer from the refrigerator. I mentioned Maria, who was playing beside the swimming-pool with one of the Frosch daughters. His eyes lit up. 'She's beautiful. And do you know, she's even grown up to look like me. It's remarkable. Elizabeth adopted her when she was a baby and crippled. But she was operated on and she's fine now. I'll get her for you.' He bounded over to the doorway and projected his baritone across the lawn. 'Marreeah. Marreeah.' She pretended not to hear and went on playing. 'She'll be in a minute,' said Burton resuming his seat.

'I can't envisage a permanent separation from Elizabeth. I can't imagine life without her. I love her very much. However, if she wants to take off, she takes off. Who knows what goes on in the feminine secretive mind? There isn't another woman in my life. And as far as I know, there isn't another man in Elizabeth's. We'll be back together soon.'

I asked about his drinking. He changed the subject. 'I took marijuana once. Its effect was most extraordinary. It made me incapable of movement. Not like drink at all. You know marijuana is Spanish for Mary Jane? You didn't? Well, Mary – mari: Jane – juana. See?'

Maria entered sheepishly and loped over to her father. 'Daddy, I'm going in to see Mommy,' she said, half looking at him. He smiled, equally sheepishly, up at her. 'I'm coming with you.' She turned towards the stairs. 'You know you can't,' she chided him gently, and went to pack. A few moments later, Burton called up after her, 'Are you packing my clothes, too?' She replied no. 'You'd better.'

His mind strayed back to his wife, probably now beginning to stir in her hotel suite. 'We argue all the time. She's a splendid child and I'm very fond of the lady. The frightful thing is that I'm amused by all this. Disturbed naturally, but wildly fascinated.'

Our conversation was interrupted by another entrance. Two ladies, grey-haired and in their late fifties, early sixties, came in from the garden. Burton introduced them to me as Mrs Gwen Jenkins, widow of Ivor, and her sister-in-law, Mrs Gwynneth Thomas. All three began to talk animatedly together in Welsh. From time to time, the two women looked up, and smiled in my direction. Burton suddenly turned back to me. 'I'll tell you what. I'll write an appraisal of Elizabeth for the *Mail*. In my own words. You can keep the copyright.' He started up in the direction of the type-writer. His progress was halted by Gwynneth. She remonstrated with him, again in Welsh, and then turned to me and said in English as he settled back in the chair, 'He's in a wicked mood, you know.'

Burton seemed disappointed. 'All I do really is act, read and write. I'm a recluse by nature.' He looked again at his watch. Noticing it, I asked if it was time for him to ring Miss Taylor. 'Not Miss Taylor. She's Mrs Burton. It will be a very private conversation. I think you ought to push off now.'

I took my cue, shook hands all round and left. It was just after 11.30am. Plenty of time to catch the first editions of my newspaper in London and gain a great front page world scoop which was followed up even in New York. At the top of the drive the frustrated, snarling pack of journalists continued to be kept at bay by the lone policeman. It was not until nearly two hours later that they managed to effect an advance on the cottage. They appeared, suddenly, at Burton's window, catching him by surprise. He jumped up and tried to leave the cottage by a side door which was locked. Then he bounded up the stairs.

To the onlookers he appeared a man who had devoted his brightest efforts to the pursuit of pleasure and now, at the age of forty-seven, had almost overtaken it. At the top of the stairs he opened a window and shouted from it, in a scene redolent of *Romeo and Juliet*. His words were less eloquent. 'Go away,' he beseeched his pursuers. 'Go away. Can't you see that I am upset?'

With that, he shut the window, retired to bed and did not speak to another journalist for ten days. At The Regency Hotel, Mrs Burton confined herself to quarters. Only hairdressers, bellhops or maids were allowed in or out of the suite and they were scrutinized carefully by Bob Wilson. Instructions had been issued previously that, for the moment, any calls from Mr Burton should be rejected. After hours of talks with Mrs Burton, an exhausted Aaron Frosch had left her suite well past midnight. To the assembled Press, he appeared slightly unsteady on his feet. As Mrs Burton surfaced, thirteen floors below in the hotel lobby, some thirty photographers and journalists were served coffee and biscuits by Mr Caballero, the hotel manager. Most of them had been in the lobby for two days and nights. That afternoon, Mrs

Burton announced via the omnipresent John Springer, that she would be visiting her mother in California the following day and would be leaving the hotel promptly at 1.30pm. Suspecting subterfuge, the cynical Press elected to remain in the lobby another night.

On Thursday 5 July, the good weather Mr Burton had long awaited finally arrived. By noon, the temperature was in the low eighties. An hour later, some 300 people, armed with cameras, tape recorders, television booms and plain curiosity jammed the lobby of The Regency and spilled on to the pavement outside. Guests at the $50 a day hotel had difficulty getting in and out. Television cameras and lights were positioned directly opposite the bank of three elevators. An hour passed and the lady did not appear. But evidence of her presence on the premises could be found in the garage at the rear. A black limousine stood there empty, but with a sign showing the name Burton in the window.

It was clear that Mrs Burton intended that no one miss her grand exit. Had she wished, she could have slipped away by a back route from the hotel the night before and retired unmolested to California. In her absence, television and radio men in the lobby began in desperation to interview auto-graph hunters who had wormed their way into the crowd. Another hour passed and the sweaty Press continued to talk to themselves.

Behind them, on the opposite side of the lobby by the manager's office, Mrs Burton slipped out from a service ele-vator and began to cross the lobby. Her adopted daughter, Maria, still wearing jeans and striped tee shirt from the pre-vious day, hung onto her like a determined Sumo wrestler. They were ringed by four bodyguards. Mrs Burton, heavily made up and recently coiffured – hence her delay – wore a photogenic white trouser suit and gold hooped earrings.

Realizing that they had been deceived, 'hoodwinked', as one of them said, the crowd of journalists, photographers and television men pivoted and streamed across the lobby. Within seconds Mrs Burton and her entourage were surrounded, their progress at a standstill. The newsmen screamed and interjected, the photographers scuffled and wildly snapped. 'Bella, bella,' shouted one of them, leaping like a high jumper in the air. 'Look this way. Just once, please.' But his competitors soon drowned him out. 'Liz. Elizabeth. Mrs Burton. Oh Jeez, you bitch, just look into my camera once.' Mrs Burton gripped Maria more firmly. She seemed pale and somehow offended, genuinely perplexed by the commotion she was causing and had so carefully stage managed. She was a lady, after all. My private affairs, she seemed to say, should be treated with a little discretion, a little civility, for God's sake. Undaunted, her husky escorts pushed their way through the mêlée. 'I've said all I have to say,' she muttered once. And then, before lapsing into silence, she repeated it again. The hordes pressed more closely around her and it seemed impossible that she would ever reach the street. But a minute or two later she was at the front revolving door.

Outside, an American matron who had come to gape was horrified at the crush. 'Let her through,' she yelled. 'Let her through. Oh my Gahd. What will she think of New York?' They forced their way through the door, out to the street and into the waiting limousine. Park Avenue, by now blocked, was a crescendo of irate car horns. Clumsily, Elizabeth and Maria piled into the back seat and slammed the door. Inside, Elizabeth clutched the only other occupant, the faithful Eenso. She glanced out, almost carelessly, at the now angry crowd, a look of distaste in her face, a look which said: 'You animals, don't you have anything better to do?'

Then she turned away, no longer interested. Instant theatrics were her speciality. As the limousine pulled away, a couple of cameramen kicked it in frustration.

Meanwhile back in Los Angeles ... The Beverly Hills Hotel was a flat, pink edifice with a swimming-pool, two tennis courts presided over by the former Wimbledon champion Alex Olmedo, and a number of secluded bungalows in the grounds. It had a renowned bar called the Polo Lounge, where the city's starlets would seek out the stars, and it was in the green and pink Polo Lounge that the Burtons' only previous separation had ended. One night in January 1970 they quarrelled publicly in front of Bumbles, a Hollywood discotheque, and Elizabeth went home with her socialite friend, Mrs Edie Goetz. Harsh words had been exchanged by the couple earlier, with Burton becoming openly abusive about his wife. For two days they did not speak but on the third Elizabeth returned to The Beverly Hills Hotel where they were staying, walked up to Burton's table in the Polo Lounge, and punched him on the nose. He then invited her to sit down and have a drink and the quarrel was officially over.

By the evening of 6 July, the Polo Lounge contained a nucleus of British journalists. The American Press, having decided the Burtons had been overplayed, had been called off. Thus only the intrepid British remained on the trail of the elusive Mrs Burton. Both the *Mail* and the *Daily Mirror*, then Britain's largest circulation newspaper, drank in the bar that evening and that morning Bill Lovelace arrived. A *Daily Express* photographer who had spent considerable time with the Burtons around the time of their marriage, Bill had just missed Mrs Burton in New York, but expected to see the lady here and obtain her full co-operation for exclusive photographs and interview. The trail, for the moment, was cold but that day I had encountered Eddie Fisher in the hotel grounds. He looked old beyond his years. In an effort, perhaps, to look younger, he wore a red golf blazer, half-moon spectacles and a white shirt open at the neck, revealing a cluster of gold medallions and chains. Fisher had been staying at the hotel for some weeks and the word was that he was having difficulty meeting the bill. When asked if he had seen the lady lately or even knew where she was holed up, he recoiled. Maybe he remembered the painful saga ten years earlier when Elizabeth had leaked to the Press that he was demanding $3 million in alimony and divorce settlements. 'Elizabeth Taylor?' he parried as if trying to place her. 'No, I haven't seen her. Not in a long time.'

But through the usual devious sources we learned that Mrs Burton was staying at the home of Edith Head, the Hollywood costume designer who has won more Oscars than she cares to remember. Bill Lovelace had actually managed to get her on the telephone, a conversation he was later to describe as 'short'. 'Hello, Bill Lovelace,' said Mrs Burton. 'No I don't want to have any photographs taken. No I don't want to talk about it. Goodbye, Bill Lovelace.' Lovelace would try again, but clearly Mrs Burton had resolved to keep silent about the affair.

On the night of 6 July, twenty-four hours after her flight from New York in a private plane put at her disposal by George Barrie, the head of the Fabergé group who had produced her last film *Night Watch*, Mrs Burton was again with Peter Lawford. They went to a Beverly Hills discotheque called the Candy Store and were pictured leaving by a UPI photographer. It was the last time she was to be seen publicly in Los Angeles. But during her fourteen-day sojourn on the coast, she revisited old friends. Donald Crisp, the ninety-five-year-old British actor who had played her father in her first film, *National Velvet*, now lives in a Los Angeles home for retired actors. Elizabeth spent seven hours with him the day before she left California to fly to Rome for her reconciliation with Burton. As she left the home, she turned to the matron. 'Please reserve a room for me, I'll be back,' she said. There were tears in her eyes.

But by the evening of 8 July, despair had settled upon us occupants of the Polo Lounge. It was evident that there would be no cosy disclosures from Mrs Burton. We were called off and rebased ourselves. If we had stayed a week longer we would have found Mrs Burton with her children, Liza Todd (her daughter by the late Mike Todd) and Maria, Peter Lawford and his two children and Elizabeth's childhood friend, Roddy McDowall, visiting Disneyland.

Meanwhile, Mr Burton was still in Quogue. Now and again he telephoned his wife to inform her that he had indeed given up the demon drink, his drinking being the reason she had put forward for the separation. During that first week apart, Aaron Frosch had celebrated his client's forty-ninth birthday with a dinner-party and was pleased to note that Mr Burton had not even touched a glass of wine. 'He toasted me with TAB,' Frosch told Mrs Burton. On 13 July, Richard ended his Long Island holiday and flew to Rome. He was to be the house-guest of film producer Carlo Ponti whose wife, Sophia Loren, was due to appear in Burton's next film, the Ponti movie *Assassination in Rome*.

Rome has never had happy associations for Burton. After *Cleopatra* he resolved never to see the place again. Also the paparazzi regard him as a prime target; he could not eat or drink in public without interruption. 'The Italian Press is the worst in the world. The photographers appear out of the soup. It's most harrowing,' he told me. But he seemed in a contented frame of mind when he landed at Leonardo da Vinci airport and was driven to the Villa Ponti, an hour away.

Rid of his troublesome charge, Aaron Frosch was congratulating himself on successfully patching up the Burtons' problems. On 12 July, he had informed me of a reconciliation. 'All differences between Richard and Elizabeth have been resolved. His drinking has now ceased. He has not been drinking and his intention is not to drink.' A trifle wearily, he added: 'And I hope they live happily ever after.'

The usual statements were issued to the Press. And, as ever, the Press prepared to honour the occasion. The historic reunion would take place in Rome. The time: 1.30pm. The date: Friday 20 July. The venue: Leonardo da Vinci airport.

On the Wednesday before, Mrs Burton began to pack her bags in California. She had not seen her husband for fifteen days and, according to Frosch, she was 'eagerly looking forward to seeing him again'. But that day at Edith Head's home her mind was on other matters. The separation had strengthened rather than weakened her resolve to be rid of her husband. She had decided that her career would only blossom again without his malign influence. Alone, she would resume her throne as the Queen of Hollywood. And, besides, she had again discovered the joys of being a single woman. In Beverly Hills she had lost weight, regained her figure and now looked ten years younger. She packed Maria and Liza off to the Hawaiian island of Kauai where her oceanographer brother, Howard Taylor, had a house; he looked after them for the remainder of their school holiday.

Mrs Burton booked first-class seats on the direct BOAC 747 flight to London on Thursday; there she planned to transfer to a chartered jet for the final leg to Rome, and 'reconciliation' with Richard. Bill Lovelace booked an adjoining seat, trusting that his airborne proximity would

weaken her resolve not to be photographed. It didn't and
he clambered out at London twelve hours later, his cameras
still in their cases. Mrs Burton changed planes, leaving the
hapless Lovelace to follow by a later schedule. He missed
extraordinary scenes in Rome.

Burton had travelled from the Moscow Film Festival to a
smaller, similar affair at Taormina in Sicily. Throughout he
was accompanied by a New York physician, Dr William
Hitzig of Park Avenue, on the recommendation of the solicitous Frosch. He appeared to be drinking again. One afternoon in Taormina he sank to his knees, dramatically
clutching his chest. 'My heart. My heart,' he croaked, search-
ing for support. A friend helped him up. 'It's not your heart,'
he chided gently.

About an hour before Mrs Burton's jet, chartered at a cost
of $2,500, was due in Rome, Burton arrived at Leonardo da
Vinci in a Rolls-Royce Phantom equipped with darkened
'purdah' windows. Despite these, he could be discerned
through the glass wearing his customary polo neck; he
appeared distracted and the vulturous Press hung about
moodily in the hope of getting a statement. But what statement? In Moscow, Burton had perpetrated the myth that
there had been no real separation. 'What separation?' he had
snapped at an American newsman. 'The whole thing has
been made up by the newspapers.' Soon most of the Press
sensibly retired to the bar.

Some minutes later, Mr Burton decided to leave the car.
For reasons best known to himself, he entered the airport
building and almost immediately ran headlong into a cluck-
ing throng of journalists. He swayed when he saw them and
seemed to bend at the knees. The journalists pressed forward, ready to pounce on their prey. Mr Burton sagged.
'Help me back to my car,' he said in the manner of a man

who had decided that, if he were going to pieces, he was going to do it damn well. 'I don't feel well.' Three of the journalists complied, whispering questions en route. None smelled drink on his breath.

Less than an hour later, Mrs Burton arrived in her eight-seater jet which lingered on the tarmac some twenty minutes before she actually appeared. Dressed in tight fitting denims to accentuate the loss of 20 pounds in weight, she descended the steps and regally approached the car, a swarm of photographers recording her every step. Mr Burton, anxiously staring out of the window, did not move from the back seat. His wayward wife opened the door herself and tentatively climbed in. As the crowd of cameramen, using infra-red lenses and film to pierce the darkened glass, surged round, Mr Burton lunged at her. They embraced and, with tears welling in their eyes, the happy couple drove away.

The Villa Ponti is in Marino, fifteen miles outside Rome along the Appian Way. The property itself is an almost impregnable fifty-room fortress standing in 6 acres. It boasts an elaborate alarm system to protect the two Ponti children from kidnappers, including such devices as electronic beams, 8 foot high barbed wire, trained guard dogs and heavily armed ex-policemen on twenty-four hour patrol. It was here that Carlo Ponti hoped the couple would have a successful reconciliation. He had a lot tied up in his wife's next film and wanted Mr Burton to iron out his problems before beginning work. Once again the international Press gathered together in Rome. Once again we hoped to tie up the ends, disperse the mists and close the chapter. The city had played Cupid to their romance once before, and an encore was demanded.

I arrived from New York early on Monday 23 July and checked into a room at The Grand Hotel on the same floor as Bob Wilson. Bill Lovelace had preceded me by three days but his new plea to Mr Burton was still going unanswered. I wrote to Mr Burton, and handed the letter to Bob Wilson for delivery. Awaiting successful outcomes to our missives, Lovelace and I bided our time, seeking consolation in local bars and filing uneventful stories.

Despite its apparent impregnability, the Villa Ponti is overlooked to the south by a little hill. Here, among a clump of trees, 700 yards from the house itself, an industrious Italian photographer with a formidable lens had concealed himself for three days after the arrival of Mrs Burton. By Monday morning he had taken the pictures he sought. Mr Burton crying. Mrs Burton being comforted by Sophia Loren. Mrs Burton in tears beside the swimming-pool with Mr Burton standing somewhat to the side. The gates remained closed and the long silence continued. Clearly all was not well in Paradise. And the malaise permeated to the waiting Press.

John Springer was in Rome, also at The Grand. He had arrived in anticipation of a Press conference at which his newly reunited clients would display their happiness. But soon Springer began to have doubts about the validity of the announcements of a successful reconciliation. Also, it appeared, he had witnessed a distressing scene at the villa when Mr Burton handed his wife a letter, only to grab it back when she burst into tears and tore it to pieces. What did the letter say? Who was it from? Mr Springer was not saying.

Burton spent Monday and Tuesday at the villa having costume fittings for yet another film to replenish the coffers. This one, from a Pirandello novel, was provisionally entitled *The Voyage* and Vittorio de Sica was slated to direct. Shooting, in Naples and Sicily, would take ten weeks.

Mrs Burton also had costume fittings but ventured into

town. She stopped by Bulgari, the jeweller, and picked up a few trinkets. Her first appearance before the cameras was scheduled for Wednesday 1 July. Her project, *The Driver's Seat*, from a book by Muriel Spark, cast her as a woman who plans her own murder.

On Wednesday, I received a handwritten reply to my letter from Mr Burton. His hand seemed querulous, not that of a composed man. 'Dear Nigel Dempster,' he began, explaining why he had not been able to see me. 'Forgive what seems like my discourtesy but I am deep in costume fittings and conferences about the film with Sophia and Carlo Ponti which starts in a couple of weeks and there is the usual hustle and bustle – Italian style! Sorry can't see you. Sincerely Richard B.'

Meanwhile, John Springer prepared to return to New York. He felt redundant in Rome and, besides, he did have other clients. By Wednesday evening Bill Lovelace, still without a reply from Mrs Burton, had had enough as well. He returned to London. He had followed Mrs Burton for three weeks, travelling nearly 25,000 miles at a cost of $7,500 and had not a single photograph to show for it. It had been a bad few days. It had been a bad three weeks. There were other fish to fry.

But I decided to give it one last try. A face-to-face confrontation with Burton, whatever. I learned that on Thursday morning he was due to drive into Rome for final post synching on a film he had started two years earlier, *Tito: The Fifth Offensive*, but which had needed some additional material. Bob Wilson seemed chary of telling me exactly which studio Burton would be visiting, so I was forced to follow him from Marino.

I arrived just after dawn in Marino and parked my rented Fiat 100 yards down the road from the entrance to the drive of the Villa Ponti. It was going to be another hot day, certainly in the low eighties. At 8.45am a black chauffeur-driven Mercedes pulled into the drive. At 8.10am Carlo Ponti, alone and at the wheel of a modest family car, drove out towards Rome. Twenty minutes later the Mercedes reappeared. As it passed me I glimpsed Burton, in a white polo neck and tan lightweight suit, hunched in the back. He appeared intent on some reading material and did not notice as I tucked my car behind his.

He did not glance up during the twenty-five minute journey to the outskirts of the city and paused in his reading only to light cigarettes. Near the Coliseum, the Mercedes branched off the main street and into a cul-de-sac. It stopped outside the National Recording Studios and the chauffeur hurried from his seat to open the passenger door opposite. I had pulled up behind and beat him to it.

Burton, climbing clumsily from the car, looked stunned at the unheralded confrontation. Surely I had realized, the look said, that the note had dismissed me? His appearance was almost unrecognizable. The face was strained, heavily blotched and mottled, his eyes heavily creased and watering slightly. They narrowed. 'Who the hell are you?' he barked. I smiled at his tactic. 'I want to ask you five questions. I'll be brief. I know you're a busy man.'

Burton started towards the studio door, furling his script into a weapon. 'You can ask one,' he said, generously. 'Well,' I countered, 'is there really a reconciliation? Those pictures outside the villa seem to point the other way.' Burton had achieved the safety of the doorway. He stopped just inside, his left hand curled around the edge of the door. 'Of course there's a reconciliation,' he said like an actor who has learned his lines but failed to grasp their meaning. 'Why do you want to know?'

I replied: 'A separation is announced to the world. Then a reconciliation. Then you both disappear without further comment. Quite naturally, the world is curious.' Burton seemed disconcerted by my logic. His eyes rolled, the voice cracked. 'It's none of their bloody business. But you can tell the world we're happy.'

Three days later Mrs Burton moved out of the Villa Ponti and into The Grand Hotel, announcing through her lawyers that she and Mr Burton were seeking a divorce.

Mrs Burton, now calling herself Elizabeth Taylor, duly started work on *The Driver's Seat* on Wednesday 1 August. Mr Burton's film had been delayed until late September owing to the illness of Vittorio de Sica. He returned to New York, alone, on 29 August for talks with Aaron Frosch. Miss Taylor had been pictured, on several occasions, in the embrace of Dutch-born Henry Wynberg, a former Los Angeles second-hand car salesman of obscure origins, whom she met during her separation period in Los Angeles.

Following Elizabeth's divorce from Burton in Switzerland in 1974, she did *not* marry the generously endowed and lisping Wynberg. Instead, she and Burton remarried the following year in Botswana. She became Mrs Burton all over again, but for one year only, divorcing for good in 1976.

In between his two marriages to Liz, Burton did not pine. In October 1974 I revealed in the *Mail* Diary that just four months after his divorce, Burton was in love again, with thirty-eight-year-old Princess Elizabeth of Yugoslavia who had apparently been happily married to Old Etonian merchant banker, Neil Balfour, eight years her junior and a man with political pretensions.

Balfour, whose elder brother, Christopher, was a director of Christie's, the St James's auction house, moved out of their listed King's Road house (next to the imposing residence of Viscount Lambton and his wife, Bindy) and left the field to Burton. His son, Nicholas, then four, remained with his mother but she could not contain Burton's drinking and, despite announcing plans to marry the star, Princess Elizabeth, a first cousin of the Duke of Kent, finally left him in March 1975, saying: 'I still love Richard, but I cannot bear a repeat of his last performance. He was hopeless and didn't make sense any more.' Within two months she was back living with a forgiving Neil, who halted proposed divorce proceedings. But their marriage was holed below the water by the very public affair and they eventually divorced.

Only weeks after his romantic remarriage to Elizabeth in Botswana, Burton was drinking heavily again and he confided in Peter Lawford, of all people, that the remarriage had been 'an act of folly'. By January 1976 they were separated and the marriage dissolved six months afterwards.

Being single again, Burton was in a position to do Formula One racing driver James Hunt a tremendous favour. Known as Hunt the Shunt, and destined to become world champion driver in 1976, the Wellington-educated James had married retired barrister's daughter Suzy Miller on 19 October 1974 at the Brompton Oratory, Knightsbridge. They had moved to Marbella (where they had first met in a bar) to take advantage of the tax situation and protect James's burgeoning income, but he had quickly become disenchanted with his marriage. James telephoned me with the news and added that he wanted her out of his life, and as cheaply as possible. 'I'm willing to give her an airline ticket to anywhere in the world and a couple of grand. That's all,' he told me ungallantly.

On a skiing holiday in Gstaad in February 1976, Burton met Suzy and they soon became inseparable. To say James was relieved is an understatement. By the summer he was in love with Jane Birbeck, a twenty-three-year-old who he nicknamed 'Hottie', and Suzy obtained a 'quickie' divorce in Haiti shortly after Burton ended his marriage to Elizabeth. Burton and Suzy duly married in August, a union which lasted six years.

For his fifth wife, Burton chose BBC TV continuity girl Sally Hay, whose father, Jack, had been a sub-editor on the London *Evening News*. They met on the set of the £6.5 million TV epic on Wagner and married in Las Vegas in July 1983, just thirteen months before Burton died of a stroke at the age of fifty-eight, after being taken ill at his villa in the village of Celigny, overlooking Lake Geneva. Burton was buried locally and Sally moved to London, where she bought a spacious house close to Hyde Park off the Bayswater Road. She inherited the bulk of his reported £3.6 million estate and, through shrewd investment, had more than doubled it in less than a decade. She has worked in television, on the Kilroy programme among others, and has never remarried.

Epilogue: Keats did not supply the epitaph for the Burtons' marriage. Subconsciously Burton had done that in the *Daily Mail* article he alluded to in our conversation at Quogue. The last paragraph reads: 'The body is nothing. Idiocy is all. Sanity is a fool. And the woman wins. Always.'

The Lady from the Labyrinth

PATRICIA KLUGE

Palm Beach has been called 'God's Waiting-Room' because of the advanced age of its multimillionaire inhabitants who soak up the Florida sunshine, mainly during the winter months, and belong to clubs with quaint names redolent of another, more discreet age, like the Bath and Tennis.

Even the best local hotel, The Breakers, was founded by a railroad king and it was here that American media magnate, John Kluge, later billed as the world's richest man, planned to entertain the Prince and Princess of Wales at a charity evening in November 1985 with his statuesque Baghdad-born wife, Patricia.

For Mrs Kluge, who towered over her diminutive German-born husband and at thirty-six was three and a half decades younger than him, it was to be her crowning achievement, the ultimate recognition of her integration into polite American society which began auspiciously with her April 1981 marriage at St Patrick's Cathedral in New York, the ceremony being conducted by Cardinal Terence Cook. They celebrated by adopting an infant son, John Jnr, in 1983.

The charity evening was to be in aid of the United World Colleges, a project close to the heart of octogenarian Dr Armand Hammer, the head of Occidental Petroleum who was chief benefactor of the colleges, a major philanthropist and contributor to causes dear to the heart of his young friend, Prince Charles. Patricia Kluge, who with John had become close to Hammer, was on the board of trustees and had been invited by him to become ball chairman with tickets top priced at $50,000 a couple.

Although Los Angeles-based Hammer and his third wife, Frances, were not due to attend, the Kluges were looking forward to the event, John occupying the place of honour next to Diana with Pat being seated beside Charles. Couples paying $50,000 for their tickets were offered the added incentive of being photographed with the Royal couple. In Palm Beach, life does not come much grander than that.

This upcoming idyll was to be destroyed when I was approached in September 1985 by a former Soho police officer who had known Patricia in less salubrious times. He told me that she had been born in Baghdad to an Iraqi mother and British father, Edmund Rose, and had married Russell Gay, who owned the soft porn magazine *Knave*, in June 1973. For two years, Patricia dispensed sex advice under her name. The column, featuring a scantily clad picture of her, offered information about such matters as the sexual skills of different European nationalities. She had also, I was reliably informed, worked briefly as a belly-dancer at the Labyrinth Club in London's Bayswater.

Accordingly, I sent out to a second-hand magazine shop in the Charing Cross Road which turned up some back issues of *Knave* which included Patricia's contributions over a two-year period (she divorced Gay in November 1976). Among the explicit photographs of her adorning her ghost-written column happened to be one with a snake. Armed with this information and background, the *Mail* Diary set about contacting the Kluges and finally traced them to Albemarle, their sumptuous estate near Charlottesville, Virginia. Variously described as having either 4,000 or 12,000 acres with a magnificent forty-five-room main house, it had cost Kluge (who owned America's fourth largest network of TV and radio stations and was in the process of selling it to Rupert Murdoch for $2.4 billion) in the region of $20 million.

Patricia was nothing but frank when confronted with her past and told me of Gay: 'He was a strong personality and I was in love with him. I was only nineteen when I met him and I became his obsession. If I hadn't met him, this would never have happened. I was working as a receptionist for shipping man Ravi Tikkoo at the time. I don't think Armand Hammer knows about my past, although my husband and all our friends do. I was married to the kind of man who made me do these things.' As an afterthought, she confided that the royal couple were not strangers and added: 'I have met Prince Charles and Princess Diana on about five occasions.'

The Diary item, illustrated with the *Knave* logo, an apparently topless Patricia as well as a photograph of the Kluges with Frank Sinatra's wife, Barbara Marx, and, for good measure, Armand Hammer shaking hands with the Heir to the Throne, was set to run on Friday 20 September. The previous afternoon Dr Armand (who died of cancer at ninety-two in December 1990) was busy threatening senior executives and directors of the *Daily Mail* with closure of the paper should the item run. It was, he assured those he talked to on the telephone from California, a tissue of lies and he cautioned discretion.

Being telephoned by Dr Armand was considered serious enough for the column to be put under the microscope and at one stage it was almost pulled. But the evidence, in particular the old copies of *Knave* magazine, was too compelling and Patricia's quotes on the matter added weight. Publication went ahead and, needless to say, Hammer failed to close down the *Daily Mail*. The fall-out was immediate: with the American press following up my scoop, the Kluges found themselves banned by Hammer from any association with the charity event (in 1982 Dr A had paid $5 million to set up the Armand Hammer United World College of the American West in Montezuma, New Mexico, to the opening of which Prince Charles was flown in September 1982 in Hammer's private jet).

But if living well is the ultimate revenge, Patricia quickly outflew the swallows. For the housewarming at Albemarle – the estate boasted 120 workers – the guest of honour was ex-King Constantine of Greece and his wife Queen Anne-Marie, and other guests included Sir David and Lady Carina Frost and Lord and Lady Romsey – and the couple continued to entertain liberally, showing off their many acres, which included a golf course and croquet lawns. They also imported wild birds, such as pheasant, for shooting parties but that stopped when their aristocratic gamekeeper, Irish baronet Sir Richard Musgrave, was convicted of conspiring to kill at least 400 predatory birds and animals – hundreds of hawks and owls, foxes and even neighbours' dogs were snared or beaten to death, their feet chopped off to prove the kill. Said an unrepentant Musgrave after the case: 'I guess I'll be the first criminal in the family since Charles I.'

And in the summer of 1987 the Kluges' well-appointed

yacht, the *Virginian* (previously owned by bi-sexual magazine mogul Malcolm Forbes and then called the *Highlander*),
welcomed aboard the Prince and Princess of Wales for a
five-hour cruise around the Balearics after the Royal couple
boarded in Palma, Majorca, during an Iberian holiday with
King Juan Carlos and Queen Sofia. Pat then scored another
victory with the British Royal Family: she hired their carriage
driver David Saunders, paying him £50,000, to set up a
carriage driving museum and centre at Albemarle; he had
previously been employed by Prince Philip and had run the
Sandringham Driving Centre.

As a coup de grâce, she further infiltrated the House of
Windsor by entering into a three year, £300,000 sponsorship
deal of the Royal Windsor Horse Show which is run from
the Queen's Mews at Windsor Castle. This virtually guaranteed her a photo opportunity with Prince Philip during the
prizegiving ceremony. And there was more to come.

Around Christmas 1988, the Kluges bought 19th-century
Mar Lodge (built in 1896 for Edward VII's daughter, Prin-
cess Louise) and became the Deeside neighbours of the
Queen and Prince Philip who lived across country at Bal-
moral. With thirty bedrooms and 8 miles of fishing on the
River Dee (the Queen Mother's favourite stretch of water),
Mar Lodge had been on sale for £7 million and reputedly
boasted 3,000 head of deer and antlers in the ballroom.

Back in Albemarle, following the disgrace of Sir Richard
Musgrave and his exit from the States (via Concorde, paid
for by Kluge), the estate had been allowed to return to the
wild and the shoot abandoned, much to the chagrin of regular guests. Musgrave's successor, Paul McGagh, said as the
hawks, foxes and other predators had the run of the acres
with their pick of pheasants roaming free: 'You can assume
it will be shut down. I gather the whole damn thing is being

transferred to Britain.' The idyll was not to last long: in April 1990 Saunders, whose marriage had broken up because of his association with the Kluges, was fired after moving his operations to Mar Lodge; Pat and John separated after he discovered through the *Mail* Diary that she had become involved with Governor Doug Wilder of Virginia, America's leading black politician, and Mar Lodge was ravaged by fire and put on the market for an ambitious £10 million.

In 1991 the Kluges finally divorced. They had given £400,000 to Governor Wilder's campaign for election in 1989 and in return Pat had been appointed to the board of visitors to the University of Virginia, which had sparked a minor riot among students. Kluge had become wise to her friendship with Wilder, a divorcee eighteen years Pat's senior, when the pilot of his three-engined Falcon 50 told him that it was a coincidence that, whenever the craft took off, it was only minutes behind the Governor's official plane!

Despite their many sightings together, Wilder, grandson of a slave and a Korean War veteran, told me: 'We're only friends', but Kluge persevered with the divorce, moving to a small house at Albemarle 3 miles from the main residence where he let Pat and John Jnr live, attended by scores of staff. But reports that she received the equivalent of £100 million a year in a settlement were wide of the mark. A more accurate estimate was an annual payment of £500,000, the use of the yacht (since sold in 1997 to JCB heir Sir Anthony Bamford for £14 million) and the continued residence of Albemarle. According to friends, she was keen to become involved in the movie industry, launched the Virginia Festival of American Films and planned to become a movie producer.

After a decade of fame, Patricia Kluge has adopted a low profile, giving up her sponsorship of the Royal Windsor

Horse Show after Mar Lodge, with its 3,500 red deer, was sold to the nation with a £4 million contribution from the Easter Trust and £10.2 million from the Heritage Lottery Fund (Kluge was reported to have settled for just £5.5 million) and lives quietly at Albemarle, her every movement apparently monitored by Kluge, who was eighty-four on 21 September 1998.

Wilder, mooted at one stage as vice-presidential running-mate to Texan billionaire Ross Perot in the 1995 Presidential Election, is out of the picture and Pat's last known escort was Gary Lieberthal, who bred horses nearby in Virginia and was a TV producer.

Patricia was thought to have made £50 million from astute investments, but friends in England, like interior designer Lady Charles Spencer-Churchill, sister-in-law of the Duke of Marlborough, have lost contact. 'Haven't heard from her in years,' she says, succinctly. 'It's almost as if she doesn't exist any more.'

Blunting the Sword
of Truth

JONATHAN AITKEN

The news in March 1998 could not have been bleaker for Jonathan Aitken, once hailed as the golden boy of British politics. Both he and one of his twin daughters, Victoria, then seventeen, had been arrested and questioned over alleged perjury during his aborted libel action against the *Guardian* and Granada's World in Action programme; his Sandwich house had been sold for £500,000; he faced the prospect of moving out of his magnificent Westminster home, and his return to the business world, as a £150,000 a year consultant with GEC, was being terminated.

Jonathan's old antagonist Anna Ford told me she felt no pity. Now a BBC newsreader and presenter of the Radio 4 Today programme, she had famously emptied a glass of white wine over his patrician head at a Chelsea cocktail party given by Lady Melchett in June 1993 (along with Angela Rippon, Anna had been fired by Aitken from TV-am).

'The person I feel sorry for is his mother Penpy [Jonathan's widowed mother, Lady Aitken]. She's eighty-six and is seriously frightened that she'll never see him again. The maximum for perjury is life and if found guilty he's likely to be sentenced to seven years. Also, she may have to move out of her flat which is across the courtyard from his Westminster house because everything is being sold to meet the legal bills.

'The trouble is that Penpy never remonstrated with him when he was young, she never shook her finger at him and he thought he could do anything he wanted.'

Almost three decades earlier, my old pal Jonathan (we had met in the Sixties through his cousin, Sir Max Aitken, then proprietor of Beaverbrook Newspapers where I worked) was facing a similar crisis in his life and he offered me an intriguing invitation.

It was early 1971 and his career, he told me, was 'in ruins'. He wanted me to join other friends and supporters for a buffet supper at his top floor flat in Phillimore Gardens. The flat itself was part of a large, detached house, divided into three; his mother occupied the ground and garden floors and his actress sister, Maria, the middle. He explained we would have a few drinks, eat and then offer him advice as to his future.

Back in the late Sixties it looked as if Eton- and Oxford-educated Jonathan, born in August 1942 and the son of the late Sir William Aitken, Tory MP for Bury St Edmunds, had it made. A foreign correspondent for the London *Evening Standard*, he was the author of an early bestselling book, *The Young Meteors*, and had fought the Labour-held Meriden constituency in Warwickshire in 1966. His reward, in December 1967, was to be adopted as the Conservative candidate for the ultra-safe Yorkshire seat of Thirsk and Malton for which Robin Turton, the MP since 1929, was not seeking re-election.

The adoption process had not been without problems: liberally minded Jonathan was one of sixty-five people whose signatures were attached to an advertisement in *The Times* that July calling for reform of the law on smoking cannabis and former Grenadier Guards officer Lt Colonel Lewis Starkey led the opposition at Thirsk and Malton. However, Jonathan's candid answers at a packed meeting of 800 and his youthful good looks (many present were women of a certain age) won the day and he was adopted by a big majority.

But just over three years later, he was dropped by the constituency after being sent for trial and charged under the Official Secrets Act over an ill-advised article on the Nigerian Civil War in the *Sunday Telegraph*. It had come about because Colonel Douglas Cairns, Britain's senior observer of the Nigeria–Biafra war, had sent a copy of a report prepared by the defence adviser to the British High Commission in Lagos to Major-General Henry Alexander, Britain's first observer of the war, who had retired to Yorkshire in December 1969.

From Yorkshire, Alexander had invited Jonathan to dinner. He wanted to convince his future MP, an avid supporter of the breakaway state of Biafra, that Nigeria was winning the war. He lent him the document on the understanding that it was confidential and would be returned the next day. But Aitken kept a copy and in early January 1970 his agent telephoned the *Sunday Telegraph* who agreed to pay £500 for the information in the document. Sadly, it was published on 11 January, the day after Biafra collapsed and the war ended.

Notwithstanding, Jonathan, Cairns and the *Sunday Telegraph*'s editor Brian Roberts were summonsed under the Official Secrets Act and Aitken's association with Thirsk and Malton was all but over. When the case came before the

Central Criminal Court in January 1971, Jonathan was supported by powerful friends who gave evidence on his behalf. Among them were the new Speaker of the House of Commons, Selwyn Lloyd (whose private secretary Aitken had been between 1964 and 1966), and, absurdly, Hugh Fraser, younger brother of war hero Lord Lovat and the Secretary of State for Air from 1962 to 1964.

Why absurdly? It was common knowledge that Jonathan had been enjoying a lengthy affair with Fraser's wife, the biographer Lady Antonia, daughter of the Earl of Longford. For this reason Hugh Fraser was dubbed 'saintly' by the newspapers; he must have known of the liaison but stood by his wife, the mother of six children. Both were portrayed as staunch Roman Catholics. When Hugh Fraser celebrated thirty years as Tory MP for Stafford and Stone in 1975, a somewhat sickening photograph was taken of the Fraser family and published in a broadsheet newspaper with a caption eulogizing their happiness and devotion to family life.

Clearly the author either knew nothing of Jonathan Aitken and the affair, cared less or was playing possum. (By coincidence Sir Hugh, after his divorce, was involved with Lady Melchett, widow of former British Steel chief Lord Melchett.)

Although Aitken and his co-defendants were cleared on 3 February 1971 after a seventeen-day trial and costs estimated to be in the region of £50,000 awarded to them, his effortless rise had taken a nose-dive. Hence that invitation to Phillimore Gardens.

It was a strange gathering, which included the likes of Bernard Levin, and I was surprised to find Lady Antonia Fraser acting as hostess for Jonathan. After some wine and supper, Aitken asked for silence and told the thirty or so guests about his problems. He ended by saying: 'You are my friends and I need your advice. What should I do now?' I broke the ensuing silence by raising my hand and saying, 'I suggest, Jonathan, that your cause is not helped by your choice of companion. In the circumstances, I would advise you to split up with Antonia. It can only harm your career.'

Instant uproar – not least from Antonia – and Jonathan spluttered that he could not agree less and ushered me to the door. Clearly my comment was the last thing that he wanted to hear and the affair continued for another couple of years with Fraser seemingly condoning the cuckolding – Aitken was a regular guest of the Frasers at the family estate in Beauly, Inverness-shire.

(By a strange coincidence Aitken was to save Hugh's life in October 1975 when a terrorist bomb exploded under Fraser's Jaguar XJ6, parked outside his house in Campden Hill Square, Kensington. The explosion killed one passer-by, his neighbour Professor Gordon Hamilton-Airley, who was walking his poodles, Binny and Emmy Lou. Aitken's telephone call to Fraser at 8.45am delayed the departure of Fraser and his houseguest, Caroline Kennedy, daughter of the late President and Jackie O, who was attending an arts appreciation course at Sotheby's. Both would have been killed instantly.)

Despite the sour ending to his party, I remained on friendly terms with Jonathan who was adopted as prospective Tory candidate for Thanet East in December 1972 (his cousin Timothy Aitken, a grandson of Lord Beaverbrook, later told me that it was he who had applied but through a mix-up Jonathan received a reply, went along and was selected).

Jonathan was duly elected at the February 1974 General Election and in January 1975 I wrote in the *Mail* Diary that Jonathan was supporting the candidature of Hugh for leadership of the Tory Party and hinted at his friendship with both Frasers – the article bore the headline Hugh and Mr A and Lady A – although by this time Antonia had moved on. Jonathan had lost her to actor Robert Stephens.

In August 1974 Robert, whose seven-year marriage to actress Maggie Smith had broken down, told me for a *Mail* Diary item why he had become close to Antonia, dubbed Lady Magnesia Freelove by *Private Eye*: 'I have been seeing Lady Antonia quite often on business. She has written a play which she is quite keen for me to direct and we have been discussing it.' It was a feeble excuse but, without evidence or acknowledgement of an affair, we had to swallow it and ran the item without comment.

Robert in turn was to lose Antonia to Harold Pinter and, in April 1975, acting on information received, the *Mail* Diary lead item carried the headline: 'Why Antonia is Delighted at the Success of Harold Pinter'. It went on to reveal that Antonia had seen the first night of Pinter's play *No Man's Land* at the Old Vic from a seat in the stalls bought by him, and that his wife Vivien Merchant, the mother of his sixteen-year old son, Daniel, had been absent. The cat was firmly out of the bag and events proceeded apace. On 25 July, a deeply hurt Vivien finally named Antonia in her divorce. Separation for the 'saintly' Hugh and Antonia followed.

As the news broke, I went to interview Robert Stephens who was appearing at the Open Air Theatre in Regent's Park in *A Midsummer Night's Dream*. At the end of the matinee before a sparse audience on a warm summer's day, I waited outside his dressing-room; after a decent interval, he opened the door in response to my knocking, towelling the sweat from his brow.

With total frankness, he told me the romance with Antonia had ended in March, after a year, when she confessed she was in love with Pinter. He added: 'I asked Antonia what was going on and she told me about Pinter. I had heard rumours and asked her about them. I stayed with Antonia and her family in Scotland for the New Year's holiday. But when we returned to London in January, I noticed a change. I am not surprised our affair finished. There was never any question of a marriage between Antonia and me.'

Back at my office on 29 July 1975, I telephoned Jonathan to find out more as I was writing the whole of page 3 of the *Daily Mail* about the situation. While discussing his four years with Antonia, he pointed me in the direction of several of her other admirers, namely Robert Stephens, ex-King Constantine of Greece, Rupert Lycett-Green and Viscount Lambton, all of whom featured in my report.

This led to a curious campaign against the *Mail*, editor David English, other senior executives and me, masterminded by *The Sunday Times* managing editor Mike Randall (a former *Daily Mail* editor) and joined by staunch Catholic Paul Johnson. *The Sunday Times* foolishly rang all executives at the *Mail* putting footling personal questions to them and leader writer Chris Nicholson replied memorably: 'No comment and my no comment is a no comment.'

Apart from his political ambitions, Jonathan continued to harbour hopes of a print journalistic career – he had a freelance contract with Yorkshire Television. To this end in 1972 he began working for Associated Newspapers, the deadly rivals of his family business, Beaverbrook Newspapers, which published the *Express* titles and the London *Evening Standard*. When he became involved with the *Standard*'s only competition, the now defunct *Evening News*, he told me boldly: 'I am in line to become editor.'

In fact Jonathan's journalistic career was on the wane and his ambitions, at least for the *News*, unachievable. On the romantic front, he was much more successful and among his conquests was Lord Ogmore's voluptuous daughter, Elizabeth, whose marriage to actor Richard Harris had ended in divorce in 1969; Earl Howe's beautiful but bird-brained youngest child, Lady Charlotte Curzon; and the Marquess of Reading's daughter, Lady Jackie Rufus-Isaacs, who had enjoyed a dalliance in the late Sixties with the Earl of Snowdon during his marriage to Princess Margaret.

Realizing also that he had to secure his financial future – great-uncle Lord Beaverbrook gave him nothing and Sir William left just £5,000 when he died in January 1964 – Jonathan forged ties with Saudi Arabian Prince Mohammed, an association which was to cost him dear two decades later.

In February 1977 word reached me that Carol Thatcher, whose mother Margaret had succeeded Ted Heath as Leader of the Opposition in February 1975 and was poised to become Prime Minister, had fallen in love with Jonathan. Then twenty-three and due to qualify that month as a solicitor, Carol was a keen skier and planned to spend six weeks celebrating the passing of her law exams in the Swiss resort of Verbier. I telephoned Jonathan and asked him what he intended to do with Carol, who was reputed still to be a virgin.

He told me that he was planning to fly to Switzerland and seduce her. When I suggested that this course of action would guarantee banishment from Mrs Thatcher's political inner circle and would also ensure that he was never given office in a Tory Government headed by her, he replied: 'On the contrary. Margaret will be eternally grateful to me. Just you see.'

The seduction duly took place, over a weekend, and Carol was head over heels in love. But Jonathan was not to be pinned down and was soon ignoring his conquest. In April

Mrs T took the pining Carol on an official visit to China and then she travelled on to Australia where she was put up in his eyrie in The Windsor Hotel in Melbourne by local entrepreneur Peter Janson. She worked for a while as a 'jilleroo' on a property in the Northern Territory and in September 1977 announced plans for a journalistic career. Two months later she was accepted as a £91 a week cadet trainee reporter on the *Sydney Morning Herald*.

Carol's seduction had exactly the opposite effect on Jonathan's plans. After Mrs Thatcher became the Prime Minister in May 1979, he found himself in the political doldrums, adding to his woes when he was quoted as saying that, such was Mrs T's appreciation of foreign affairs, she thought 'Sinai was the plural of Sinus'.

But by this time Jonathan had fallen in love. In June 1979 he telephoned me with the news that he planned to marry Lolicia Olivera Azucki, adding that she was born in Yugoslavia, held a Masters degree from Lausanne University and worked as a partner and adviser to a firm of discount brokers in Lausanne. He invited me to meet him at The Grosvenor House Hotel, close to his Upper Grosvenor Street, Mayfair, office, on 24 June to take delivery of a photograph of him with Lolicia, a shot of the couple relaxing on the beach in Marbella the previous year.

At Grosvenor House he elaborated on their relationship. 'I don't think I am putting it too highly when I say she saved my life,' he told me, dubbing her Florence of Arabia. They had met three and a half years earlier at a party in Geneva and, at Christmas 1977, when Jonathan became critically ill with typhoid in Abu Dhabi, he was nursed back to health by Lolicia. 'She has a good strong character and she keeps me in order,' he added.

They married on 16 November at St Margaret's, Westminster, with a reception at the House of Commons in The Speaker's State Apartments, courtesy of George Thomas (later Viscount Tonypandy). On their honeymoon, they visited his old friend, ex-President Richard Nixon, for dinner at his Californian estate beside the Pacific in San Clemente, before travelling on to Hawaii.

Their first children, twin daughters Alexandra and Victoria, were born in Lausanne prematurely in June 1980 and the family moved back to Jonathan's Connaught Square, Bayswater, house. This was sold a year later for £280,000; at the same time Penpy's Phillimore Gardens mansion went on the market for £1 million.

The Aitkens then moved to No. 8 Lord North Street, a large Georgian house close to the Houses of Parliament, which had been put on the market by the *Financial Times* for £250,000 (the newspaper had bought it from a director, the Earl of Drogheda, who had continued to live there). Later a property investment presented itself which Jonathan jumped at: across his courtyard at No. 8 was North Court, a block of fourteen flats with its own garden and Aitken bought it from Westminster Council for an estimated £300,000 – the original asking price had been £670,000. He annexed the gardens for his own use and put Penpy into the ground floor flat, a 30 yard walk from his own drawing-room.

Meanwhile, Jonathan's business career was booming thanks to Prince Mohammed of Saudi Arabia and his trusted lieutenant Said Mohammed Ayas (who rose to prominence when it was revealed that he paid for Aitken's notorious Ritz Hotel bill in Paris in September 1993 which formed part of his aborted libel action in 1997). Jonathan's Middle East connections also included Syrian-born Wafic Said, a confidant of Prince Mohammed, who became a major shareholder in Aitken Hume, the finance company co-founded by Jonathan and his cousin Timothy in 1981. And it was with Timothy that Jonathan took control of TV-am, resigning in February 1988 after it was disclosed that the Saudi Royal Family had an undisclosed £2.1 million stake in the company.

Jonathan's family was also growing. A son and heir, William, was born in September 1982, and Jonathan, then forty, took up marathon running, perhaps to compensate for his fading youth. By coincidence we were both staying at The Windsor in Melbourne, home to Carol Thatcher a decade earlier, for the Melbourne Cup in 1987. Seeing me kitted out for an early morning run around the city, Jonathan asked if he might join me. For the next four days we set off around the streets every morning (including a circuit of the famous Melbourne Cricket ground), with Jonathan timing the run on a stopwatch. After the third day he said as we got back to the hotel: 'Good, that was three minutes faster than our initial run!'

But success in Parliament was to elude him for another five years. When Mrs T was ousted in November 1990, promotion to John Major's Government seemed tantalizingly close. It came two years later when Jonathan, now perceived as a multimillionaire with solid Middle East connections, was appointed Minister for Defence Procurement and subsequently Chief Secretary to the Treasury in 1994, a position from which he resigned on 5 July 1995 to sue the *Guardian* and World in Action for libel 'with the sword of truth' over his business dealings with the Arabs and that thorny weekend at The Ritz, where the hotel's owner, Mohamed Al Fayed, had spotted Aitken in the lobby and noted that Ayas was also registered at his hotel. The implication was that improper deals were taking place between a Government minister and a Saudi commission man.

The case, which is estimated to have cost Jonathan a £2 million chunk of his fortune, came to a dramatic halt when he announced that he and Lolicia were divorcing; it was further revealed that Lolicia's claim that she had settled part of The Ritz bill could not have been true since she had been in Switzerland at the time, and the defence was able to produce an airline docket and car hire bill to prove her whereabouts.

Facing up to having to move out of North Court and the loss of her son's liberty, Penpy said: 'We have talked about prison. I have a deep groaning feeling inside about how horrible it is going to be for Jonathan. I have come to terms with it. I have to. It is just one of those possibilities. He is paying such a terrible price for such a small mistake, all over a silly hotel bill. Jonathan was a wonderful child, who grew up into a brilliant man who has many friends. He has made one terrible mistake, which he will regret for the rest of his life.'

Anna Ford, among others, noted that, when Victoria left Lord North Street for an appointment with the police, she was escorted, not by either of her parents, but her actress aunt, Maria. 'What does that say to you?' asked Anna.

But Penpy continued to defend Jonathan as a parent, saying: 'He feels desperate about her involvement. It is on his conscience because he is a devoted father who loves his children. They are his first concern. They are close to their grandmother, too. I am a port in the storm.'

Cast-iron Cad

JAMES HEWITT

I n a secret then shared by a very few, the Princess of
Wales, less than a decade after her fairytale marriage to
the Heir to the Throne in 1981, was in love; according to
my information, she was infatuated with an officer in the
Household Cavalry. My only problem was that I had to find
out her lover's identity.

There was one obvious candidate: eligible bachelor Major
David Waterhouse of the Life Guards was conveniently
stationed at Hyde Park Barracks in Knightsbridge, a short
walk from Diana's Kensington Palace apartment. David,
born in July 1956, was the son of a former Life Guards major
and nephew of the Duke of Marlborough. That he was close
to the Princess was well known. They had been photographed together on several occasions, the first time at a
David Bowie concert at Wembley in June 1987 (when he
was mistaken for another Diana escort, Philip Dunne), and
later, after an evening at the local Kensington High Street

cinema, when he had vaulted a barrier to escape the paparazzi.

When David, not considered by relatives to be a classic ladies' man, was seen frolicking with Diana after a dinner party at the Knightsbridge Mews house of high street newsagents heiress Kate Menzies in November 1987, the incident seemed to confirm most people's suspicions.

On Prince Charles' thirty-ninth birthday (he was on Duchy business in Devon and Cornwall) Diana had dined with Kate, often regarded as her closest friend, with Waterhouse in tow; on leaving, they had playfully fooled around in the cobbled mews outside, the major, behind the wheel of his car, pretended to ram the Princess. The scene was captured by freelance photographer Jason Fraser who was then asked by the tearful Princess for the film.

She told him: 'I must have that film – you don't know what this could do to me. I feel so trapped. Please, please.' He gave her the innocent spool and said later: 'She said thank you very much, got into her car without even saying goodbye. Her tears turned off as soon as I handed it over, she stopped blushing and her tone became clipped. The transformation was remarkable. I realized I had been taken for a ride.'

David (who had ridden in the Sovereign's Escort at the wedding of Andrew and Fergie at their personal request) had also been invited to Highgrove in August 1990 for a day with Diana, while Charles was in Majorca with his close friends Lord and Lady Romsey, and in January 1991 was sent to the Gulf as the Allied forces prepared for the invasion of Kuwait, commanding a £1.5 million Challenger tank. As a squadron leader, he was designated as a 'battle casualty reserve' and remained in constant contact with the Princess.

In fact Diana's mind was on the impending Gulf War,

brought about by Iraq's invasion of Kuwait and its subsequent plundering, but not so much on Dave Waterhouse.
The object of her affections, I was to discover, was another
Life Guards officer. His name was James Hewitt and he had
become friendly with the Princess when he was chosen in
the late eighties, while serving near Windsor Castle at
Combermere Barracks, to give her and Prince William riding
lessons. In 1989 Diana was photographed shyly presenting
James with the Captain and Subalterns Cup after he led his
team to victory in the Army polo competition at Tidworth,
during which he had taken a crashing fall, injuring his arm.
Prince William, then seven, had been the first over to him,
saying: 'James, James, are you all right?' Obviously by then
he had become close to the Princess and her children.

Carrot-haired Hewitt was the only son of a former Royal
Marine captain John Hewitt, and his mother Shirley ran a
riding school overlooking the River Exe at Topsham in
Devon. A few weeks short of his thirty-third birthday (which
fell on 30 April), Hewitt had apparently been engaged to
Emma Stewardson, whose family was involved with the
Loseley Park dairy business from its former stately home
headquarters near Guildford, and she telephoned me out of
the blue at my office in early 1991.

Emma, who was then twenty-nine, said she had been send-
ing Fortnum and Mason parcels to her great love James in
the Gulf but feared that she had lost him to the Princess of
Wales. She explained: 'We were meant to be having lunch
– I live very close to the main entrance to Highgrove – when
James telephoned and cancelled saying he was busy. The
next thing I knew, I was looking out of the window when
he drove past in his open TVR sports car into Highgrove
for a date with Diana. He's told me that she loves him and
I don't know what to believe. He's become obsessed by her,

Top: Post-Prince Andrew and pre-
daughter Tatiana, Koo Stark being
interviewed by me for the BBC.

Above: Doll and pins by Lichfield who
took this photograph in his Aubrey
Walk studio.

Right: Princess Michael of Kent
welcomes me to her Kensington Palace
terraced house, next door to the
Princess of Wales.

Prince Philip, bearskin askew, looks glumly at the world.

Sacha, Duchess of Abercorn, a close friend of Prince Philip, suitably dishy at the Theatre Royal, Drury Lane in 1969.

David Frost and his wife Lady Carina ('Keeks'); they married at Chelsea Registry Office in 1983.

Before she died in Los Angeles in 1994, Lynne had lost her looks and her figure.

'Frostie' and man-eater Lynne Frederick, his first wife.

Princess Margaret with film director Bryan Forbes and Peter Sellers in the 1960s, before Sellers married Lynne Frederick.

Above: PR man Max Clifford and star client Antonia de Sancha during the Mellor affair.

Above right: Palestinian-born Mona Bauwens – Mellor took a shine to her and bombarded her with telephone calls after their first meeting.

Gap-toothed Lothario David Mellor and his former wife, Judith, the mother of his two sons.

The Hon. William Shawcross and his third wife, Countess Olga Polizzi, daughter of Lord Forte, celebrate their 1993 marriage at The Waldorf.

Norman Lamont, before getting a black eye in a Bayswater mews scuffle with the boyfriend of Olga Polizzi.

Richard Burton and Elizabeth Taylor during their first marriage.

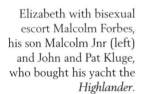

At $1 million a picture each, private jets were *de rigueur* for Liz and Burton.

Elizabeth with bisexual escort Malcolm Forbes, his son Malcolm Jnr (left) and John and Pat Kluge, who bought his yacht the *Highlander*.

Armand Hammer, mysterious boss
Occidental Oil and benefactor of
ince Charles, as well as patron of
n and Pat Kluge.

John and Pat Kluge step out in
their finery at another million-dollar
bash.

Patricia Rose (later Kluge) snuggles up to her first husband, Russell Gay, and friends.

Lady Magnesia Freelove, photographed by Lichfie during her marriage to th saintly Sir Hugh Fraser.

'Young Meteor' Jonathan Aitken with his Yugoslav-born wife, Lolicia.

'It was you,' says Carol Thatcher to her first love, Jonathan Aitken.

Charged with perjury, Jonathan Aitken faces an uncertain future; below, with twin daughter Victoria who has escaped prosecution over his aborted libel action.

Above left: Lovelorn Diana presents a polo cup to James Hewitt while Prince William looks on.

Above right: 'Cad' James Hewitt in full Life Guards fig.

The author meets 'cad' James Hewitt at Daphne's.

Marcia Williams, later
Lady Falkender, private
and political secretary to
Harold Wilson.

'Goodbye' – Harold
Wilson bids farewell to
No. 10 in March 1976.

Happily married – Earl and Countess Spencer.

Happy families. Charles and Victoria with daughters Kitty, Eliza and Katya.

Outside the Cape Town divorce court – Countess Spencer and her estranged husband's ex-mistress Chantal Colopy.

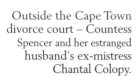

Cartoonist Sally Ann Lasson spilled the beans over her Paris tryst with Earl Spencer.

Lord White – Gordy – and his American-born wife Victoria on the polo field.

totally infatuated with the Princess. I'm convinced they're having an affair and that it's been going on for a long time.' According to Emma, who had been working for an estate agent in Gloucester, she had been engaged for four years to Millfield-educated Hewitt, like his rival Charles a four-handicap polo player. But both his parents – who had recently separated – denied this, telling me in a call that they would have surely known had their son intended to marry.

Perhaps Emma had been looking to sell her story, but I made no financial offer and, in any case, the facts of an affair with Diana would have been extremely difficult to prove. Instead, after ferreting around in Royal circles for a few days, on 25 February 1991 I published a lead item in the *Mail* Diary revealing the concern Diana felt over Hewitt's partici-pation in the battle. With the item I printed the photograph of Diana, accompanied by Wills (Prince William), presenting the polo trophy to James. Emma had informed me of the existence of the snap. On the Monday morning that the item was published, I received a telephone call at my desk through the switchboard. The anonymous caller had a clipped, upper-class voice and I would have guessed that he was an Army officer. 'Your story about James Hewitt and Diana this morning,' he said. 'Bingo! You've hit the jackpot. It's undying love.'

Less than three weeks later I heard more about James. He had been performing deeds of derring-do in the Gulf and was in daily contact with the Princess. On Friday 15 March I was confident enough to lead the *Mail* Diary with the news that Diana was tuning into her wireless at 5am to hear news of the war and had been receiving first-hand reports from Hewitt. He had been based in Sennelager, Germany, after a stint at Hyde Park Barracks and had left Germany for the

Gulf on Boxing Day 1990 as commander of the Life Guards A Squadron.

The latest news for Diana had been that Hewitt, in his own Challenger tank, had led a 100-hour dash from Saudi Arabia on the commencement of the ground war and was now sitting astride the Kuwait to Basra road in charge of the Royal Scots battle group. He had helped wipe out 300 Iraqi tanks, several hundred artillery weapons and had taken more than 8,000 prisoners. Another fact came my way: Hewitt had been receiving letters and gifts from a lady who signed herself 'Julia' or plain 'D'. The benefactress, I was quickly informed, was none other than the Princess of Wales.

Now we know from Diana herself that her marriage to Charles was effectively over after an official visit to Portugal in February 1987. The spectre of Camilla Parker Bowles loomed too large for the Princess and, on their return from Portugal, she moved Charles into his dressing-room at Highgrove and they never shared a bed again.

The story has changed so many times that it is unclear when Hewitt actually saw the Princess for the first time. For instance, when he attempted to sell his side of things in October 1994, he put the fateful meeting as being in 1989 and claimed: 'For three years I was the man in her life. We were deeply in love. She even contemplated leaving Charles.' He added she was trapped in a loveless marriage, claimed he had given Diana her first orgasm and boasted that she had showered the modestly paid officer with gifts of clothes. That latter part, at least, is accurate. In the infamous Squidgygate Tape, when a New Year's Eve 1989 telephone conversation between Diana at Sandringham and James Gilbey on his mobile was intercepted by a retired Abingdon bank manager, Cyril Reenan, Diana tells Gilbey: 'Well I've decked people out in my time. Gilbey says: Who did you deck out? Not too many, I hope. Diana replies: James Hewitt. Entirely dressed him from head to foot, that man. Cost me quite a bit. Gilbey: I bet he did. At your expense? Diana: Yeah. Gilbey: What, he didn't even pay you to do it? Diana: No.'

But these days the 'official' version from Hewitt is that they met in 1987 after she had stopped sleeping with the Prince of Wales. According to Hewitt the fateful meeting took place as she approached her twenty-sixth birthday (she was born on 1 July 1961) and he has claimed: 'We were introduced by a mutual friend at a party and started talking about riding. She told me how she had lost her nerve a long time ago and had always thought about trying to regain it. I said that I thought I could help and I started giving her lessons. Naturally I had to clear our meeting through the Army and we began by riding together weekly in Hyde Park. It was all very surreptitious. Obviously there were protection officers about but we looked like any other couple riding in the park.

'When I first knew her I was as unaware as anyone else who wasn't a close friend, how unhappy she was. I found her interesting and intriguing. She is great fun with a good sense of humour. She enjoyed riding because I am a very good instructor.'

As Diana's affair with Hewitt progressed without publicity or fanfare, her family still refused to believe that she was having an extra-marital physical relationship. Her father, Johnny Spencer, remained loyal to his youngest daughter to his dying day and to any inquiry from friends, during the tortuous years of her dalliance, on the matter of lovers he would only reply: 'My daughter Diana has only ever slept with one man, and that is her husband. In any case, the trouble with her, she tells me, is that she doesn't like sex.'

Diana's brother Charles also stoutly defended his sister's honour and said to me in February 1993: 'Hand on heart, I can tell you that Diana has only slept with one man in twelve years, has only slept, in fact, with one man in her life. She's not interested in that at all. I know that Prince Charles is the only man she has ever slept with. James Gilbey would have loved to have slept with her, but I can assure you he has not and nor has James Hewitt.'

When the tape was finally published – in August 1992 – part of it was suppressed. That part contained this revealing exchange: It's just like sort of . . . Gilbey says. Playing with yourself? Diana suggests. What? says Gilbey. I said it's just like – Diana says: Playing with yourself, Gilbey finishes the sentence. Yes, she says. Not quite as nice. Not quite as nice, he says. I haven't played with myself actually, not for forty-eight hours. Not for a full forty-eight hours.

From the tape it would appear that Hewitt's idyllic days, if not exactly over, were numbered but he claimed the relationship went on into 1991 and was effectively ended by my disclosure and the Gulf War. When he finally returned to Britain from his base at Sennelager, the grand passion was truly over. Still a captain, although referring to himself as major, Hewitt was having problems with the exams which would guarantee him promotion. He failed them miserably the first time and, by the spring of 1993, he had failed them again. He left the Army clutching a £40,000 cheque and a pension of around £5,400 a year after tax, reflecting almost seventeen years' service, telling me: 'It's not the end of the world. I've enjoyed my Army life very much and will miss it. I would consider almost any job.'

At the same time as all this was going on, Emma Stewardson was also suffering. Her engagement to twenty-six-year-old Wiltshire antiques dealer, Mark Kimberley (he was five years her junior), was called off and he said to me: 'We became engaged a few months ago, but it didn't work out.' It was at this time that Emma revealed her knowledge of James and Diana and said to me: 'I believe James first met the Princess of Wales when he was involved with the ceremonial at her wedding. The riding lessons and all that came later.' Without Diana and short of cash, Hewitt reacted like a caged animal. He had secrets to sell but was unable to realize his assets. He wanted to be seen as a gentleman, but there was no cash in that. He took up with chubby-cheeked journalist Anna Pasternak, who offered him a profitable way out. The deal was that she would write a Mills and Boon-style book of Hewitt's passion for the Princess which might or might not be regarded as the official version of their affair. Pasternak would claim that he had nothing to do with it; Hewitt would not be seen to benefit financially. Either way, there was around £300,000 in it and Hewitt was hungry.

Princess in Love, by Anna Pasternak, educated at St Paul's Girls' School and Oxford and a great niece of Boris Pasternak, the author of *Doctor Zhivago*, was a syrupy publication which began serialization in the *Daily Express* in March 1994, regurgitating all Hewitt's claims about his affair with Diana. Yet other newspapers 'revealed' that Hewitt had tried to sell them the story and had, eighteen months previously, enlisted the help of PR Max Clifford. 'The Major' hoped for a £3 million deal, but was to be disappointed. Although vague on dates, the book was finally published in October 1994 and suggested that Hewitt's relationship with Diana began in late 1986 or early 1987. Soon he was publicly boasting of a five- rather than a three-year affair. It was all very confusing to historians on the trail of the story. In the *Daily Mail* Paul Johnson wrote an article headed: 'The Death of Honour'. That said it all.

Around the time of publication Hewitt, somewhat mysteriously, managed to buy Eversfield Manor, a Georgian
mansion at Bratton Clovelly on the edge of Dartmoor near
Okehampton. It had been put on the market, with 18 acres,
for £245,000 by Judge Bruce Markham-David, who had
lived in the Grade Two listed property for eighteen years. He
moved into the six-bedroom, three-bathroom house, which
boasted a stable block, with his sister Syra and mother Shirley who had decided to quit her £170,000 village house near
Topsham. There – if we are to believe the former officer's
account of the 'five-year' affair – according to Anna Pasternak, Diana had spent many a night in a rickety bed with
Hewitt, washing up in the kitchen and acting like an ordinary
housewife.

The relationship was finally given validity when Diana
bared her soul in a Panorama interview with Martin Bashir,
broadcast in November 1995. He asked her: Another book
that was published recently concerned a Mr James Hewitt,
in which he claimed to have had a very close relationship
with you, from about 1989 I think. What was the nature of
your relationship?

Diana: He was a great friend of mine at a very difficult,
yet another difficult time, and he was always there to support me, and I was absolutely devastated when this book
appeared, because I trusted him, and because again, I worried
about the reaction of my children. And, yes, there was factual evidence in the book, but a lot of it comes from another
world, didn't equate to what happened.

Bashir: Were you unfaithful?

Diana: Yes. I adored him. Yes, I was in love with him.
But I was very let down. There was a lot of fantasy in the
book, and it was very distressing for me that a friend of
mine, who I had trusted, made money out of me. I really

minded about that. And he'd rung me up ten days before it had arrived in the bookshops to tell me there was nothing to worry about, and I believed him, stupidly.

The Hewitt I know is a vain fool, given to wild fantasies. His plummy voice makes a mockery of his middle-class background. I finally met him in October 1996 when he introduced himself to me at a cocktail party at Daphne's restaurant in Chelsea. I commiserated with him over a reported collision at a roundabout near his Devon home, which was not his fault, and his subsequent arrest for drink-driving. He seemed friendly and grateful. But in February 1997 I found this meeting, which he had solicited, translated into a *Mirror* exposé about him trying to pull a girl (who was also a *Mirror* reporter) he claimed to have met at the same Chelsea party where I was 'bothering' him. What a buffoon.

In his own defence, Hewitt had often called himself a 'cad', which few would disagree with. His efforts to turn his Devon house into a profitable riding centre have failed and even his mother's sale of an article for around £40,000 to *Hello!* in August 1996 barely covered the cost of repairs to the roof of the manor. The death of Diana on 30 August 1997 saw Hewitt in his true light, yet again. Barely six weeks later he was trying to sell another book about his 'five-year' affair with the Princess, while publicly stating: 'The world has lost a very special person who touched the hearts of millions. I would like to say how much I loved and admired her.'

When his sometime fiancée, Italian beauty Anna Ferretti, was caught out attempting to sell sixty-two letters he had received from Diana (as the writer the copyright remained with her, publication would have been impossible) to the *Mirror* for £150,000 in March, first it was claimed that

Hewitt had burned 'between fifty and seventy' intimate messages sent to him by the Princess. Within days it was reported that he wanted £5 million for them (even though he had supposedly destroyed them) and had even, at one stage, contemplated selling the cache to Dodi Fayed, whose brief summer 1997 romance with Diana ended in the tragic Paris car crash.

The *Mirror* returned the letters, which Hewitt claimed had been stolen from his Devon house by Ferretti (by now an ex-fiancée) to Kensington Palace and Hewitt took legal action to regain possession, saying: 'They cannot keep items stolen from my house. It is true that, after Diana and I ended our relationship, she asked me to burn the letters but I couldn't. They are part of my life. They mean so much to me. I have been asked numerous times to sell them but always refused.'

Now said to be on his uppers with a bank overdraft and standing orders unpaid, Hewitt has a goldmine which he is unable to profit from, simply because of the copyright problem. That is a situation which Diana, who eventually came to despise her foppish former lover, would surely have found amusing.

'PM Ruined my Christmas' says Diarist

HAROLD WILSON

'**W**rits are the Oscars of my profession', I once famously told an interviewer, but the news from No. 10 Downing Street on the morning of 17 December 1975 was distinctly unwelcome. Harold Wilson was about to become the first incumbent Prime Minister in history to issue a writ for libel against a journalist – me.

Some hours earlier around 1.8 million copies of the *Daily Mail* had been printed and distributed with my Diary lead concerning Harold (who had started his second term as Labour premier in March 1974) and his intention to resign in the New Year from No. 10. He objected to my scoop, it transpired, because of one word in the headline and a sentence in the body of the nine-paragraph text. After a telephone consultation with the PM, his solicitors, D. J. Freeman and Co., duly hand-delivered a letter to my office with the following demands: 'The proprietors and editor of the *Daily Mail* and Mr Dempster should publish a full retraction and apology tomorrow. They should make a statement in open court in terms which will be agreed. They will undertake not to publish the same, or similar, alleged libels. And they should suggest a suitable sum of money in addition to paying Mr Wilson's costs.'

In time-honoured fashion, the *Daily Mail* editor David English and the proprietors ignored these demands and our legal department simply sent a note back to D. J. Freeman and Co., acknowledging their letter. There the matter lay while I was ordered to produce a memorandum detailing the circumstances behind the item, which, in any case, had been fully checked for legality the previous evening by our night lawyer.

What on earth was all the fuss about? The headline, taken from the copy by my sub-editor Peter Donnelly (a Labour supporter, as it happened), included the word 'tired' in quotation marks. Harold had had to deal with the alcoholic antics of his Deputy Leader George Brown and the repeated references to his behaviour in *Private Eye* as being 'tired and emotional', a convenient euphemism for drunkenness which has been much bandied about since.

Thus Wilson quickly came to the conclusion I was labelling him an alcoholic. But what really got to him was the article's sixth paragraph which read: 'Friends have noticed that since he returned to power his drinking consumption has increased and he had become something of a late-night brandy addict.'

This information, along with an (unused) snippet that Harold also enjoyed a Churchillian penchant for a cigar while he was always photographed puffing a proletarian pipe, came from the *Mail*'s political editor, the late Anthony Shrimsley, and could not be faulted but it added to the sting that the Prime Minister would be leaving office early for reasons other than political.

What D. J. Freeman and I could not have known was that Wilson already had made up his mind to resign in March 1976, as my item predicted, and had informed only his likely successor and Foreign Secretary, James Callaghan, of his decision, along with his wife Mary and his political secretary Lady Falkender (Marcia Williams).

Thus an inspired, but hitherto insignificant, Diary item suddenly became of national importance, thanks to Harold's excitable reaction and I quickly found myself headline news.

Both the BBC and ITN included in their evening television bulletins the story of the libel writ. When I made my way by taxi, attired in a dinner-jacket, around 7pm that day to the City for a pre-Christmas dinner at the Haberdasher's Hall, my heart sank as we went down Fleet Street and the *Evening Standard* (then owned by the rival *Daily Express*) billboards proclaimed: 'Prime Minister to Sue over Gossip.' That was the work of my long-time antagonist Charles Wintour, then editor of the *Standard*. It was misplaced revenge but served only to add to my mystique.

The story had started, as so much did in the *Daily Mail*, in the upstairs bar of our local, the Harrow, to which Peter Donnelly and I repaired with a colleague or two between finishing the column, putting it to bed (this was in the days of hot metal typesetting) and getting a pull of the page from the compositors.

That week Roly Orton, the *Mail's* long-time Leicester corr (short for correspondent, Roly was known as Orton of Leicester), sought me out on a visit to The Street of Shame for a drink.

A bluff, genial, old-fashioned journalist, Roly had toiled in the provincial vineyards for years and supplemented his income from local newspapers by feeding items to the nationals, in his case, the *Daily Mail*. He was a highly reliable source and the story he had for me was arresting.

Roly had been at a dinner in Leicester attended by James Callaghan. After the meal, according to Roly, an expansive Callaghan had regaled a few people gathered at the bar with the news that Harold Wilson had told him he intended to resign. He would reach the milestone age of sixty in March 1976, by when he would have served ninety-two months during his two periods as Prime Minister, a record for a Labour leader.

I questioned Roly closely about the circumstances of the Callaghan visit to Leicester, and how he was when he passed on the information, and quickly became convinced that I had a great exclusive; it was the sort of story, known as 'a flier', which sat well in the Diary of a newspaper rather than on the front page, where it would have needed full corroboration and quotes, unlikely, in the circumstances, to come from No. 10 hostile to the Tory press.

I talked it over with my deputy, Richard Lay, who had introduced me to Roly Orton, and we decided to go with the information after confirming that Callaghan had indeed been at the dinner. A call to Tony Shrimsley added substance to the item and it was duly printed, but with far-reaching consequences that could not have been foretold.

I did not have a pleasant Christmas or New Year, with the threatened Wilson litigation hanging over me. As the winter waned, by early March there was not news for me of a comforting nature. As spring approached, Wilson seemed more secure than ever at No. 10 and it appeared that I had goofed. Newspapers are unforgiving places for mistakes and the full weight of the Prime Minister's ire was fairly placed on my shoulders, and my shoulders alone. I was not very happy.

Then in mid-March my luck turned. My old friend Princess Margaret, whose romance with Roddy Llewellyn (unemployed and seventeen years her junior) I had broken in the *Mail*, was to be divorced after less than sixteen years of marriage to the photographer Earl of Snowdon. I got wind of this and was preparing to splash with the news when my colleague John Edwards dashed into my office on the main editorial floor of the *Mail*. 'Wilson's resigned,' he told me breathlessly. 'You were right. You're off the hook.' It was 16 March, a day I will never forget, and the following morning the *Mail*, along with every other Fleet Street publication, led its front page with the tumultuous news, relegating the Princess's divorce to an inside page.

For many years Harold's reasons for quitting while seemingly at the height of his powers and influence were to remain a mystery. One theory was that he was being blackmailed by the KGB, who had photographs of him in bed with a tart in Moscow on a visit to the Soviet capital in the early Sixties, and another that he announced his resignation to spare the Royal Family's blushes, thus banishing Margaret's embarrassing news. Neither was anywhere near the truth. In fact, Wilson was tired, but in the conventional sense, and the Alzheimer's, which was to kill him eventually in May 1995, was already beginning to take hold.

Quite simply, he sought a retirement with his devoted wife Mary near their elder son, Robin, a don at Oxford just as Harold had been in his younger days. Naturally, I then heard no more from Wilson or D. J. Freeman and the writ went into abeyance, much to my gratification and that of the *Mail*'s legal team. Harold had been ill-advised in his action, which had only served to confer a measure of heroism on the *Mail* Diary and his legal assault was born of a certain antipathy to me which stemmed from the dealings of his political and private secretary, Marcia Williams, her brother Tony Field, and a seedy Wolverhampton 'businessman' called Ronald Milhench.

In April 1974 the *Mail* had revealed that Harold Wilson's signature had been forged on a letter to aid a £1 million land speculation deal. The letter, on Wilson's personal House of Commons writing-paper, was addressed to Milhench, then thirty-two, and a Jack the Lad widower who lived in Wolverhampton with his two children. Their mother, Kathleen, had mysteriously drowned, leaving Ronnie to collect £40,000 in insurance. Officially an insurance broker, Ronnie had been involved for more than a year in the purchase and attempted re-sale of 95 acres of industrial redevelopment land at Ince-in-Makerfield, Lancashire. In February 1973 he had contracted to buy the site for £951,000 from the Field family who had paid just £175,606 for the land six years earlier.

It was a sordid story which reflected badly on Harold Wilson's private office at No. 10. Linked to the 'slag heap affair', as it came to be known, were Harold's eminence grise, Marcia Williams, her brother Tony, sister Peggy, Philip Moore-Clague (an Isle of Man property dealer) and undischarged bankrupt, Victor Harper.

Through his company, Todaro Ltd, Milhench paid £10,000 an acre for land which had cost Mr Field's company less than £1,000 an acre. In March 1971 Mr Field got planning permission for the land and Ince Council spent £180,000 of ratepayers' money building an access road to the site. In February 1973 Mr Field finally found someone to buy the land – Ronald Milhench, who said he was dabbling in property for the first time. It was in his desperation to get a bank loan to complete the purchase of the land and sell at a profit that Milhench, who had worked for the Sun Life Assurance Company of Canada after leaving the British

Army as a staff sergeant, forged Harold Wilson's signature.

Milhench then used the letter bearing the signature, and which referred to the land deal, to try to sting £25,000 from the *Daily Mail*. The forgery fooled no one and in November 1974 Milhench was sentenced to three years in prison after admitting forging a document, attempting to obtain £25,000 from the *Mail*, attempting to obtain a further £10,000 from another company and, curiously, possessing a sten gun and two loaded pistols in a public place without authority.

On behalf of the *Mail* and its editor David English, I had formed a relationship in 1973 with Milhench and had visited his home, Whitegates Lodge, in Richmond Road, Wolverhampton. As he settled in jail, it was put on the market for £30,000, double what he had paid for the seven-bedroom property three years earlier.

Somehow Harold put two and two together, made five, and got it into his mind that I was behind the exposé which had embarrassed him and Marcia, hence his alacrity to sue me for libel in December 1975. As it turned out, it was a grave error by a brilliant man, but understandable in the circumstances. Marcia was his crutch and ran his private office (giving rise to unfounded rumours about their relationship), and her position was being undermined by the *Mail*. One of his first reactions had been to create her a Life Peeress in 1974 when she became Baroness Falkender; this led to her being lampooned in *Private Eye* as Lady Forkbender.

Nor did it help matters that Marcia had been having an affair with Walter Terry, the *Mail*'s political editor from 1971 to 1973 and a married man, by whom she had borne two sons. All in all, Wilson became convinced of my involvement and sought to punish me.

It was another five years before I met Marcia and became a close friend of hers. By then Wilson and Mary were in an

Oxford property owned by publisher and former Labour MP, Robert Maxwell, who had promised to 'look after' the former PM. One saw the occasional forlorn photograph in newspapers of Harold – now Lord Wilson of Rievaulx – standing at a bus stop with Mary in an Oxford suburb making their way into the centre of town.

Marcia – who was much reviled for her so-called Lavender List of Honours marking Harold's resignation – was living in a mews house near Bryanston Square, north of Oxford Street, and employed her sister Peggy as her secretary. One of the mooted honours, thrown out by the honours committee, had been a peerage for the highly controversial Jimmy Goldsmith, which was watered down to a knighthood. The quid pro quo, it was said, was a directorship of his food companies for Marcia after Wilson's resignation, but that never came about and, up to his death in 1997, Goldsmith denied the arrangement. Nevertheless Marcia prospered, bringing up her sons, Timothy and Daniel, without the aid of Walter Terry, who remained with his wife Mavis and their two children.

Marcia and I finally met at a black-tie charity dinner in Greenwich which began with a boat ride from Charing Cross pier down the Thames. After dinner I suggested to Marcia that we visit Annabel's and there we bumped into my old friend Taki Theodoracopulos (Taki, who pens the *Spectator* column, High Life), who was delighted to meet Marcia at last. With his date for the evening, Emma Soames, we moved on to Taki's South Kensington house and eventually I dropped Marcia back at her place around dawn.

We kept up the friendship, meeting occasionally, and in 1981 she invited me to the House of Lords where she was giving lunch for two mutual friends, Joan, Lady Hodge, and former RAF Battle of Britain hero Dennis Wilde. I arrived before Marcia's other guests and was shown by a liveried flunkey to an alcove where she was seated and invited to order a drink. No sooner had it been served than there was a flurry in the room. Harold Wilson had arrived and made his way unerringly to Marcia's side. He sat down, briefly acknowledged me after Marcia made the introduction, saying: 'Harold, you know Nigel, don't you?' and began perusing the menu while Marcia made it as plain as she could that he was not invited to stay for lunch.

'The trouble with Harold,' she said to me as the unwelcome guest lit his pipe, 'is that he still thinks I work for him.' Shortly afterwards Joan and Dennis arrived and, when a waiter took our order, Harold added his. Looks passed between Marcia and the waiter, who asked somewhat pointedly: 'Shall I add another chair to your table, Milady?' She nodded.

As we sat down to lunch, Harold was served with soup and began eating while the rest of us attempted to have a conversation. He had said little and, while showing no embarrassment at my presence, steadfastly refused to look at me. But help was at hand and midway through his soup, his wife Mary appeared in the Lords dining-room and made for her husband. 'What are you doing here, Harold,' she demanded. 'You are meant to be catching a train to Huddersfield.' And before he could finish his soup, she whisked him away, much to Marcia's relief.

'He seeks me out and there's nothing I can do about it,' Marcia told us after Harold's chair and table setting had been removed, allowing us to enjoy the rest of lunch. 'He suddenly appears, sits down and refuses to believe that he isn't welcome.'

When Harold was buried on 6 June 1995 in the Isles of Scilly, where he had a bungalow for many years and had once given a Press conference on the beach while on a summer holiday, Marcia walked behind the coffin to its interment beside Mary. Ironically, even in death there was the faintest hint of discord, but from another quarter. Harold was buried alongside a boatman from the Scillies, Lloyd Hicks. Asked if the late Mr Hicks would have joined in the many tributes to Lord Wilson, a former friend replied: 'He couldn't stand him.'

The Rise and Fall of Champagne Charlie

CHARLES SPENCER

F riday mornings are not the most exciting of times in a national daily newspaper, what with the weekend beckoning and given the different composition of Saturday editions in Fleet Street, now an area of major circulation battles.

Friday 1 February 1991 was no different as I sat in my office overlooking Kensington Church Street, until my telephone rang sometime before noon and I found the Princess of Wales's brother, Viscount Althorp (later Earl Spencer), on the other end. After exchanging pleasantries – we had been friends for eight years – he said: 'Do you want a scoop?' The story Charles Althorp had to tell me was not a pretty one. But he said he felt he was about to be betrayed by an old girlfriend and wanted to strike first. He informed me that Sally Ann Lasson, a writer and cartoonist whom I also knew well, was planning to sell her story of an affair with him for £5,000 to the *News of the World* and he felt if it appeared in the *Daily Mail* on the Saturday it might spike her guns.

Charles, then twenty-six and five years younger than Sally Ann, explained that the previous March, with his six-month old marriage to former model Victoria Lockwood in difficulties (she had another man, he claimed), he had taken former flame Sally Ann to Paris for a tryst.

Charles and Sally, who was very attractive and skinny but chain-smoked madly, had been lovers before he met Victoria in 1989 and proposed to her after a whirlwind romance. They had married in September 1989 at Althorp, the family's 8,500 acre Northamptonshire estate with Charles's old Eton and Oxford friend Darius Guppy as best man.

'I have told my wife everything and we've agreed to put this behind us,' Charles said to me. 'I have caused Victoria more grief than I would wish her to have in a lifetime with me and I accept full responsibility for the folly of my actions. Sally Ann was extremely jealous when I married Victoria. She had made it clear that she always wanted to be my wife.'

Knowing Sally Ann's marriage to songwriter Dominic King had ended in divorce, it was to her, as an older woman in the same boat, that he turned in March 1990 when his relationship with Victoria (then twenty-four) entered what he called 'an extremely unpleasant patch'.

He went on: 'It was a foolish move in retrospect. But with a failed marriage behind her, I thought she was in a position to give advice. One afternoon when I sincerely thought my marriage was over, I asked her to come to Paris with me and we had our second one-night stand. The experience so sickened me that I did not stay a second night and returned to London.'

Charles added that Sally Ann began telephoning him after he got back and they eventually had a meeting in Mayfair in July 1990. He told me she was 'furious' when he disclosed to her that his marriage was, by then, becoming increasingly happy (Victoria was pregnant with their first child). 'She demanded I make her my mistress. After that there were more calls but from mid-August until December I did not hear from her.'

When Sally Ann contacted him in December, she informed Charles that some workmen at her new Knightsbridge apartment had run off with her money. 'She was desperate for £5,000 immediately. She wondered if I could help raise it. I was totally unreceptive to this request. Then early last month (January 1991) she told me she was suicidal because her father was ill and she had financial problems. I heard nothing more until Thursday when she informed me she had sold a story about me.'

Many Fleet Street observers felt that Charles had shot himself in the foot by going public with his confession and Sally Ann, who was thirty-one and worldly wise, made the most of the move. My scoop enabled the *News of the World* to print her allegations, since they now had the corroboration they had sought and Spencer even gave the Sunday newspaper a statement which read:

'In September 1986 I had a one-night stand with Ms Lasson but did not see her for eighteen months after that. During this time, she on several occasions telephoned me with obsessive messages. In late 1988 I saw Ms Lasson again twice but no further physical relations took place. Once or twice we spoke on the telephone, but it was not until May 1989 that I saw her again, just prior to meeting my wife. Ms Lasson was extremely jealous when I got engaged and married to Victoria in a whirlwind romance and she made it clear that she had always wanted to be my wife – a thought that had never occurred to me.

'In February and March 1990 my wife and I went through an extremely messy patch in our marriage, and a separation seemed possible. I talked to Ms Lasson about my marital problems – a foolish move in retrospect but, with a failed marriage behind her, I thought she might be in a position to give advice.

'On the afternoon of 28 March, after a particularly unpleasant series of quarrels with my wife, I rang up Ms Lasson and asked if she would come to Paris with me for two days.

'I sincerely thought at the time my marriage was over. We went to Paris and had our second one-night stand, four years after the first. The experience so sickened me that I did not stay the second night in Paris but returned to London, eager to patch up my marriage. This my wife and I were able to do to such an extent that today, a month after the birth of our first child, we are deeply in love.

'Our marriage is the most important thing in our lives. Ms Lasson began behaving in an irrational way. She demanded at the beginning of July 1990 that I go round to her flat to discuss the whole matter. I went and explained how my marriage was increasingly happy. She was furious, demanding she be my mistress and that I "keep" her, as her funds were, according to her, running low.'

Sally Ann, a close friend of Lorna Bunn, the third wife of the 'Master of Hickstead' Douglas Bunn (and who committed suicide in January 1995), was suitably outraged by this statement and replied: 'I don't know what he means by saying the experience of a night with me in Paris so sickened him that he returned to London. I won't be tacky and go into the detail of sex but I will say that when we made love on that occasion in Paris he was more romantic and sensual than I had ever known him.

'How can making love in Paris not be romantic? But, as his sombre wedding pictures show, he's not the most demonstrative of men. He has a problem with being tactile, sensual and touchy.

'Sickened is a tacky word to use about a weekend you arrange with another woman in Paris. Unless he means that's how his wife felt when he confessed to her two days ago. The first time we made love was not a one-night stand – it was at the end of a long friendship [she had interviewed him in the summer of 1985 for the A Life In The Day feature in *The Sunday Times Magazine*]. I deny ever leaving what he calls obsessive messages on his answering machine. He has rung me far more than I have ever called him.

'We had lunch together on New Year's Eve 1988, which is hardly the time when you meet a casual girlfriend, and we had been speaking on and off since November. I never said I wanted to be his wife. When he was droning on about his marriage problems in October of last year I said: "If you're so unhappy with her why didn't you marry me?" And he said: "Because I would have made you unhappy."

'I wanted him to use his title, wealth and position to spread a little philanthropy. I wanted to make him a cross between the Earl of Shaftesbury – the peer who saved little boys from being sent up chimneys – and the stylish Cary Grant. He told me: "I know you want me to be a Cary Grant – but I just can't be."'

And Sally Ann had the last word when she revealed that the last words she heard from him were in a telephone call when he told her: 'You'll be the loser – you're stuffed.'

The Paris tryst with Sally Ann and the unhappiness in his marriage became known to sister Diana, who felt she had an antidote. She had been lent Necker, the British Virgin island owned by her friend Richard Branson, who normally rents out the 74 acre paradise for £10,000 a day. He bought the island for £200,000 in 1976 and has spent an estimated £13 million on it.

Diana invited Charles and Victoria to share the freebie family holiday (flights were included) along with her mother Frances and sisters Sarah and Jane and their children, who would be company for William and Harry: all were on their school holidays. By any account the magic of the Caribbean worked wonders for the Althorps and, on her return, Victoria confided she was pregnant. Almost nine months later Lady Kitty was born, sprouting the tell-tale Spencer red hair, a fact which Victoria apparently relayed in a telephone call to her former boyfriend from her hospital bed.

Victoria was five months pregnant with twins when her father-in-law, Earl Spencer, died at the end of March 1992. Charles had become increasingly distant from his father because of Spencer's remarriage to Barbara Cartland's daughter, Raine, the previous wife of the Earl of Dartmouth. Among the nicknames Charles gave his stepmother were 'Acid' Raine and when his father married her in 1976 he used to chant along with his sister Diana: 'Raine, Raine, go away and don't come back another day.'

Diana was skiing at Lech, in Austria, with the Prince of Wales and their two sons when she heard of her father's death. She had only left England a couple of days before after being assured that Spencer, who was hospitalized with pneumonia, was making a good recovery. Leaving the 'boys' to continue their holiday, Charles and Diana flew back to England for the funeral at Althorp on 1 April.

That the couple were estranged was common knowledge but the manner of their arrival at Althorp was significant. While Diana was driven to the Northamptonshire estate for the service, Charles was flown in by a Royal Flight Wessex helicopter. His brother-in-law did not seem best pleased to see him and, back at historic Althorp House after the service, the Prince of Wales sought out the new Earl Spencer, who told me:

'He asked if he could talk to me alone and we went into the Library. He didn't seem to appreciate how I felt at my loss. We had just buried my father and he kept telling me how lucky I was to have inherited so young. He said: "Gosh you are lucky. I wish I'd inherited when I was young. My parents don't trust me with anything." The problem with Prince Charles is the way he was brought up.'

With that, the Prince of Wales returned to Highgrove in his helicopter while Diana remained at Althorp for a champagne buffet. Charles Spencer, who was to inherit the bulk of his father's £88 million estate, spent little time in eradicating all traces of Raine from Althorp. First he sent her packing with a curt note and then he removed the portrait she had commissioned of herself at the cost of £7,500 in bright pink from pride of place on the Staircase Salon among Gainsboroughs and Van Dycks. It had been painted by one Carlos Sancha.

'I found the inventory and went round looking for what had vanished,' said Spencer. 'There were around 200 items which had been sold to pay for the renovation of Althorp. I remember most of them well – whenever I went up and down Bond Street I used to see them in antique dealers' windows. I reckon Raine sold paintings, furniture and family papers worth around £16 million although she didn't get that sort of money. I was told that £3 million had been spent on Althorp – there was gold leaf everywhere and all the floors had been carpeted. It was like a bordello.'

According to legend, Charles and Diana put all Raine's possessions into black dustbin liners and, on Friday 3 April,

Raine visited the mansion for the last time to remove her goods – and the portrait which was destined for the West Yorkshire home of her eldest son, William, Viscount Lewisham.

Charles remained with Victoria in The Falconry, their 19th-century house in the park, until after the birth in July at the Lindo Wing of St Mary's, Paddington, of daughters, Eliza Victoria, who weighed 4 pounds 15 ounces and Katya Amelia, who was 5 pounds 4 ounces. As the daughters of an earl, they carried, like their elder sister Kitty, the courtesy title of Lady and the burgeoning family moved into Althorp, which boasted seventy bedrooms, in the autumn.

But having children was not a panacea to patching up an ailing marriage and Charles was to say much later, when he was trying to divorce Victoria in South Africa: 'Deep down, I've always known my marriage was a mismatch, a terrible error, an impulsive whim that I compounded by adding more and more children to my family. Part of the problem was having an immature wife, one who is incapable of dealing with a husband of strong character, except by going on an alcohol binge or resorting to drugs.'

Life and the future appeared rosy for Charles when I met him at The Connaught Hotel for lunch in the restaurant on Friday 11 February 1983. Then achieving fame as the brother-in-law of the Prince of Wales, Charles had just left Eton and had secured a place at Magdalen College, Oxford. An Eton contemporary, Jamie Palumbo, son of the future Arts Council chairman Lord Palumbo, had telephoned me suggesting a meeting. He added: 'I feel that Charles will need help and you are the person to provide it.' Charles was a shy, reserved young man while Palumbo, who drove a Ferrari and enjoyed the fruits of a moneyed background, made the running, explaining that his friend would be increasingly in the public eye and should have a sage Fleet Street figure to turn to. I immediately saw the attractions of such an arrangement and did my best to convince Althorp that he could trust me as a friend. Before leaving The Connaught, we exchanged telephone numbers.

After he went up to Oxford in September 1983, lunches together in London were to follow – usually at Wilton's – and among the complaints Diana's brother had about his early press were that newspapers insisted on labelling him 'Champagne Charlie'. He told me, after a false report appeared that bouncers at Boodle's, an Oxford nightclub, had accused him of not paying for his champagne: 'It's most unfair – I'm hardworking, rarely go to parties at Oxford and never drink champagne. I hate the stuff.'

Among the stories that the *Mail* Diary carried with his compliance was the identity of his first girlfriend, pert Oxford secretarial student Lucy Stiles. But the romance fizzled out in May because, Charles told me: 'We both were worried that it was leading into an early marriage.'

In any case Charles had started a course at the London Stock Exchange, working for the Queen's brokers, Rowe and Pitman, prior to spending three months driving across North America. He intended to return to London in August, where he was living in his mother's flat in Victoria, before heading for his first year at Magdalen.

Settling into Oxford, he bought his first home, a £210,000 house in Notting Hill which he was advised to sell in November 1984 because police warned him he could be a target of the IRA and the property was vulnerable to attack. In fact the only attack on Althorp came from a different sort of Irishman, Dublin-born Bob Geldof who discovered that the viscount was paying court to his longstanding girlfriend, Paula Yates. One bunch of flowers too many was delivered to the Geldof house, also in Notting Hill and, when Althorp followed them up with a personal visit, he was met by a volley of abuse from Geldof who warned him to 'keep away'. Charles later claimed to me that the relationship with flirtatious Paula had been a physical one and clearly Geldof's reaction seemed to bear that out.

But despite my advice and help, bad publicity seemed to haunt Charles. He was reproved for visiting the Hippodrome, described as a 'nightclub full of homosexuals' and swigging champagne as 'grossly fat American drag star Divine performed on stage', and was then accused of being involved in a brawl in a London restaurant with a party of twenty. It was claimed that he offered a bottle of champagne (that drink again) to the first person to debag a quite blameless patron, DJ Tony Blackburn. Then there was the matter of being fined for speeding at 94mph on the M1.

'I can't seem to do anything right,' moaned Charles to me but his interest in the Hippodrome was sparked by a burgeoning friendship with Peter Stringfellow, who also entertained Althorp at his nearby Covent Garden club, Stringfellows, a haunt for the demi-monde.

It was 'Stringy' who was Charles's star guest at his twenty-first birthday party in May 1985 at Spencer House, the ancestral family London home in St James's overlooking Green Park. Despite a guest list which included the Prince of Wales and Diana among the 320 invitees, Stringfellow jumped on to a chair in the ornate dining-room after midnight and announced the engagement of his own twenty-two-year-old daughter Karen to twenty-five-year-old Mark Young, the manager of the Hippodrome. The birthday boy took the interruption in good heart and guests, who included most members of the Royal Family, sank 300 bottles of Mercier champagne. The bash, which set Charles back around

£50,000 and ended at 6am, also featured Simon the Robot, transvestite singer Ruby, his backing group Ebony and the Hippodrome's gay compere Bradley, a motley crew with whom Spencer would find little in common today.

If Charles, then busy as a roving correspondent for American network giant NBC, blames the start of his misfortunes on his choice of wife, his choice of best man, Eton and Oxford schoolfriend Darius Guppy, was to cause him as much anguish in years to come. Prior to his marriage to Victoria in September 1989 at the Church of St Mary the Virgin, Great Brington, where generations of Spencers repose in a vault, he had confided in me: 'I am absolutely sure I am doing the right thing. We have only known each other six weeks, but she's the girl for me.' Charles and Diana came with William and Harry (a pageboy), there was a reception for 450 following the marriage ceremony conducted by the Archbishop of Canterbury, Dr Robert Runcie, at Althorp House and it was, perhaps, a portent when rain bucketed down as the happy couple left the church in a 1760's horse-drawn carriage, the same one in which Earl Spencer's mother and father had been driven to the 1937 Coronation. The deluge did little for the bride's silk and antique gold lace wedding-dress, trimmed with old Russian sable. Once inside Althorp, Guppy disappeared and, when it came to the best man's speech, he was nowhere to be seen. Eventually a search party traced him to a loo, but the moment had passed.

Almost two years later Charles Althorp returned the compliment when Darius (who had also read history at Magdalen at the same time as Charles) married model Patricia Holder at Chelsea register office, with Victoria carrying baby Kitty. Just two weeks earlier, Althorp had provided £250,000 towards Guppy's bail of £500,000, after the impossibly handsome Jermyn Street jeweller had been charged with fraud involving £1.8 million. This followed his claim in March 1990 that he had been robbed, along with partner Benedict Marsh, of gems worth £1.25 million when gunmen burst in on them in their New York hotel.

I had heard about their company, Inca Gemstones, when Ben Marsh's father, Peter, a leading figure in the advertising world in the Sixties and Seventies and once married to Coronation Street star, Pat Phoenix, contacted me. 'Any chance of a mention in your column?' he asked. 'My son Ben and his friend Darius Guppy have started this company and it would give them a boost if you could write something in the *Mail* Diary.' It was a small favour which I was happy to grant but little did I – or Charles Althorp – realize where it would all end up.

In February 1993 Guppy and Marsh were found guilty of conspiring to defraud a Lloyd's of London insurance syndicate between August 1989 and April 1990, of conspiring to steal from Inca Gemstones between August 1989 and January 1991, and of conspiring to commit false accounting between April 1990 and January 1991. The pair were jailed for five years and each fined £533,000 (to be paid within six months or they would face a further three years in jail). Guppy's heavily pregnant wife (daughter Isabella was born in May) ran up to him, kissed him and said: 'I love you, darling.' The trial, at Snaresbrook Crown Court, had lasted fifty-eight days.

While his friend languished in jail (he was eventually released from Ford Open prison in February 1996 after agreeing to repay £200,000 to creditors) Charles, now the 9th Earl Spencer, was blessed with a son and heir, Louis Frederick, in March 1994. In keeping with Spencer's love of cricket he made Allan Lamb, the South African-born

Northamptonshire and England cricketer, a godfather to his lad, who carried the courtesy title of Viscount Althorp. Known as 'Lamby', Allan and his wife Lindsay lived a few miles from Althorp and the cricketer occasionally turned out for Spencer's team who played on the estate.

It was at Lamby's fortieth birthday party barbecue in June 1994, in the garden of his Northamptonshire home, that nemesis struck for Spencer in the shape of mother of two Chantal Collopy. Married to a Cape Town clothing manufacturer, Don Collopy, Chantal was also at the birthday bash with her husband (Lindsay Lamb was godmother to her younger son, Callum) – and so was Earl Spencer. Don feared the worst when he saw Spencer monopolizing an obviously flattered Chantal, who said later: 'Charles came over to me in Allan's kitchen and asked: "Chantal, are you happily married?" I replied: "Aren't we all supposed to be?" We carried on chatting for about ten minutes and he mentioned he'd had an affair before. I said I lived a million miles away and I had two children. I didn't really want to strike a close friendship. But we met up again another night when a whole group of us went to Annabel's club in London. He whispered in my ear that he had found out where I was staying and was going to call me at 11am. He called briefly in the morning and then in the afternoon – all the chaps had gone to watch cricket at Lord's – and he asked me if he could ring me in South Africa and I gave him my number. I was terribly flattered by his attention. When he called me the first time, Don was there and didn't seem worried. Charles called me every day that week and I think it was after that I started falling in love with him. I was not a young girl – I'd just turned thirty-five – and to have these feelings really confused me.'

Don and Chantal finally separated in June 1996, five

months after Spencer had moved his wife and children to Cape Town, claiming he wanted to give Victoria – who had been treated at Farm Place, Ockley, Surrey, for bulimia and drug addiction – 'breathing space, to see in which direction they're going.' But two months later he announced that his six-year marriage was over and, while Victoria moved to a luxurious bungalow with the children and nanny, Charles remained in the house he had bought for £625,000 in Constantia, in the shadow of Table Mountain.

Don finally learned of the affair when he taped his wife's telephone calls and confronted her with the evidence. He moved to a bachelor pad in the Hout Bay area of Cape Town, overlooking the ocean, and he and Chantal shared their two sons. In the meantime Spencer was juggling his own visiting rights – he used to have his kids at weekends – with trysts with Chantal. But it was an idyll that was not destined to last. I heard, and reported in the *Mail* Diary, that on a pre-Christmas visit to Althorp, Chantal was unceremoniously dumped. She said: 'He telephoned me in a terrible state, he was an emotional wreck. He said: "Chantal, I've realized that I am never going to accept your children and I never want anyone else's children running around here. I have to end this relationship." I was devastated. He was always using my children as a means of getting in and out of the relationship. He had only recently told me in a letter how much he cared for me and how he wanted to spend the rest of his life with me. You can imagine how confusing it was.'

Chantal retreated to the £46,000 house Charles had bought her, the middle in a row of three next to the official Cape Town residence of President Nelson Mandela, and attempted to put her life back together again. She told me: 'Charles says coming to South Africa has been wonderful for the children and I've noticed how they've blossomed in the Cape. But they'll all go back eventually and be educated in England. Where Victoria is, so are the children and where the children are, so is Charles. Louis is down for Eton and will go to boarding-school when he is eight or so.'

In March 1997 Charles was host in Constantia to his sister Diana. They had fallen out over Diana's hopes of having a country retreat on the Althorp estate and had hardly spoken for two years after Charles had gone back on his word offering her a house, citing the probable breach of security and invasion of their privacy. She was long divorced from the Prince of Wales but I was reminded of a conversation I had had with Charles in February 1993 when he explained her future. On her official separation from Charles he told me: 'Diana will continue doing her public duties and, when two years are up, she'll stop and get a divorce. She'll drop out of public duties. As for a financial settlement, she's not a greedy person. She'll lead a classic Sloaney life. She's looking for someone to love her, she wants more children. A title or someone famous is not necessary. I imagine Prince William will make a very good King. He's very grown up for his age, and while children always get spoilt, he's got a very moulded character.

'As for the Royal Family, it's all over as far as she's concerned. There's no vengeance, remarkably, possibly because our parents went through a particularly unpleasant divorce and subsequent unhappy life. Prince Charles has been amazed at the lack of vengeance. Diana is reorganizing her life, but at the moment she's not 100 per cent there. As I see it, and I am a big fan of Diana's, she's not as half as manipulative as she's painted out to be. She's shrewd rather than manipulative. If Ken Wharfe, her detective, tells her the photographers want a particular angle, she does it.

'As for the marriage, she feels she did her best. She feels uncertain about the future of the Monarchy. She wants William to be King but Charles is not certain he wants to be King. Diana offered to step down when they separated, but the Queen was desperate for her to stay. Diana is very determined not to let people down. The Queen and Prince Philip have been very supportive.'

Apart from an official photo call opportunity with President Mandela, Diana enjoyed a Press free week in the Cape with her brother (as he mentioned at her funeral). One day he took her to lunch at Meerlust, a 17th-century winery half an hour from Cape Town, owned by bachelor Hannes Myburgh. Charles had become friendly with Hannes after making a documentary on him and Meerlust, which produces arguably the best red wine in South Africa. A posse of security men was employed to keep photographers at bay and Charles and Diana eventually escaped by the back gate after a peaceful day.

In March 1997 I revealed that Charles had fallen for Josie Borain, perhaps South Africa's most famous fashion model. Josie, a year older than Spencer, had been in New York where she had been the muse of Calvin Klein (it was reputed that her multimillion dollar contract stipulated just 100 days work a year). Born in Johannesburg, she had returned to South Africa and settled in the Cape following an abortive romance with former Springbok motorcross champion Grant Maben. After they separated she produced his son, Peter Raven Maben Borain, who almost died following the birth, and said: 'Relationships and me just don't seem to work. Grant and I were both very impulsive and I've jumped into lots of boiling water without first dipping my toe.'

Josie moved into a stone and thatch property in Hout Bay, a ten-minute drive from Constantia, and was quickly accepted as Spencer's new love. On the August 1997 night that Diana and Dodi Fayed were killed in the car crash in Paris, Josie was the first – and only – person allowed into Spencer's compound. She accompanied the earl to the Westminster Abbey funeral service for his beloved sister where his address, which pointedly accused the Press of hunting down his sister and killing her, and threw down a challenge to the Royal Family over the upbringing of William and Harry, was greeted by applause both inside and outside the Abbey.

If Spencer's love–hate relationship with the Press had reached a new low, worse was to come two months later when he made the most foolish move of his adult life, suing Victoria for divorce in Cape Town. Far from being compliant, Victoria stunned her estranged husband by turning up in court with, of all people, his former mistress, Chantal Collopy, and then, through counsel, accused Charles of having a dozen affairs while she was at Farm Place.

The case was a fiasco for the earl who was portrayed as a very rich man, with a family fortune in excess of £100 million, while Victoria was struggling to survive on a £5,000 overdraft. Spencer soon caved in and Victoria accepted a £2.1 million divorce package, later suing her London solicitors for another six figure sum because she felt she had been badly advised. Had the divorce taken place in London, she estimated she would have received many more millions.

If Spencer thought the court proceedings – his attempts to muzzle the South African Press failed miserably and Fleet Street sent down its finest to cover the shenanigans – were the nadir, worse was to follow. Josie left him in the New Year after months of rumblings about their romance. She told me in January about reports that she had been dumped in favour of documentary film-maker Bonny Rodini: 'Not true. I have not been dumped. I do the dumping in relationships. As for Bonny, I understand she and Charles might be working on some film project together.'

In February Charles put his Constantia home, described as a 'Gentleman's residence', on the market for £1 million and shortly afterwards Josie, who had briefly worked as fashion editor for *Fair Lady*, the leading South African magazine, announced that she was returning to her native Johannesburg with her fifteen-month-old son. By an extraordinary twist, Chantal and Don, who had divorced in November 1996, had become reconciled. Now living in Durban, while Chantal remained in Cape Town, Don telephoned his ex twice a day and she said: 'Don and I want to make our family whole again. I would like us to get remarried, but at the moment we are just talking about living together. It's early days yet. There's a lot to sort out. Don's pride was hurt and things were very bitter between us.'

And dropped too was the legal action between Collopy and Spencer. Don had sued the earl for £22,000 for 'alienation of affection', while Spencer had countersued for £66,000 for defamation and invasion of privacy. Both agreed to end the litigation.

In April Victoria was herself back in England, looking for schools for Kitty and the twins while Spencer presented a gloomy image as he fought off accusations of trading on his sister's memory. He had been vilified for charging rubberneckers £9.50 each to visit Althorp and walk around the island where Diana is buried (visitors were first welcomed in July and August 1998); later, 15,000 people paid £39.50 each for an al fresco concert in the deer park at Althorp on 27 June in aid of Diana's Memorial Fund.

'He's taken after his grandfather, who was an unhappy man, living at Althorp and hating the world – he even once yanked a cigar from the mouth of Winston Churchill in The Library,' says a family friend. 'I fear Charles is permanently destined for sadness.'

Third Degree Battery Man

GORDON WHITE

The late night call from a journalist friend in Aspen, Colorado, concerned an inquiry about a rich Englishman who had spent the previous night – that of Christmas Day 1991 as it happened – in the local jail. He had been charged with third degree battery after his girlfriend had been admitted to the Aspen Valley Hospital with bad bruising. She claimed that her assailant was her host in Aspen. The man in jail was called Vincent Gordon Lindsay White. The caller from Colorado asked if I knew anyone of that name.

I did indeed, but the person was better known to me and to the public as Lord White of Hull, a 6 foot 5 inches tall Yorkshireman who was due to celebrate his sixty-ninth birthday in May. For seven years he had been involved with Californian model Victoria Tucker, who was forty years his junior, and they had flown by private jet to Aspen from their Beverly Hills home to stay in the house of their old friend, sometime actor George Hamilton, which they had rented for two weeks for £60,000. Although he had been knighted in 1979 and ennobled in Margaret Thatcher's resignation honours list in December 1990, 'Gordy' White had been booked under his original name and after, a night in the Aspen jail, released on £500 bail. If convicted he faced two years in jail or the equivalent of a £2,500 fine.

Precisely what had happened? My research turned up the following scenario, confirmed several years later by the Life Peer's younger daughter, Sita White, who, admittedly, bore no love for Victoria. While in Aspen, Victoria had left the house every morning to go skiing but reappeared in the afternoon with few visible signs of having taken to the slopes. White had become highly suspicious, not least because he knew that an old flame of Victoria's, Tom O'Gara, whose family ran an Ohio company which made all the armoured vehicles for American Presidents, had also taken a house in Aspen for the Festive Season. Victoria had left Gordy a year or so earlier but had eventually returned to his side. When he discovered her movements, a quarrel ensued and she was admitted to hospital with severe bruising and accused White of attacking her, hence his arrest by Officer Tom Glidden at Hamilton's house on 435 North Second Street.

When White left jail, he found that Victoria had fled and had gone to Vail, another Colorado skiing resort three hours away, and was taking no calls from White, who denied any involvement in her bruising. He told me: 'I do not beat women. I never touched her.' They were eventually reconciled at White's Los Angeles mansion in the New Year after Victoria received a cheque from White for $200,000 in anticipation of their marriage. She informed Aspen police that her injuries (more than twenty contusions) had been caused by a fall on the Aspen slopes – the Black Run is used for World Cup competitions. She added that any previous statement she might have made to the authorities had been while she was sedated and dosed with painkillers. Due to re-appear before an Aspen court on 28 January, White was relieved when all charges were duly dropped.

The couple married in Bermuda in July 1992 and when I caught up with Gordy there he told me: 'We've been together for seven years. I've proposed three times and Victoria has finally accepted.' Forgotten were his words when the subject of marriage to her had previously cropped up: 'Never marry a young girl – they want babies.'

I had become close to White, variously known as Gordy and The White Knight, some thirteen years earlier in none too promising circumstances. He had come to my annual picnic in a car park on the Thursday – Gold Cup Day – of Royal Ascot and was incandescent with rage. Pointing his finger at me as rain washed away the carefully laid out picnic he said: 'You wrote that I am James Hanson's acolyte. Look it up. I'm no one's acolyte. I'm his equal partner.'

By now White, the financier who built up the American arm of the Hanson conglomerate which was at one stage valued in excess of £14 billion, was taking refuge in the front of the catering truck as the heavens continued to empty and the dressed cold salmon, neatly laid on a trestle table beside the van, looked like swimming away on its own. Gordy had been brought to the picnic – to which a couple of dozen friends were invited annually – by property man David Olivestone and it was clear the lofty Yorkshireman was intent on seeking me out. In the circumstances I felt it wise to apologize for the unintended slur and as, the paths of the car park became rivers, we sipped champagne and ate what food we could, provided by Scott's, the Mount Street restaurant.

It had been a strange year for White. He had moved to a junior suite in the Pierre Hotel, New York, with just $3,500 to build a new fortune after the Stock Market crash of 1973, accompanied by his second wife, actress Virginia North (who was said to hail from North Virginia) and their son, Lucas, who was born in October 1974. He was knighted in the Queen's Birthday Honours List (Hanson had already received his 'K' in his pal Harold Wilson's resignation honours list in 1976) and had lost his wife to Brazilian playboy, Roberto Shorto. She told me for a Diary lead in August 1979: 'Gordon and I have been discussing a divorce for six or nine months and have done it in Bermuda, where we have been resident. We lived together for ten years, it is totally amicable and we remain dear, dear friends.'

From Venezuela, where he was visiting his first wife, Elizabeth, and their daughters, Carolina and Sita, Gordy said: 'I hope things work out for Virginia. It [the divorce] has been a tragic thing which has been pending for some time. She's a marvellous girl, and we are very, very fond of each other. Lucas will remain with her.'

Roberto Shorto was the most unsuitable man to run away with, as Virginia was later to discover (she eventually took out a court order barring him from harassing her). The brother of Denise Thyssen, then the wife of Baron Heini Thyssen, who owned the world's finest private art collection, Shorto traded as an art dealer and lived in Chelsea. He had a two-year-old daughter, Maxine, by his marriage to Sir James Goldsmith's niece Dido, which had been dissolved in 1978. Staying with the Thyssens in Marbella, Roberto added: 'My friendship with Virginia has nothing to do with her divorce. She has been staying here with me for a few days and we shall be going back to London when we can get on a plane.'

Although resident in Bermuda for tax purposes – he had even bought a burial plot on the island in 1972 to comply with regulations – White lived in California where his intimate coterie of friends was headed by George Hamilton and David Niven Jnr, known as 'Niv' and the matinee idol's elder son. He was accompanied everywhere by the American Edward Collins, who was a director of Hanson in America and acted as White's *chef de cabinet*, a role he had once fulfilled for Huntingdon Hartford, the libidinous heir to the A&P (Atlantic and Pacific) grocery stores fortune. While Hanson (Gordy had met him in the Fifties through James's elder brother Bill, a noted equestrian who had died young from cancer) looked after the business in Britain from swish offices in Belgravia, White preferred the relaxed life in the States and rented a house for £30,000 a month in 128 acres of Angelo Drive, Beverly Hills, where the Union Jack was hoisted daily. In New York he owned one floor of a discreet block on the corner of Madison Avenue and 72nd Street. As part of his divorce settlement he bought Virginia a £150,000 Chelsea apartment.

Born in May 1923, Gordy had one failing as he entered the dating game following his divorce: he was going deaf and told me he could no longer hear what anyone said in night clubs. He called women 'armpieces' and found Hollywood stars irresistible – in the Fifties, when he was an actors' agent, he had escorted Jean Simmons, while Hanson was engaged for 354 days to Audrey Hepburn – and at Royal Ascot in 1981 he arrived with his new squeeze, veteran actress Mary Tyler Moore, recently divorced from her husband Grant Tinker with an estimated £4 million settlement. He was also linked with Elizabeth Taylor, Linda Evans (of Dynasty fame), model Cheryl Tiegs and even Joan Collins but they were red-herrings.

Racing was one of Gordy's abiding passions and he had two dozen horses in training in England which ran with varying degrees of success. His colt, Hardgreen, had finished 6th in the 1979 Epsom Derby and his greatest Turf success was to win the Group One Champion Stakes at Newmarket with Legal Case. And it was through racing that Gordy eventually made his successful play for a Life Peerage, putting him on a par with his partner James Hanson. Through the Hanson Group's Ever Ready battery subsidiary, he entered into a three-year deal to sponsor the Epsom Derby from 1984 at a cost of £2 million. It gained him a marquee beside the winning-post – where Hollywood stars and battery salesmen were entertained to lunch and tea – the opportunity to present the Derby trophy and, most importantly, have tea with the Queen and other members of the Royal Family. A peerage for an outlay of a couple of million (it was increased to £5 million when renewed for a further three years in 1987) and the chance to have some fun appeared cheap at the price.

But while the likes of Dyan Cannon, Valerie Perrine, Roger Moore, George Hamilton and Michael and Shakira Caine were flown into Epsom by Air Hanson's Sikorsky helicopters for the big day, the reward seemed as distant and unlikely as ever as Victoria became the regular lady in White's life. He bought the *Galu*, a 176 foot yacht which he based in the Mediterranean and chartered out at £74,000 a week (it was on sale for £8.5 million) and a £4 million house in Tite Street, Chelsea, to ease the burden of staying in London but marriage to Victoria in the 1980s seemed a long way off. He even told me in betting parlance: 'I'll give you 33/1 against it happening.' But no one then could have foreseen the incident in Aspen and Gordy's reaction to the situation.

Following the wedding in 1992, Gordy and Victoria moved into a $4 million Bel Air house called White Cliff, with fine British and European hunting and racing oils. The *Galu* was chartered out for a year for around £3 million to Aussie media magnate Kerry Packer; the Tite Street mansion was sold and the couple settled down to sedate married life in California where Victoria, then a successful model, had started off as the girlfriend of local restaurateur, Joe Stallini. Royal Ascot and the Derby seemed a million years ago and even the Park Avenue apartment was disposed of.

In early August 1995 Gordy was in London with Victoria having spent six weeks in Britain. He was feeling unwell. It was decided to fly home to California but on the private jet he suffered breathing problems and, rather than land, he continued the journey, breathing from an oxygen container. When he reached Los Angeles, he was taken by ambulance to the UCLA Hospital and his former wife, Virginia, and their son, Lucas, then twenty, flew to his bedside. He became unconscious and never recovered, dying on 23 August. He was seventy-two.

Victoria inherited an estimated £16.5 million, including £6.5 million cash, the Bel Air house and its contents, as well as another property in Santa Barbara. On New Year's Eve 1996 she married Tom O'Gara at his 980-acre beef farm outside Sun Valley, Idaho, much to the fury of Gordy's daughters, Sita and Carolina. His son, Lucas, who inherited the bulk of White's £70 million fortune, refused to be drawn into any controversy. Victoria sold the Bel Air property – where O'Gara was to be found just five months after Gordy's death – and in October last year had a son, Jack, shortly after their application for a £2 million, eleven-room Park Avenue duplex was turned down.

Back in California, where she lives in a $1 million house

given to her by her late father, Sita White remains horrified by her former step-mother and says simply: 'It's all terribly distressing to say the least.'

'I Khan't go on
with it'

SITA WHITE

I was lunching at Royal Ascot on Wednesday 17 June
1992, in the box of leading owner-breeder Robert Sang-
ster and his wife Sue, which overlooks the Paddock, when
I heard the news. The Hon Sita White, the younger daughter
of Lord White of Hull, had just given birth to a daughter,
Tyrian, weighing 7 pounds 2 ounces, in Cedars Sinai hospital
in Los Angeles where her father had bought her a $950,000
property in West Hollywood.

There was only one problem: Sita was unmarried and we
all knew there was no chance of marriage to the baby's
father. He was, she told family and friends, Imran Khan,
then the Pakistan cricket captain and a man with political
aspirations. She had fallen in love with Imran – they had
met at Tramp nightclub in Jermyn Street – a few months
after her marriage to Italian photographer Francesco Venturi
had collapsed. Sita and Venturi had married in September
1986; they had a £50,000 wedding reception dinner-dance

for 500 at the Duke of York's Barracks in Chelsea and Sita's father had presented her with a £500,000 house in The Boltons, South Kensington.

In social circles it was no secret that Sita (then twenty-four) was infatuated with Imran, whose paramours had included artist Emma Sergeant, Lady Lisa Campbell (sister of Earl Cawdor and descended from Macbeth) and Viscount Linley's longstanding girlfriend, Susannah Constantine. At 10am one day in 1987, I had spotted them near my house in South Kensington in Sita's blue convertible BMW at the traffic lights on the junction of Fulham Road. Rather tellingly, Imran was still wearing a dinner-jacket and Sita a party frock. They had obviously spent the night together and were heading back to his Chelsea eyrie half a mile away. The romance escalated when Imran invited Sita to his home in Pakistan and she was naturally devastated when their relationship finished after 'several months'.

Sita said that Imran ended their relationship by writing to her, explaining that he was still in love with Emma Sergeant, daughter of financial journalist Sir Patrick Sergeant. But after moving to California in 1990, Sita asked Imran to father her child; he agreed and spent one 'final' night with her in the autumn of 1991 at her home. She said, after I revealed in the *Mail on Saturday*, 20 May 1995, that Imran was the father: 'It wasn't ugly, it was beautiful, I know it sounds incredible and taken out of context of how I felt about him, people may think it's a bit tacky. But it's not. Imran had wanted a boy. He was disappointed when I told him we had a baby girl. But I adore her. Imran and I are not close any more. Tyrian was the image of him from the moment she was born. She is a lovely little thing and I am wild about her.'

But three years earlier there was a concerted effort by Sita and her father to ignore the fact that the baby's father was Imran Khan, and Gordy White, who did not approve of inter-racial marriages, told me: 'I'm not proud that my grand-child's father is a Pakistani.' But he was supportive of Sita and when she first informed him she was pregnant he said: 'Well, love, don't worry, this is the Nineties. Single mothers are OK.' She stayed with her father until the eighth month of the pregnancy but when he visited her in hospital after the birth he took one look at the baby and told Sita: 'This is not a white child,' and walked out without another word.

So what went wrong? According to Imran, Sita became jealous when he fell in love with Jemima Goldsmith, daugh-ter of Gordy White's close friend Sir James Goldsmith. They married in May 1995 in Paris (Imran was forty-two, Jemima twenty-one), followed by a civil ceremony in Richmond, Surrey, and a dinner reception for 250 at the Goldsmith home, Ormeley Lodge, in nearby Ham Common. Although he was in London, Lord White had turned down the invi-tation and told me pointedly: 'I do not know Mr Imran Khan. I have never met him.'

Three months later White was dead, leaving a shattered Sita to cope on her own with her myriad problems, but bolstered by a trust fund of around £1.9 million and annual income of £100,000. However, she felt slighted that Imran still refused to acknowledge that he was Tyrian's father and had explored the possibility of bringing paternity proceed-ings against him in California.

In October 1996 (two months before Jemima had her first child, son Sulaiman) Sita married actor-model Alan Mar-shall, thirty-two, in LA, with her brother Lucas giving her away in a white wedding, but her situation was not improved when Marshall moved out after less than a year and divorce proceedings were instigated. And when Imran, now retired from cricket and attempting to become a political force in his native country, was forced to deny paternity after his main political opponent, Nawaz Sharif (destined to become Prime Minister) of the Moslem League, accused him of having an illegitimate daughter, Sita blew a fuse and expressed fury at the statement Imran issued: 'My alleged scandal with Sita White is the brainchild of Nawaz Sharif and his disciples as I have never been involved in any affair of any sort with the lady.'

Her response was instantaneous – driven by the news that he had accused her of selling the story to a London newspaper for £60,000 – and she rang from California to tell me: 'How dare he deny he's her father? I've never demanded a penny in child support and he's never paid anything. I'm going to do whatever it takes to prove him guilty.'

In private, Imran explained that it was a capital offence to have an illegitimate child in Pakistan and he dare not admit anything, even though he and his Movement for Justice party had failed to win a single seat in the February 1997 general election. His back was clearly up against the wall and all Jemima would say was: 'I know all about this. It's nothing to do with me.' Meanwhile, as Imran resolutely refused to visit California to submit to a blood test, Sita told me: 'I'll bet $20 million he's the father of Tyrian.'

In August 1997 a Californian court officially declared Imran the father of Sita's child and Sita, whose outgoings for Tyrian totalled $76,000 to that date, said: 'He challenged me and called me a liar, so I had no alternative but to take legal action to establish paternity of Tyrian. Is she to go for the rest of her life not knowing who her father is?' And when Imran arrived in London following the death of his father-in-law, Sir James, he dared not leave Ormeley Lodge as a writ server for Sita was positioned outside the Georgian mansion. It seemed only a matter of time before the net would finally close in on Khan and Sita appeared to be holding all the aces.

Then, on 12 November 1997, on the eve of the St John's, Smith Square, memorial service for James Goldsmith, Sita had a change of heart and telephoned me from Hollywood, asking me to pass on a message to Imran and Jemima. She told me: 'I'm dropping the action. I can't go on. Imran has called me four times this week and explained his problems. The suit alleging paternity comes up soon in London and Imran wants me to drop the action. I have decided to do so. If he wants to participate in the future of Tyrian, the door is always open.'

For the first time Imran spoke on the matter and said to me: 'I'm glad it's all over. The sins you commit are between you and your God. The friendship between Sita and me was personal but my political opponents have been making capital of this.' What helped change Sita's mind? Imran had finally spoken to Tyrian and Sita said: 'After they talked, she turned to me and said: Daddy sounds a bit like the Lion King [in the animated Disney film]. I really don't think I need speak to him any more.'

Fergie and her American Friends

SARAH FERGUSON

I t was late Sunday afternoon, 16 March 1986, when word
reached me from a Royal source and friend of Sarah Ferguson that the announcement of her engagement to Prince
Andrew was imminent. Just six months earlier she had been
madly in love with widower Paddy McNally, twenty-two
years her senior, and had given him an ultimatum while
staying at the Villa d'Este on the shores of Lake Como for
the Italian Grand Prix at Monza in the second weekend of
September: 'Marry me or else,' she said, telling him he had
five days to make up his mind. The father of two teenage
boys, Sean and Rollo, McNally had politely declined.

And now she was about to become a member of the Royal
Family.

The Queen and Prince Philip had returned to Britain on
Friday the 14th from a tour of New Zealand and Australia
and Fergie's father, Major Ronald Ferguson, was due to leave
for Australia the following Wednesday to see his eldest

daughter, Jane, and her son, Seamus. Perhaps most telling was the fact that Sarah's mother, Susan Barrantes, was due to arrive in London on the Monday from the Argentine. Needless to say the Buckingham Palace Press Office had been unhelpful – they prefer to announce engagements themselves – but I stuck my neck out and convinced the editor that the couple were engaged and it would become official during the week.

Just to cover myself I put in a telephone call to Paddy in Geneva. He and his first wife, the late Anne Downing, who had died of cancer in 1980 (she was nicknamed Twist because her knickers were always in one), were old friends and I told him bluntly that the front page of the *Daily Mail* in the morning would be carrying my exclusive of the engagement of his former flame and the Queen's second son. 'Will I get egg all over my face?' I asked him. He paused for a moment or two and in an act of great comradeship allayed my fears. 'You'll be all right.' I was mightily relieved. On Monday 17 March, the *Daily Mail* front page, with a Nigel Dempster Royal Exclusive by-line, carried the banner headline: 'Engaged!' with a second deck stating: 'They will announce it to the world officially this week.' My reasoning was simple: Ronald Ferguson wanted to be around for comment and it could not wait much longer lest it interfere with the Queen's sixtieth birthday celebrations on 21 April. As Ferguson was at Heathrow catching his flight to Sydney, Buckingham Palace made the official announcement, confirming my scoop. Andrew, who had just completed a two-year tour of duty as the helicopter pilot on the frigate HMS *Brazen*, gave his fiancée a large oval-shaped ruby, to match her hair, surrounded by a cluster of ten diamonds and set in a band of 18 carat yellow and white gold.

No one could have been more delighted than Paddy, the

youngest of four sons of Doctor Patrick McNally (a former RAF Wing Commander) and his wife, Mary. Paddy began his career in motor racing journalism with *Autosport* and then became a tax exile (his wife Anne was extremely rich) in Switzerland where he worked for the Philip Morris tobacco giant whose Marlboro brand sponsored the McLaren team and was the major investor in Formula One. Later Paddy was to come under the wing of F1 owner Bernie Ecclestone, taking charge of placing the advertising hoardings at all the Grand Prix, and make himself a multimillion pound fortune

His near four-year affair with Sarah Ferguson began in late 1981 after she split up from Kim Smith-Bingham, whom she had met while he was working on a polo ranch in the Argentine. He had moved to Verbier, the Swiss ski resort where Paddy had an eight-bedroom chalet known as 'The Castle', to sell skis and clothes and rent out equipment. She was still involved with Paddy when she was asked to spend Royal Ascot in the third week of June 1985 with the Royal Family at Windsor Castle. Inspired by the Princess of Wales, the invitation actually came from Lt Colonel Blair Stewart-Wilson, Deputy Master of the Royal Household, and a delighted Paddy (he saw the Royal connection as a feather in his cap) personally drove Sarah in his brown Range Rover and dropped her off at the castle's private entrance. There she was met by a footman and a lady-in-waiting who showed her to her room and assigned her a maid. On the bedside table was a card giving a list of mealtimes and the table placement for lunch before the races and dinner afterwards. Sarah noticed that she would be seated next to Prince Andrew. It was the start of an improbable relationship which finally blossomed into romance – and marriage.

But Sarah was not done with McNally: she joined him for

a summer holiday in Ibiza at the £2 million villa of Viscount Cowdray's elder son, Michael Pearson. Then came Italy and that September 1985 ultimatum which finally paved the way for her marriage to Andrew. The wedding took place on 23 July 1986 and Paddy, who enjoyed a front row pew with his parents and his elder brother Peter, then financial director of LWT and his wife Edmee, joined thirty-five friends for lunch at Brinkley's restaurant in Hollywood Road, off the Fulham Road. Paddy's host was Old Etonian Ben Holland-Martin, an escort of Princess Margaret, and his date was Becky Few-Brown, who had once gone out with Ben and had taken over Sarah's role in McNally's life.

On the wedding day Andrew was made Duke of York and Sarah became Duchess and Her Royal Highness. Less than four years later Becky married the Marquess of Blandford, elder son and heir of the Duke of Marlborough, with Paddy as best man (he gave the couple a new Range Rover as a wedding present) and McNally's reputation as a latter-day Professor Henry Higgins was complete.

Although the Yorks had two daughters – Princess Beatrice was born in August 1988, followed by Princess Eugenie in March 1990 – Sarah was less than content. She claimed that in the first two years of marriage Andrew spent just 90 nights at home with her, such was the onerous nature of his duties in the Royal Navy. Seated next to the Duchess for dinner one night in early 1990 at The Ivy, the top floor of which had been taken over by Lord Palumbo, an old friend of the Ferguson family, and his wife Hayat, I was asked by Sarah, who had been getting an increasingly hostile press, where she had gone wrong. 'Well,' I replied, 'there's the matter of your house at Sunninghill, which reports say is costing £5 million to build. In this day and age when people are finding it difficult to make ends meet, might it not have been less inflammatory and good public relations to have moved into an existing building or announce the real cost, which I suspect is rather less?'

Sarah looked at me as if I was mad and replied: 'Don't people want Andrew and me to be happy?'

When Sarah was eighteen weeks pregnant with Eugenie, she was already out of love with her husband, as I was to reveal. On the morning of Thursday 2 November 1989 she had been flown from Gatwick to Houston for a six-day visit to America, accompanied by her lady-in-waiting, Helen Spooner, the wife of a banker, her equerry, Major William McLean of the Coldstream Guards, and Geoff Crawford, the Australian-born assistant Press secretary to the Queen who had been seconded to the Yorks. Waiting to welcome the Duchess and her party was Lynn Wyatt, then the most vibrant hostess in Texas at whose mansion, Allington, at 1620 River Oaks Boulevard, they would be staying.

Mrs Wyatt had been born Lynn Sakowitz and her family, now headed by her brother Robert, had set up a chain of stores to rival Neimann-Marcus, the Dallas emporium famed for its gimmicky Christmas List (his and hers submarines had been featured one year). In the Fifties Lynn, who was born in July 1935, had married New York real estate heir Robert Lipman, at 6 feet 7 inches a giant of a man, who was four years older and they had two sons, Steven and Douglas, before separating. Lipman himself was a strange figure. A nascent hippy, after the separation he moved to London, where he rented a furnished flat in Belgravia's Wilton Place and became known as 'Bob'. He took drugs, spent his nights at discotheques and on the evening of Saturday 16 September 1967 was at a Chelsea restaurant, having quit his flat and booked into a West End hotel for a fortnight.

That morning Lipman had smoked opium and cannabis,

and in the afternoon had visited the studio of a photographer friend and sniffed amphetamine. He progressed to another apartment where he smoked hash and bought some acid for $25. Around 9pm he went to another flat and smoked cannabis with several friends. After 11pm they went to a restaurant where they were joined by Claudie Delbarre, an eighteen-year-old French blonde whom he had been dating for about a month. She had come to London to work as an au pair before gravitating to the role of hostess in a night-club bar in Romilly Street, Soho. She was available to go home with customers ready to pay cash for sex. After dinner the couple went back to his hotel for a joint, then went on to the Speakeasy disco in a mews near Bond Street. At 4.15am they were at Claudie's Chelsea apartment in Walpole Street and shared some LSD and made love. Later that day Claudie was found dead with head injuries and 8 inches of the corner of a bedsheet stuffed in her mouth.

After settling his hotel bill, Lipman, who had left Claudie's flat at 6.15am, fled the country for Scandinavia as the police began their search for him after a witness said he had been seen leaving a night-club shortly before the alleged murder of Claudie. Scotland Yard detectives found he was heading for Lisbon but the trail went cold in Denmark. He eventually turned up in New York, admitted himself to a £100 a week clinic in Hartford, Connecticut, to cure himself of drug addiction and was arrested in March 1986 by the FBI. After being extradited to Britain, he was held in custody at Brixton jail, charged with Claudie's murder. His trial began at the Old Bailey on 7 October 1986 and, after four days, Lipman was found guilty of manslaughter during an 'LSD trip to hell'. He said he had no memory of the killing.

Lipman was sentenced to six years in jail and went back to America when he was released with one third of the sentence commuted for good behaviour. He made no attempt to contact Lynn or their two sons; Lynn had by then married Texas oilman Oscar Wyatt in 1963 and he had adopted the boys, giving them his surname. According to Steve Wyatt his real father had died in the early eighties in Vienna after 'falling under a train', a story I printed on 20 January 1991 after learning it from American model Denice Lewis, with whom Steve had lived for three years, until parting from her on Christmas Eve 1987 in Aspen, Colorado (she retaliated by running up a $51,000 bill on his credit card).

Naturally Sarah knew nothing of this sad history when she first set eyes on Steve in November 1989. Bronzed and smiling, with a body hardened by exercise, Steve exuded sex appeal. Sarah had never met anyone like him before. On that first evening she attended the Houston Grand Opera as part of the British Opera Festival, and danced with Steve at the party afterwards. At the weekend the Wyatts flew Sarah down to their 20,000 acre ranch near Corpus Christi and she was able to show off to Steve by taking the controls of the helicopter, one of many craft owned by Oscar's company, Coastal Corp, which was said to control 5 per cent of America's consumption of oil and gas reserves. At the end of her five-day visit to Texas, during which she presented a trophy at a polo match, she was welcomed to a school by six hundred pupils dressed in red, white and blue and singing 'Deep in the Heart of Texas'.

The Royal party was then flown privately by Oscar to New York, along with Lynn, and booked into The Plaza Athenee Hotel, as guests of the Wyatts. Among Sarah's outings was a meal at Mortimer's with John Bowes-Lyon, the Queen Mother's great-nephew and who lived at the New York home of designer Halston, and a dinner party for

Norman Mailer, to whom Sarah said: 'I am so happy to meet you but I must admit I haven't read any of your books. Tell me, how many have you written?' When Mailer replied at least twenty, Sarah said: 'Really? Then I am absolutely determined to read one. Which do you recommend?' He suggested *Tough Guys Don't Dance* and, when the Duchess asked what it was about, Mailer replied succinctly: 'Pussy.'

Sarah returned home on 9 November with a mountain of excess baggage – she said the fifty parcels and packages contained 'Christmas presents' – but could not get Steve out of her mind. They kept in touch and by chance discovered they would both be in Yorkshire in early December. Steve had been invited by adman Frank Lowe, whose agency Lowe Howard-Spink had billings in excess of $1 billion a year, to Constable Burton, a 3,500 acre sporting estate north of York which he had rented from Charles and Maggie Wyvill. Fellow guests would include the Earl of Lichfield, banker Nicky Villiers, actor Nigel Havers, Christie's head Charlie Allsopp, Wayne Eagling, the Canadian-born principal dancer of the Royal Ballet, and Brian Alexander, a former beau of Princess Anne and younger brother of Earl Alexander of Tunis. For her part, Sarah had an official engagement on Friday 8 December, attending the gala premiere of *Showboat* at the Grand Theatre, Leeds, as patron of Opera North, and decided she wanted to join Steve at Constable Burton.

Lowe, who sold his agency to American giant Interpublic the following year for £136 million, was to tell me later about the shooting-party which Sarah gate-crashed: 'I'd known Steve for a few years and we'd been shooting together in places like Mexico and Texas and the first I knew he was a friend of the Duchess of York was when he asked me if she could come for dinner on the night of 7 December. I agreed reluctantly because that sort of presence can spoil a jolly party. I wasn't very pleased with Steve but there wasn't very much I could do without being rude.'

Sarah duly arrived, looking very pregnant, and left early the next morning for London where she had a lunch date. That afternoon she returned to Yorkshire, with another lady-in-waiting, Carolyn Cotterell (who was similarly pregnant). The show in Leeds began at 7pm and Sarah made a fuss about not staying late afterwards. Instead, with a police escort, she was driven the fifty miles from Leeds to Constable Burton where she and Carolyn arrived towards the end of dinner. She had telephoned Maggie Wyvill to say there had been a 'technical hitch' with her airplane, which was taking her to Sandringham for the weekend, and could she come over?

The photographer Patrick Lichfield was one of the first to go to bed but when he awoke the next morning he found that there were two extra guests for breakfast. 'As far as I knew, Sarah and Carolyn were due to return that night to East Anglia but I was having an early breakfast when suddenly the door opened and there was Sarah still wearing the long black evening dress she had arrived in the night before. She told me the plane had not been able to take off so she had been forced to stay the night'.

As the guns prepared to go out for the day at 9.30am, Lichfield suggested a 'group piccy' on the steps of the impressive 18th-century mansion. He told me: 'I thought it would look great with Sarah wearing her black cloak and I posed the various people around her, placing Steve at her feet to her left. As I was snapping away, Maggie took some photographs with her own camera, which was just as well. As I was getting out of my Range Rover later, my camera fell out and the back sprung open. The film never came out so all the snaps of the occasion were Maggie's.'

When the full extent of Sarah's involvement with Steve Wyatt became known two years later (after a cache of imprudent snaps of them together were found in his former London apartment in Cadogan Square and brought to the *Daily Mail* offices), Maggie received offers of £120,000 for her negatives but refused. For safety's sake she also removed a framed enlargement which had hung in the front hall of Constable Burton. She told me later: 'I don't think anything untoward happened. She was nearly six-months pregnant and I gave Sarah and her lady-in-waiting a double room.'

The Duke of York was soon to meet Steve, the man his wife was always talking about. Andrew was impressed with estimates of Oscar's fortune – between $5 billion and $8 billion – and was introduced to Wyatt at Castlewood, a twelve-bedroom house near Egham, Surrey, which was owned by King Hussein of Jordan and was on loan to the Yorks while Sunninghill Park was being completed. Princess Eugenie was born by caesarean section at 7.52pm on Friday 23 March at the Portland, a private clinic near Regent's Park, and weighed 7 pounds 2 ounces. Andrew was present at the birth and left the clinic two and a half hours later.

But friends who hoped the baby would bring a new stability to the marriage were to be disappointed as the Duke's career took him away for longer and longer periods. In contrast Steve, who was working out of the Pall Mall offices of Delaney Petroleum, part of Oscar's empire, was in a position to be more solicitous and arranged a five-day holiday for Sarah from 2 May at The Gazelle d'Or, a smart French-run hotel, with villas and individual swimming-pools, on the outskirts of the walled Moroccan city of Taroudant. As company for Sarah he suggested his former girlfriend, Pricilla Phillips, a leggy American beauty who had ambitions of becoming an actress (she was later to marry Pink Floyd co-founder Roger Waters). Steve laid on a private plane but decided against joining the group himself.

In July Steve arranged another break for Sarah and her daughters. He invited them to the South of France for his mother Lynn's fifty-fifth birthday celebrations at Les Rochers Fleuries on the Chemin de Roy, their $75,000 a month rented home on Cap Ferrat. With two tennis courts and extensive grounds, it was on the market for $15 million.

There Oscar and Lynn entertained neighbours and local celebrities including David Niven and his Swedish wife Hjordis, who lived in St Jean-Cap Ferrat, as well as the greatest catch on the Riviera, Prince Rainier of Monaco who was vamped by Lynn at every opportunity, so much so, that friends told me: 'If anything happened to Oscar, Lynn's ambition would be to marry Rainier.' Among the photographs taken over the party weekend – probably by fellow guest Pricilla – were those of Steve with Princess Beatrice, then nearly two, on his lap and Steve and Sarah with their arms around each other on a swing seat. Others included Steve and the Duchess wearing black hard riding hats and riding knee-to-knee; all these were among the haul that would haunt the couple a year and a half later and lead to the official separation of the Duke of Duchess of York.

Just how close Steve and Sarah had become following the birth of Princess Eugenie can be gauged by an incident which I was to reveal in the *Daily Mail*. Sarah had been invited to a dinner party hosted by Lord McAlpine, the forty-eight-year old construction heir and Treasurer of the Conservative Party, and his wife Romilly at Le Gavroche, London's only Michelin three-star restaurant. Sarah had declined, saying she had another invitation that night, but asked if she could come on afterwards. In fact she had been requested by Steve to host a dinner, in the second-floor Buckingham Palace apartment she shared with Andrew, for Dr Ramzi Salman, Iraq's oil marketing chief with whom Oscar was closely involved. After dinner Sarah suggested the three of them went on to Le Gavroche where their arrival caused consternation.

Among the guests were Lord Palumbo, a godfather to Princess Beatrice and confidant of Major Ronald Ferguson, and his Lebanese-born wife, Hayat. When Dr Salman, whose countrymen had invaded Kuwait on 2 August and were busily looting the Emirate, was introduced to Lady Palumbo, she ignored him completely and, after two further attempts to attract her attention, she told him pointedly: 'I don't see you.'

Meanwhile Lady McAlpine was valiantly trying to seat her guests at already full tables and Alistair made room for Sarah next to himself while Romilly motioned Steve to another table. Having none of that, Steve grabbed Sarah's hand, plonked her on his lap and told the assembled throng: 'Mah woman and I sit together.' For the remainder of the evening everyone was treated to an extraordinary, tactile display by the couple, including Steve stroking Sarah's capacious thighs, which left little to the imagination.

That October Sarah, still engrossed in Steve, was feted in New York by his mother who booked her into the £1,000 a night Presidential Suite at The Plaza Athenee. Lynn took an adjoining suite so that they could attend a fund raising dinner and dance for the American Associates of the Royal Academy. For Sarah, who was thirty-one on 15 October, Lynn had come from Texas with a special present – a £12,000 travel bag decorated with portraits of Sarah and Andrew and their daughters by Texan artist Clayton Lefevre. In the bag Lynn had thoughtfully placed two pairs of hand-painted shoes by Lefevre for the little Princesses.

Built in 5 acres on Crown Estate property at an estimated cost of £3.5 million, Sunninghill Park (a wedding present from the Queen) was finally completed in October 1990 and nicknamed South York, after the Dallas soap, because of its hideous ranch-style design. Five miles from Windsor Castle, it was designed by Professor James Dunbar-Naismith, head of architecture at Heriot Watt University and Edinburgh College of Art. Initially, the interior was to be the work of an American firm whose work Sarah had admired when she had visited the Connecticut house of aviation pioneer and racehorse owner, Henrik de Kwiatkowski, but the problems of employing an overseas company became insurmountable and leading London designer Nina Campbell was drafted in.

Among the 200 friends and acquaintances invited to the housewarming party on Saturday 6 October were Michael Caine and his former beauty queen wife Shakira, Elton John, Billy Connolly and Pamela Stephenson, Imran Khan, Sir David and Lady Carina Frost and Viscount Linley. Steve Wyatt was also on the list and took along his step-cousin, fellow American John Bryan. They had been at state school together in Texas and during their senior year at high school. The timing of the bash could not have been worse: Sarah's mother Susie had lost her second husband, Hector Barrantes, after a long battle against lymphatic cancer and the memorial service had been hastily arranged for the morning of the 6th at Chedworth in Gloucestershire. While it was felt tasteless for Sarah to go ahead with her celebrations so soon afterwards, she said she could not cancel at short notice and was rewarded when Windsor neighbour Elton played a selection of his hits, dedicating them to Hector.

In December, Steve received his greatest reward for his burgeoning friendship – an invitation to Buckingham Palace for the ball to commemorate the birthdays of the Queen Mother (ninety), Princess Margaret (sixty), Princess Anne (forty) and Prince Andrew (thirty). According to a fellow guest, Wyatt, who said he had been seated next to the Queen for dinner, looked 'as if he'd died and gone to Heaven. He was on a real high and introduced himself to strangers saying: "Hi, I'm Steve Wyatt, I'm a friend of Sarah's." I got the impression that if he'd had his mobile telephone, he would have called Oscar and Lynn there and then to crow about his triumph. He'd finally made it in London.'

Sadly there were few in Royal circles who approved of Sarah's friend. Her mother said: 'Chill him,' and it was rumoured that the Queen had suggested to Sarah that Wyatt was an 'inappropriate' escort. But within a few months Steve was on a collision course again with the Ferguson family.

At a dinner party in London he met Lesley Player, a petite thirty-three-year-old married to Jim Player, a record producer who had once owned an employment agency specializing in chauffeurs. As business blossomed Lesley was given a chauffeur-driven £40,000 Bentley and the upwardly mobile couple bought a mock Tudor house on the Thames near Kingston for £450,000 and spent half again on redecorating. At the height of the property boom in 1989 it was valued at £1.2 million. A year later, however, their business had gone into liquidation and the house was repossessed. Lesley parted from her husband but discovered polo – and Sarah's father, Major Ronald Ferguson, who was then a power in the land as polo manager to the Prince of Wales and sponsorship director at the Royal County of Berkshire Polo Club, with a salary of £32,000 a year.

Lesley contrived an introduction to the Major and soon they became lovers. That did not stop her double-dating with Wyatt and after meeting him at the dinner-party, they, too, became lovers. The affair lasted for five weeks and ended after she told Ronald about it, almost at the same time that Steve, in turn, found out about the Major. Later Lesley was to sell her story of being bedded by both Sarah's father and her lover, but soon afterwards Wyatt moved to Washington, leaving behind in his £500 a week London flat 120 intimate photographs which were carelessly placed on top of a wardrobe and seemingly discarded – a time-bomb waiting to explode.

At Steve exited from Sarah's life, John Bryan (who was to become a major help to the *Mail* Diary) was making an entrance. A tall, muscular and prematurely bald man, he was a good athlete, a superb skier, above average golfer and squash player. He had been at St John's School, Houston, with Steve when they were seventeen and later became connected when Steve's uncle, Bobby Sakowitz, parted from his wife, Pammy Zauderer, daughter of a New York real estate tycoon, who then married Tony Bryan, John's English-born father.

I had met Bryan a couple of years earlier when he was escorting Geraldine, Lady Ogilvy, and we had become friendly, played squash occasionally at his club, the Bath and Racquet, or mine, the Royal Automobile in Pall Mall, followed by lunch.

He was to tell me: 'My father was head of international operations for Monsanto Chemicals and their HQ was in St Louis where we lived and I went to St Louis County Day School. Then my father left Monsanto and joined a firm in Houston, so all of a sudden we upped and moved very quickly and that's where Steve and I met. After a year he went to the University of Arizona in Phoenix and I went for a year to Boston University, then spent three years and graduated from the University of Texas with a bachelor of arts degree in economics. I subsequently went to the University of Pittsburg Graduate School of Business where I got my Masters in business administration.'

Bryan, whose father was educated at top Yorkshire Roman Catholic public school Ampleforth (*alma mater* of Andrew Parker Bowles) and had served in the RAF during the Second World War, went to work for Westinghouse's satellite and broadcasting division. Then in 1985 he joined Encom Telecommunications in Atlanta, following a management buy-out from its parent company, Scientific. 'I was with them two and a half years and came to England in late 1987 to look at some business deals and worked with an investment banking firm called New York Trust. They backed me in the acquisition of a firm called Oceanics PLC,' added John.

Over Christmas and during the last days of 1991 at Sandringham, Sarah and Andrew discussed their future and decided to separate, albeit as the 'best of friends'. The Queen asked them to wait six months before making any announcement and they agreed, although they had made up their minds that their marriage was over after less than five years. On Thursday 2 January, Sarah took their daughters to Klosters to ski for the first time, although Beatrice was still showing the effects of chicken-pox. The party included Nanny Alison, Sarah's sister Jane with her children, Seamus, ten, and five-year-old Ayesha, and they had the services of Bruno Sprecher, Prince Charles's ski guide, and an instructor, Daniel Shlegal.

But the holiday was shattered by the discovery of the Wyatt snaps by cleaners who were sprucing up the apartment. Window cleaner Maurice Marple noticed them first, recognized Steve and Sarah and took them to the *Daily Mail*, hoping for a large reward. The newspaper promptly escorted

Marple to Scotland Yard and the snaps were handed over to Sarah. The furore, however, followed her to Palm Beach where there was further trouble in store in the shape of Lesley Player who at the behest of Ronald (called 'Dads' by Sarah), had been lady-in-waiting for the three-day visit to Florida, from 16–19 January, during which the Duchess was to receive a £15,000 cheque on behalf of Motor Neurone, her favoured charity, after presenting the prizes at a polo competition sponsored by Cartier. There she told Pilar Boxford, PR for the Bond Street jewellery store: 'Oh, have you seen the newspapers? It is one thing one week, and another the next. You know Steve and I were not intimate friends.'

By coincidence the group, which included Major Ronald, secretary Jane Ambler and bodyguard Chief Inspector John Askew, were invited to stay at the South Ocean Boulevard, Palm Beach, mansion of banker Robert Fomon, silver haired and in his sixties, and his wife, Lewis. They just happened to be close friends of Steve Wyatt who had been intending to fly in for the visit, until the publicity over the photographs put paid to his plans. Much to her annoyance, Lesley was given a bedroom with Ronald. She had arrived in Palm Beach from a skiing break in Aspen, Colorado, and claimed to have no knowledge of the brouhaha back home with newspapers claiming that Prince Andrew had at last discovered the truth of his errant wife's relationship with Wyatt.

On the first night in Palm Beach there was a cocktail party where Sarah was left momentarily stranded with a group of strangers while Dads talked to a group nearby. Once back home, Ronald came in for a tongue-lashing from his daughter (whom he referred to as 'GB', short for 'Ginger Bush') and she shouted at him: 'Don't you ever do that to me again. You just can't do that, leaving me talking to people I don't even know. You've got to protect me.' A mystified Lesley asked why Fergie was so upset, and Ronald told her: 'Just before we flew out they found some photographs in Steve Wyatt's flat. The pictures are only holiday snaps, taken at the Wyatts' villa in the South of France a couple of years ago. But they show that Texan fellow in a basket-chair with his arms around her, and the one that really annoyed Andrew was little Beatrice with no clothes on being cuddled by Steve. Andrew hit the roof. He thinks they're having an affair.'

When Lesley asked Ronald: 'Has Sarah been a silly girl?,' she claims he replied: 'I'm afraid so. A very silly girl.' Some of the Cadogan Square photographs appeared eventually in *Paris Match* in March and the one of Steve and naked Bea was reproduced in the London *Evening Standard* with the headline: 'Photo that Split a Royal Couple.'

There was no going back for Sarah who pronounced herself mightily displeased with the Royal Family, claiming they had been against her and the marriage from the start. Her husband was frightened of his parents and Sarah told me: 'He's like a little boy in front of the Queen and treats her like a Monarch, not a mother. If he starts a sentence and she takes no notice, he simply stops talking. Can you imagine?'

With a father who had played polo alongside Prince Philip in the Windsor Park polo team in the Fifties, and who had commanded the Sovereign's Escort when he was in the Life Guards and stationed at Hyde Park Barracks, Sarah had long been in Royal circles; and there was a family snapshot of a freckle-faced red-head, aged around six, in a group of young royals. When her mother, Susie, was asked where Sarah and Andrew had met, she replied: 'At polo. Doesn't everyone?'

Sarah had been born two years and two months after her sister, Jane. Ronald had joined the Army immediately after leaving Eton (where, it was said, he was less than academically bright) and traced his family back to the squirearchy of Ireland with land in County Down and County Antrim in the 18th century, before the Fergusons moved to England. Ronald was the fourth generation to join the Life Guards. His grandfather, Algernon, had risen to Brigadier-General, and had served in the Boer War of 1900–1902 and the First World War, commanding the 2nd Regiment of Life Guards, and his father, Andrew, became a colonel in the same regiment, marrying Marian Louisa Montagu-Douglas-Scott on All Saints Day 1927. Her father was the fifth son of the 6th Duke of Buccleuch, Britain's largest landowner with three stately homes and more than 300,000 acres.

Ronald, born in October 1931, married Susan Wright, a niece of the 9th Viscount Powerscourt, at St Margaret's, Westminster, in January 1956 after meeting her during her debutante year. She was five months short of her nineteenth birthday. Their home was Lowood, a ten-bedroom Edwardian house in 10 acres of garden and woodlands at Sunninghill, with a staff cottage and stables and both Jane and Sarah were out on ponies almost as soon as they could walk. Ronald quit the Army in 1968, after failing Staff College exams which would have put him in line for promotion, to work for a Mayfair public relations firm which numbered Aristotle Onassis among its clients. In 1969 the family moved to Dummer Down House in Hampshire, with a 876 acre farm, following the death of Ronald's father who had bought the property in 1939. But cracks were starting to appear in the marriage thanks to Ferguson's philanderings, which included a brief affair with a young girl who had been a bridesmaid at his wedding, and Susie eventually went off with Argentinian polo professional Hector Barrantes, who was employed during the English season by meat baron Lord Vestey, patron of the Stowell Park team, named after his 4,000 acre Gloucestershire estate. During the summer of

1972 there had been a polo tournament in the South of France where both Ronald (handicap five) and Hector (handicap seven) were playing and insurance magnate Ronald Driver, patron of the San Flamingo team, remembers: 'Ronald was busy chatting up other women and at a party aboard a yacht he asked Hector to look after Susie, virtually throwing her at him. By September at another polo tournament in Edinburgh, the marriage was over. Susie was in love and Ronald eventually agreed to a divorce.'

Hector was a year younger than Susie and the son of a middle class army officer. The family had no wealth and he relied entirely on polo for income. There had been tragedy in his life in 1970 when his wife, the former Luisa James, who had been eight months pregnant, was killed in a car crash in Buenos Aires while being driven by Hector's sister. Susie was finally divorced in May 1974 and married Hector in July 1975, leaving her daughters with their father, who said: 'As their mother disappeared off to Argentina when Sarah was thirteen and Jane fifteen, I brought them up. Her departure and the divorce were a trauma.'

In November 1976 Sarah gained a step-mother when he married former debutante Susan Deptford, the twenty-eight-year-old daughter of a wealthy Norfolk farmer. Jane had married the previous month, just short of her eighteenth birthday, after falling in love with Alex Makim, a twenty-year-old Australian who had come to Europe to learn about horses and was employed at Dummer as a groom.

It was to Susie and Hector's 1,000 acre property, El Pucara, that Sarah went after leaving Hurst Lodge, a weekly boarding-school in Sunningdale, and there she met her first love, Kim Smith-Bingham. Through Kim she met her second, Paddy McNally, known as 'Toad', and whose impressive chalet was called Les Gais Lutins (The Happy

Gnomes). While Sarah became a step-mother in all but name to his two sons, Paddy did not want to marry again and felt a certain relief when Sarah started falling for Prince Andrew, whose previous girlfriends had included Koo Stark and Carolyn Herbert, daughter of the Queen's racing manager, the Earl of Carnarvon.

After their Royal Ascot idyll, Sarah said of the lovestruck prince: 'Within days he said he was going to marry me!' They were staying the weekend of 23 February at Floor Castle, the magnificent Kelso home of the Duke of Roxburgh and his wife, Janie, where he had also once taken Koo Stark, when Andrew decided the time was ripe to propose. Just four days past his twenty-sixth birthday and just before midnight, Andrew went down on both knees and asked Sarah to be his wife. 'If you wake up tomorrow morning, you can tell me it's all a huge joke,' replied Sarah, but the next morning he repeated the proposal – and she accepted. That much Sarah can recall distinctly but her wedding day in July remains a blur. Years later John Bryan, who came close to the couple when they started talking of announcing a separation in March 1992, told me: 'She says she can't remember a minute of that day.' On Sunday 15 March 1992 there was unusual activity at Sunninghill Park. In the morning Andrew, who had become a keen golfer, had a round at Swinley Forest in a foursome which included Old Etonian jeweller Theo Fennell. Among the guests for lunch that day was Bryan, now being introduced by Sarah as 'my financial adviser' and in the afternoon there were other arrivals including Sir Matthew Farrer, the Queen's solicitor, and Charles Doughty, the Eton- and Oxford-educated partner in Withers, known as solicitors to the aristocracy. He had been retained by Sarah to represent her interests and it was the first official meeting to discuss the ramifications of a separation and to establish an agenda for a financial settlement prior to a divorce.

'Andrew wanted the best for Sarah and in a sense he was on her side against the Buckingham Palace lawyers,' said John Bryan, who appeared to have the full confidence of both the Duke and Duchess. 'But from the beginning she never made any demands. She said I'll leave it to you, you tell me how much I should have for the future of me and my children. There was a difficulty. Unlike Prince Charles, who has a vast fortune, Andrew has nothing but his Royal Navy salary. No other income, no capital, no assets, nothing. We were told he had a life assurance policy worth around £600,000. The house was owned by the Queen, it was designed by her architects, she paid to build it and made all the fundamental decisions. It was not a gift to them, they were just allowed to live there.'

When the story broke of the separation – in the *Mail* on Wednesday 18 March – Steve Wyatt was contacted at his apartment in Washington and was coy about any involvement with Sarah, saying: 'I have never had any romantic liaisons with the Duchess. We are still friends but it is just a platonic friendship. I and the Duke are also friends.'

Despite their situation, the couple were to remain under the same roof at Sunninghill, but Sarah was relieved of all further Royal engagements. Andrew, completing a course at Army Staff College, Camberley, would continue to receive a £250,000 annual payment from the Civil List which paid the salaries of his staff and would, in future, undertake public engagements that had already been arranged just for him. For Sarah, there were to be unfortunate repercussions; the BBC's Court Correspondent, Paul Reynolds, speaking on the apparent authority of the Queen's Press Secretary, Charles Anson, said on the World at One Programme: 'I can only say that the knives are out for Fergie at the Palace. I have never known such anger here at what has been going on. Intimate details have appeared in the *Daily Mail* and, according to Palace officials, the Duchess must have had another briefing operation going on.' Sarah was furious and as the row rumbled over the 'knives are out' comment, which became headline news, Anson was summoned by the Queen's private secretary, Sir Robert Fellowes, and ordered to apologize. The next day, Anson (described by the Press as the 'chief knife-thrower') said in a personal statement: 'Yesterday I gave the media a short statement concerning the marriage of the Duke and Duchess of York in terms authorized by the Queen. It was that statement alone, and the factual answers to questions as to future arrangements, that were authorized by Her Majesty. As head of the Buckingham Palace Press Office, I accept full responsibility for anything said beyond that, and I very much regret that what was said should have been interpreted by the media to the detriment of the Duchess of York, to whom I have offered my personal apologies. I have also apologized to the Queen, and both Her Majesty and Her Royal Highness have been kind enough to accept these apologies.'

In fact, the separation had become inevitable because of the Duke's long absences, coupled with the Steve Wyatt factor, and Bryan said: 'Andrew was a very good man, very well-intentioned, in many ways a terrific guy, a real gent. But his occupation and being away, hardly spending any time with Sarah, leaving his wife alone to deal with the Palace without intervening, helped wreck that marriage. He had been madly in love with her almost as soon as they had met and although she wasn't in love with him in the first weeks and months, she did fall in love and made a tremendous effort on his behalf. But she made it pretty clear upfront that she didn't want to be a naval wife and Andrew kind of agreed to that. She told him: "If you're going to go some-where, I want to go too." She didn't get married under the notion that Andrew was going to leave for years and she was going to be a naval widow, or whatever you call it. She made a superhuman effort on his behalf, took on every role and responsibility. She made every effort to make everything right for him, to make sure everything was perfect, from food to guests, she organized every element of their family life.

'But when you put their diaries together you see what happened – out of 1,500 days, they probably only spent 250 together under the same roof. You'd go through four or five months and it would be six days altogether. His job ruined the marriage, and the fact that he allowed his wife to be savaged by The System. They never came to her aid, for instance, over Wyatt and the photographs when all they had to say was: Hey, Steve Wyatt is just a friend of hers, what difference does it make? But they killed her for it instead.

'Wyatt was on the make, using Sarah to further his own ends and promote his business and it was his request to bring the Iraqi oil minister to the Palace. Steve's business was not going well and you can say Sarah was naive to go for it, but it was cleared by the Palace – there was no Gulf War going on and the British were supporting Saddam Hussein. Oscar Wyatt practically set up Saddam in business, he was moving a vast majority of the Iraqi crude, his refineries were built to Iraqi specifications. Steve was ambitious but had no con-tacts of his own, he was just going into places where his father happened to have gotten in before and he wanted to return favours so he asked Sarah to have the Iraqi to dinner at the Palace. She was naive but Sarah liked him and he was nice to her. I would say the whole motivation of Steve's friendship with Sarah was to help get some business.'

It is difficult to pinpoint exactly when John Bryan moved from adviser to lover but there was a revealing sighting of him and Sarah in March lunching at L'Incontro, an expensive and fashionable restaurant in the Pimlico area of Belgravia. A fellow patron told me: 'They were playing footsie under the table, rubbing their legs up against each other and looking very intimate. If I hadn't known who they were, I'd have said they were having an affair.'

The world was still largely unaware of the exact nature of Bryan's relationship with the Duchess. There had been one mention of them together in somewhat intimate circumstances dancing at Annabel's the previous December when Taki bumped into them. He told me: 'I knew Bryan from New York. I originally met him in Xenon with Fred Hughes, who was Andy Warhol's best friend and executor, and John got me to invest $50,000 in a business deal in America, something to do with satellites. I never saw a cent again. Then I was drinking late one night at Annabel's when he punched my arm and said: "Hey, Taki, come and say hello to the Duchess" and introduced us. I believe he was her man from around that time, three, four months before the official separation and I put the incident into the *Speccie*.'

In April the whole world knew more when Bryan turned up on holiday with Sarah and her daughters in Thailand on the island of Phuket, staying at the £510 a night Amanpuri Hotel where Mick Jagger had been a guest six weeks earlier (not with his Texan wife Jerry Hall but a dark, European beauty said to have been top model, Carla Bruni). Sarah had been keeping a low profile and had not been seen in public since 23 March but her presence was missed when the Easter holidays ended and Beatrice was absent from Upton House, her school near Sunninghill. Photographs were taken in Phuket by a fellow hotel guest and the bald Bryan quickly recognized when he was snapped giving Eugenie a ride on his shoulders. But by the time the photographs appeared in Fleet Street newspapers, the party, including Nanny Alison Wardley and bodyguards Chief Inspector John Askew and Sergeant John Kerr, had moved on to the Moluccas, 1,250 miles from Jakarta, and Bryan had flown back to London where he vouchsafed: 'This was a trip planned for at least two months. Sarah needed to let off steam – to escape the hothouse – so that she could relax and collect her thoughts.'

On Saturday 25 April, in an attempt to negate publicity of his participation in the jaunt (estimated to have cost £22,000), Bryan telephoned the editor of the *Mail on Sunday* which was preparing to report on the situation. Sarah was said to be pregnant and Bryan her lover, but he had a more dramatic tale to recount. The newspaper duly changed its tack and their front page to accommodate his information and the headline blared: 'Fergie Wants to Get Back with Andrew'. Without being quoted directly Bryan, described as chief executive of health care company Oceanics, based in Frankfurt, Germany, said: 'The Duchess certainly believes there is a chance that she and her husband will get back together again. She will be coming back refreshed from her holiday, determined to examine every possibility. There will be a period when they are attempting a reconciliation. They're making a concerted effort. She will actually be taking time for a few months with the aim of having a very solid and healthy reconciliation which is still very, very possible.'

To reinforce this unlikely scenario and give it the stamp of credibility, Bryan arrived alone at Sunninghill on the Sunday and spent the day closeted with Andrew saying only that he was an 'honest broker' between the couple. He had access to Sarah's solicitor, Charles Doughty, and was in the thick of the preliminary discussions over a settlement. He claimed his business relationship with Sarah had been formalized in January 1992 and told me: 'From that time, her entire situation was reorganized, banking, personal, corporate, publishing, every single aspect of her business affairs.'

It was all hogwash, of course, but, back from her Far East jaunt, Sarah was embroiled in further problems concerning her father who had been dumped by the ambitious Lesley Player, now the focus of an investigation by *The Sunday Times* over the finances of the Ladies International Polo Tournament she had set up with Ronald's backing. A report revealed that 'a company used by Major Ronald Ferguson to raise thousands of pounds in the name of the Princess Royal's favourite charity faces an inquiry into how the money was spent. The Charity Commissioners want to know why only a fraction of the receipts from one of Britain's most prestigious polo events went to Save The Children.' They claimed that, of £80,000 paid by sponsors, just £2,100 went to the charity. Lesley, later to marry and separate from a dentist, stated that between £20,000 and £25,000 had found its way to Save The Children. In June the Commissioners finally cleared her but by that time she was penning her memoirs of her life with Sarah, Dads and Steve Wyatt which was to prove a devastating and highly profitable document.

As Fergie's romance with Bryan deepened, her thoughts turned away from Lesley to a holiday in the sun near St Tropez, a favourite watering-hole. After contacting several local estate agents Bryan found what he was looking for, the five-bedroomed Le Mas de Pignerol, a secluded villa in the middle of a forest with a swimming-pool, away from the fleshpots and paparazzi cameramen. Valued at £450,000, it was owned by Charles Smallbone, whose family had made their fortune through upmarket kitchen fittings. He rented it out at £4,000 a week in the high season through International Chapters Limited and on Sunday 9 August Sarah, her daughters, their nanny, Bryan and Scotland Yard bodyguard John Hodgkinson left Romenda Lodge, which Sarah was renting on the Wentworth estate for £52,000 a year, for Blackbushe airport in Hampshire. Bryan had chartered an eight-seater turbo-prop Kingair 200 from Gama Aviation at a round trip cost of £8,000 and the craft took two and a half hours to fly to the small airstrip of La Mole, a twenty minute drive from St Tropez. There they were greeted by Sergeant Graham Ellery, who had travelled out by a commercial flight, and two rented Mercedes.

There were also two unwelcome strangers, paparazzi photographer Daniel Angeli and an assistant, with a black van. They had been quickly spotted by Ellery who warned them, in good Scotland Yard tradition, that no photographs would be tolerated. Angeli shrugged his shoulders, muttered that this was France and made sure all his cameras were fully loaded. When the Kingair came to a standstill, Ellery approached the plane as a stewardess opened the door and lowered the steps and he went inside. He informed the Duchess that there were two paparazzi a few yards away and Sarah, clad in a blue jacket and floral shorts, responded by putting on dark glasses and a huge floral headscarf. As they left the plane, Angeli snapped away before the party sped off. Cunningly, Angeli did not move and the group were reassured when no black van appeared in their rearview mirrors. But they paid no attention to a motorbike which trailed them at a distance – it was driven by another Angeli employee and, as the two Mercedes turned off the main road five miles from the airport, the motorcyclist stopped and knew he had the group trapped. There were only three villas on the track the car had taken and all were accessible. He reported the good news back to base.

The following morning, as the villa stirred and the crickets beat out their relentless cacophony, Angeli and a colleague retraced the route of the motorbike, parked and began a painstaking crawl through matted undergrowth in the direction of the villas, half a mile away. Eventually, within 500 yards, they saw the sparkle of a blue swimming-pool; training their 1,200mm lenses, they focused on their quarry, Sarah and Bryan sunbathing while the Princesses frolicked with their nanny and the two detectives lay on loungers reading books. Settling in, the two paparazzi congratulated themselves. The villa was in the middle of a natural amphitheatre, screened on all sides by woods and, with the sun behind the paparazzi and blazing into the faces of the party in the villa, the Frenchmen knew they could not be detected. 'It was like sitting in a stadium with a grandstand view to the centre spot,' one paparazzo explained later. Over the next three days, starting at 10am and taking a break for lunch at 2pm, returning at 3.30pm, Angeli and his assistant shot roll after roll. Curiously they were unaware of the identity of the bald, athletic man their cameras captured kissing a topless Sarah, nuzzling the balls of her feet, and playing with her in the kidney-shaped pool, until they wired a set to Paris where the man was identified as John Bryan. He told me later: 'We never had the faintest idea we were being photographed. It looks as if they were at the end of the garden but we would have spotted them there. They must have been a long way away and honestly you couldn't see a thing in those woods, they were so dense.'

Bought for £60,000 for reproduction in Britain, the photographs appeared on Thursday 20 August 1992 while Sarah was staying at Balmoral with Beatrice and Eugenie at the invitation of the Queen and Prince Philip who wanted to see their granddaughters. Diana and Charles and their sons made up the party and just after midnight the Balmoral switchboard took a call from Bryan who was at his fifth floor Chelsea apartment overlooking the Physic Garden. All that day Bryan had sought to obtain an injunction banning use of the photographs but had failed. When he saw an early edition of the front page all he could say was: 'Holy shit.' He told Sarah: 'The photographs are far worse than I imagined. They show everything.'

Thursday was a grim day for the Royal Family and the Balmoral houseparty but, according to Bryan, there were no recriminations for Sarah. 'There were reports that Sarah had been asked to move out into one of the lodges, but that wasn't so.' But with various other newspapers jumping on the bandwagon and reprinting part of the Angeli set, Sarah and her daughters returned on the Sunday to Romenda Lodge. Salvation was at hand, however: the next day the tabloids had moved on and reprinted the taped conversation between Diana and James Gilbey which was quickly dubbed 'Squidgygate'.

Now holed up in Los Angeles and by all reports down on his luck and no longer on speaking terms with Sarah (after a 1996 book, *Fergie: Her Secret Life* by his Oceanics colleague, Allan Starkie, made claims that he beat her up and worse), John Bryan tells me: 'Andrew understood completely why everything happened, I think he wishes the separation and divorce had not happened. But they are happy now. They have found a good and comfortable relationship.'

Sarah, Beatrice and Eugenie have moved back into Sunninghill while Andrew, whose golf handicap is down to a highly respectable seven, was last seen romancing PR Aurelia Cecil, the marathon-running divorcee daughter of

Lord Amhurst of Hackney and whose Aurelia company has been taken over for £4.3 million. On Jay Leno's late night American television chat show in April 1998 Sarah explained their joint domestic arrangements: 'If I am going to have dinner or whatever with friends, I go for dinner away from home. We have away games. We have away matches. If Andrew wants to be with someone at home, then fine, I will move out.'

Sarah and Andrew divorced in May 1996 and Sarah, who signed up with Weightwatchers, in an effort to trim her estimated £4.2 million debt has been looking to the Queen for a further settlement to buy a house of her own with her daughters. At the time of the original settlement, Bryan revealed the financial contents to me and said: 'Sarah receives a lump sum of £600,000, half of which would be in trust and handed back to the Queen in the event of Sarah's remarriage. A further £1.4 million would be in trust for Beatrice and Eugenie, with £650,000 of this sum allowed towards the purchase of a house which would be in the childrens' names.' Given the original sums bandied about in the Press – ranging from £4 million to £10 million – the settlement could not have been construed as generous.

For John Bryan, these are not great times as he tries to reconstitute his life in the jungle of Los Angeles. Once he expected to pocket £2 million from the sale of his lover's Budgie books to television and to the movies, but the appellation 'millionaire' is no longer applied to him. By chance, Allan Starkie called me from Frankfurt earlier this year and I asked how Bryan was: 'He's the same old John and trying to make a comeback,' said Allan. 'But it's proving very difficult. Don't hold your breath.'

Special 'K'

THE AGA KHAN

Often labelled one of the world's most beautiful women, the Begum Salima Aga Khan (born Sarah Croker Poole) was in her London house at the end of May 1998 with her long-time lover, Maître Philippe Lizop, who had conducted her divorce from the Aga Khan, when she heard the news from France.

By all accounts, her ex-husband had assembled his family from around the world prior to the French Derby on 31 May 1998 at Chantilly, a short distance from his magnificent home and racing complex at Gouvieux. From New York had come his half-sister Princess Yasmin (her mother was the late Rita Hayworth), her son, Andrew Embiricos, and her boyfriend, and his even later grandfather's widow, the French-born Yaki, had flown in from her home in Aswan, Egypt. His daughter, Zahra, her husband and her brothers, Rahim and Hussein, were also present but on the eve of the Derby – in which the Aga had the fourth favourite Daymarti

– he stunned everyone by marrying for the second time.

His bride was German-born blonde Gabriele zu Leiningen, thirty-five, the former wife of Prince Karl Ernich who had made a fortune from a car dealership; they had met in summer 1997 through King Juan Carlos of Spain, an old friend of Gabriele's. Gabriele had a six-year-old daughter, Theresa, and had converted (as had his first wife, Sally) to the Moslem faith. The Aga – Karim, or 'K', to his friends – had given her the name Inaara which derives from the Arabic word meaning 'light'. Not present at the two ceremonies – either religious or civil – was Juan Carlos, sixty, who clearly disapproved of the romance. He had known Gabriele before her previous marriage and she had remained a close friend of his family. When he took her to Gouvieux to see his old friend K, little did the Iberian monarch realize what he was setting in train. After that initial meeting – K offered her the use of his Gulfstream IV jet (registration F-GPAK) to return home to Germany on business – Gabriele became closer to the Aga and by early 1998 love had blossomed.

In March 1998 I revealed that K had finally dumped Italian Milena Maffei who had been in love with him for thirty-five years, both before, during and after his marriage to Sally. He had installed Milena, daughter of the Italian industrialist Italo Maffei, on the Ile St Louis in Paris (close to his former home) and she had an apartment and jewellery shop in Porto Cervo where he had lived with Sally and their three children. In saying goodbye to Milena, K had, according to friends of Sally's, uttered the immortal words, 'I don't feel the same about you any more.' Thus he was able to concentrate on Gabriele, who has a doctorate in international law.

But back to earlier days, nearly five years ago, as I exclusively reported in the *Mail*:

'The staff at Aiglemont, a £50 million complex including

a château-style house, offices and racing stables for 100 horses at Gouvieux, just north of Paris, had never seen their boss so angry.

'A man known for his fiery temper, the Aga Khan, Imam or spiritual leader of the world's 4 million Ismaili Moslems and master of a fortune in excess of £3 billion, was incandescent with rage.

'He held the objects of his fury in his hands: after twenty-five years of marriage, solicitors for his English-born wife Sally had just served him personally with divorce papers. They did not make amusing reading.

'Her demands were breathtakingly simple: a cash settlement (the ball-park figure was £20 million); a suitable house in the place of her choosing; and retention of the jewellery collection she had amassed before and during the marriage. Insured for a conservative £17 million the latter was worth appreciably more.

'His reaction was typical and immediate. He called his own lawyers and issued instructions: "Sue her for divorce." And in London the redoubtable Fiona Shackleton (later to have the Prince of Wales as a client) of Farrer and Co., the Queen's solicitors, was retained.'

When his action became public knowledge the tables were neatly turned on Sally.

What was not revealed in the gossip columns was that his divorce papers named an old friend of Sally's, Old Etonian Charles Benson, who had once worked on the racing pages of Lord Beaverbrook's *Daily Express* for Clive Graham, another Old Etonian. As Graham wrote under the name 'The Scout', Benson was known as 'The Boy Scout'.

In the papers the Aga Khan accused Benson of 'practically living with my wife for the last fifteen years' and claimed that Sally was 'financially improvident'. On 3 October 1994, his lawyers announced the end of the marriage, making no mention of his grounds for divorce. A spokesman added: 'The Aga Khan does not normally make statements on his or his family's private lives and therefore will issue no further statement on this development.'

The former Sarah Croker Poole, known as Sally and born in New Delhi, the daughter of an Indian Army colonel who had retired to the genteel environs of London's Kensington, was shocked and saddened by these events, which finally exposed the sham of her marriage to the world. At the £25 million mansion on the shores of Lake Geneva, which the Aga had rented for her since 1984 from the fragrance heiress Pometta Firmenich, Sally told friends: 'It need never have come to this. All he had to do was buy me a house in London.'

The row over the house was to cost K an estimated £50 million. When the divorce was finalized in Switzerland in March 1995, Sally repeated: 'If he had bought me a base in London, we'd still be married.'

A friend of Sally's explains: 'She has the simple urges of a middle-aged woman. She likes to visit London, see all her old friends, watch TV and videos, go to the cinema and restaurants; but she wanted a base rather than a hotel suite. K kept on promising but never delivered and by that September her patience snapped. She went to her lawyers.'

It had started as a love match – beautiful high society ex-model meets one of the world's most eligible bachelors in a St Moritz hotel. Karim had succeeded his grandfather in July 1957 as Imam of the world's Ismailis – who paid 12½ to 25 per cent of their income to the Imamate, making him a kind of Moslem King Midas.

They married in civil and religious ceremonies in Paris in October 1969. K doted on his bride, relishing her beauty, her poise and her ability to charm his followers when he visited them in Pakistan and East Africa. She, in turn, was captivated by the jet-setting lifestyle as well as the responsibilities the position brought.

Winters would be spent in St Moritz, where K would take one of the houses of shipping magnate Stavros Niarchos (later he stayed at hotels such as The Chesa Guarda Ley, a short drive from the resort) and they would ski and party from Christmas until the beginning of March.

While the Aga was careful to remain within the tenets of his Moslem faith – he did not smoke and took alcohol, a single glass of champagne, only once a year on 11 July (the anniversary of his succession to the Imamate) – Sally was a heavy smoker and enjoyed drinking whisky and wine.

'She tried to give up when she met K but soon took it up again. He did not approve but couldn't do anything about it, though he asked her not to in front of his followers,' says a friend.

From St Moritz, the couple would move to Paris and, with the arrival of their children, they were accompanied by an ever-growing retinue of nannies, chauffeurs and household staff. Bodyguards were to come later, signifying the change in the times. Summers were devoted to racing in the environs of Paris. K had inherited stables and studs in France and Ireland from his father, the playboy Prince Aly Khan. To begin with, he had not been interested in the Sport of Kings but soon he became totally immersed.

At K's Gouvieux stables, François Mathet (nicknamed 'The Colonel') trained up to 100 thoroughbreds for the Aga whose colours of green with red epaulettes met with increasing success.

Then Sally and her husband moved to Sardinia and the Costa Smeralda where K had a succession of luxury yachts, with a Spanish chef and Italian crew. Each yacht, in keeping with his desire for speed, was designed to exceed 40 knots, more suitable to a speedboat. The first was *Silver Shark*, named after a favourite racehorse, followed by *Amaloun*, which caught fire and sank. Then K had *Kamaloun* built in Bremen, followed by *Shergar*, which was named after his 1981 Epsom Derby winner.

'In Sardinia,' a friend says, 'Sally would take a group of friends, up to thirty, out for the day on one of the boats and it would moor in one of the bays. Around lunchtime K would join the party, arriving in a speedboat. His first words would always be: "Is lunch ready?" He would then sit down, be served first and wolf the food down, finishing long before the others had been served, and then go off. He has a gargantuan appetite, which explains why he has ballooned to more than 17 stone. When he skied nationally he was around 12 stone.'

Trips were made by private jet from Sardinia to Normandy, where K owned St Crespin, another home inherited from his father. August in Deauville was devoted to racing, polo and the thoroughbred sales and K and Sally would often fly in for a day or so, returning to the Costa Smeralda at the end of the meeting.

'We're planning to start a family as soon as possible,' Sally told friends when they married. 'K wants a son and so do I.'

Eleven months after the wedding she gave birth in Geneva – to a daughter, Princess Zahra. In October 1971, Rahim, a son and heir, was born. Described as the fiftieth descendant of the Prophet Mohammed, he was followed in April 1974 by another son, Hussain.

'And that was the end of our love life,' Sally told a girl-friend later. 'After Hussain was conceived, K became less attentive, particularly physically.' How things had changed since the early days. 'K was very tactile, couldn't keep his hands off Sally either in private or public,' says a friend. 'And even after their love life evaporated, he made a great display of touching Sally when they were on official business for the Imamate. It was all a charade.'

Another friend says: 'It was a charmed life and, for the first few years, Sally could not have been happier.' But while Sardinia had the sun, the yachts and the sea, it also had Milena Maffei.

Milena was two years younger than Sally. She spent much of her time between Paris and Milan, her summers on the Costa Smeralda at Porto Cervo. Her home was directly across the water from K's and a friend says: 'It was in eyeline, perhaps 100 or so yards away and everyone knew if she was there or not by the light blue shutters. If she was in, the shutters were open, and they were closed when she was away. The shutters came to haunt Sally.' Milena became even closer to K in 1977 when she moved into a £200,000 apartment in Paris on the Ile St Louis. Writer Taki Theodoracopulos, whose wife, Princess Alexander Schoenberg, is a close friend of Milena's, says: 'Milena was with him in the early days, close to him during his marriage and never gave up. She didn't marry and have children and has virtually devoted her life to him.'

Then there was Pilar Goess, who supplanted Milena in K's life and whom Sally saw as even more threatening. Half-American and brought up in Tennessee, Pilar claimed descent from Empress Maria Theresa of Austria. Her father was an Austrian nobleman who, she said, had known K for twenty-six years and had met him when he photographed the Aga skiing in Kitzbuhl. She had worked as a model and had appeared naked in a 1977 edition of German *Playboy*.

K's wooing of Pilar followed the usual pattern and among

the generous gifts of jewellery was a pink diamond ring, the cost of which was variously estimated at anything from £100,000 to £1 million. Pilar herself put its value at £500,000 – and she lost it at the McDonald's fast food outlet at a Wyoming airport that winter. It was eventually found between cardboard platters, empty ketchup satchels and cola cups in a rubbish bin and Pilar continued to wear it on her engagement finger. When asked who had given her the bauble, she made a habit of replying, archly: 'It's a present – from God.'

'Sally knew what was going on but she couldn't do anything about it,' a friend says. 'She felt trapped. She had jewellery, but no personal money as such, and couldn't move without K. She became philosophical and dedicated herself completely to her children. She became a mother hen and never looked at another man. Talk about an exotic bird trapped in a gilded cage . . . that was Sally and she couldn't do a thing about it.'

To their intimate circle, the marriage had long been one in name only. The Aga did not appear to care that his wife, the mother of his three children, knew about his mistresses. Clues were abundant, the staff at their various homes gossiped and Sally was left in no doubt about his infidelities. But she hung on, seemingly mesmerized and unable to act, until she was forced into action.

She had moved to Geneva from the magnificence of Aiglemont, with its panoramic views from the back of the main house to Paris in the distance, so that she could be close to her daughter, Zahra, and sons, Rahim and Hussain, who were at school in Switzerland.

'Also, she came to hate Aiglemont,' a friend says. 'She used to say: "I don't like the place. I feel ill at ease there." Moving to Geneva solved the problems of being too close to K, who was indifferent to her. Now at least she had her own home, where she could entertain friends. She told them she hated K and was terrified by him. 'He used to fly into terrific rages, although of course he never harmed her physically.'

In the end Sally was unhappy in Geneva, too, and yearned to return to London. This was to be the undoing of her extraordinary marriage. In the spring of 1994, after being shown round various properties in London in the £3 million to £8 million bracket by agents including Andrew Langton of Aylesford, she fell for a property overlooking Hyde Park and the Bayswater Road. It had originally been put on the market, at an overly ambitious £10 million, by the Israeli art dealer Ronald Fuhrer. By the summer of 1994 the price had come down to a more reasonable £3.5 million and the Aga made a tentative offer of £3.2 million, complaining about plumbing matters.

The offer did not tempt Fuhrer and Sally saw her dream home slipping away. She told friends: 'He kept promising to buy it, but then found reasons to bring down the price which the vendor found unacceptable.'

In Sardinia that summer, together but apart, the Aga told Sally the property would be hers by the autumn, but held back on exchanging contracts. Finally her patience snapped and she went to her lawyers. (Ironically the Aga Khan did eventually buy the property for her but, because of an unexpected turn in her love life, she now prefers to be based in Geneva.)

As the proceedings advanced (and Charles Benson was dropped from the case for lack of evidence), Sally dispensed with her London lawyers and employed French legal expert Maître Philippe Lizop, a Gerard Depardieu-lookalike not yet turned forty.

'Lizop became very gung-ho,' says a friend. 'He encouraged her to play hard-ball, advising her to hit K with everything, and this excited her.' Soon their relationship had moved beyond being strictly that of client and lawyer. While exploring all avenues of attack, Lizop discovered a fascinating fact: the Aga had lost control of his £14 million Gulfstream IV jet after a writ had been attached to it at Le Bourget airport, Paris. It was the subject of a dispute with the Société de Banque Occidentale, which claimed that it had lent $100 million to a company controlled by the Aga to acquire The Hôtel Meurice in Paris, part of the Ciga chain in which the Aga also had a stake. Ciga, owner of thirty-six luxury hotels in six countries, including the Aga's own on the Costa Smeralda, was experiencing trading problems and owed around £406 million. It was eventually sold to the American Sheraton hotel chain.

Lizop's news that the Aga had problems made Christmas 1994 all the more poignant for Sally, who spent it in a Gstaad hotel with the children, although she was mysteriously absent on Christmas Day itself.

By February 1997 Sally, according to friends, was becoming increasingly reliant on Lizop. During the summer Sally moved out of the Geneva mansion – the property had been clad in scaffolding, in anticipation of the termination of the lease – into a smaller house, also rented. She also sold part of her jewellery collection; she had intended to dispose of 250 pieces but twenty-three were withdrawn because, after legal intervention by the Aga, they were deemed to be historical Islamic treasures. In any case, the sale realized £17.77 million. Curiously, since the divorce Sally has discarded virtually all of her old friends. Although a godmother to Charles Benson's daughter, Honor, Sally failed to attend her confirmation service at Heathfield, her Ascot school, in

March of last year and has remained closeted in Geneva.

One of Sally's oldest friends comments: 'It was the Duchess of Windsor who said: "No woman can be too rich or too thin." That's Sally but I very much doubt that she's happy with it.'

How did it all begin? We turn the clock back to 1968. For everyone, there is a time to settle down. And for Sally Croker Poole, a month shy of her twenty-ninth birthday, New Year's Eve 1968 in St Moritz was as good a time as any. Her marriage to the coal-rich Marquess of Bute's youngest brother, Lord James Crichton-Stuart, had just been annulled after nine years, on the humiliating grounds of non-consummation, and she was staying at The Palace Hotel as a guest of the Greek bachelor playboy, Yanni Zographos.

As midnight approached and the owner, Peppo Vanini, primed his DJ to play 'Auld Lang Syne' for the formally suited throng, Sally was introduced to the Aga Khan. It was later described as love at first sight. Together, they danced into the dawn of 1969.

Darkly handsome, slim and an expert skier whose ambition was to represent Britain in the Winter Olympics, sadly the Aga Khan failed to be selected in 1960 and 1964. He was, of course, incredibly rich. Also, Sally noted with a growing feeling of anticipation, he was refreshingly unmarried and had just celebrated his thirty-second birthday.

Both had enjoyed numerous previous romantic involvements. As K's old adversary Taki puts it: 'While he never really sought men friends, there were always girls. Wealth and position are powerful aphrodisiacs.'

The most complicated of his relationships was with Baroness Annouchka von Mecks, who helped him celebrate his twenty-fourth birthday in Gstaad. Three years later, at the beginning of 1962, she was confident enough to describe him as 'my husband'. For his part, he said: 'Actually, I have no marriage plans and intend not to marry for a long time yet.'

He started to involve himself in business matters and in the winter of 1965 Annouchka moved to London. But she was soon back. Friends would contact her at K's Paris home. Within weeks, she knew she was pregnant. While she refused to reveal the identity of the father, the relationship with K petered out. 'She went away by herself for a weekend and when she came back she found all the locks had been changed. K's butler was left to deal with the matter,' says a friend.

In January 1966, she produced a baby son. On the birth certificate, the father is described as 'unknown'. The dark haired, brown eyed baby was given the first names Karel Ismaal Aly Edouard Darius.

By the time Sally met K, she, too, had quite a history. She had gone from a girls' boarding-school to finishing school and then been pushed into London society by her socially ambitious mother. She did the debutantes' Season but the family did not have money and she had to earn a living.

She modelled through the Sixties for the Peter Hope Lumley Agency under the name Sarah Stuart and was often featured on the lists of the world's most beautiful women. As a teenager, she had been wooed by David Niven. Later, 'Niv' was to claim to his family that it had been an on-going affair.

When her marriage to Lord James Crichton-Stuart in June 1959 showed no signs of fulfilment, she became involved with Charles Benson. But Benson was married and the relationship, in Sally's words, became 'too hot to handle', so they parted.

Within a year, she was the constant companion of another Old Etonian, Jimmy (later Sir James) Goldsmith, who lived in Paris and was making his first £1 million in the pharmaceutical business with his brother, Teddy. When *that* affair had run its course, Sally fell in love with Philip Martyn, a free-spending man-about-town whose main claim to fame was as a backgammon hustler; he once claimed, but later denied, he was world champion in 1972.

'They [Sally and Philip] were never totally faithful to each other and while Sally spent most of her time living with him, she always had her own place around the corner,' says an old friend. Among her flings, one which particularly annoyed Philip, was with Gordon White, who was then building up the Hanson conglomerate with his pal James Hanson. In later years, Gordy was very proud of the connection.

Italy's richest man, Fiat boss Gianni Agnelli, also fell under Sally's spell for a time. But the Aga was in full pursuit; there were constant telephone calls, invitations to join him on the ski slopes and generous gifts of jewellery. He was not without reservations. For instance, he was anxious as to how his followers would regard his choice of a British woman, described as a 'model', which might be interpreted derogatorily. Sally was equally apprehensive. 'He wants me to convert to Islam,' she told friends. 'And I'm not sure I can handle the changes that life as wife of the Aga Khan will bring.'

But when K proposed in the summer of 1969, she felt ready to take the plunge. She underwent a two-week course in the Ismaili Moslem religion and in July, by then officially engaged, she joined her future husband in Sardinia where his £80 million development of the Costa Smeralda was taking off. Prophetically, she arrived just in time to watch the historic moon landing on a television set in the office of the Harbour Master in Porto Cervo.

The civil and religious wedding ceremonies were set for October. Sally converted to Islam, taking the title of the Begum Salima. There was a reception at K's Paris home at No. 1 rue des Ursins on the Ile St Louis, which he had inherited, along with Green Lodge, Chantilly, on the death of his playboy father Prince Aly Khan, who was killed when he crashed his Lancia in May 1960 while driving in the Bois de Boulogne.

The guest of honour at the afternoon reception (champagne, caviar and finger snacks) was Princess Margaret. But when Sally accepted K's proposal, she was all too aware that there were old rivals for his affections, most prominent among them the Italian-born Milena Maffei.

Sally became resigned to Milena's intrusion into her marriage and told friends: 'She's always shadowing me. I go to the races and there she is, a few yards away. She has always tried to jeopardize my marriage. I just wish she'd leave K and me alone.'

But it was not to be. By the time Sally was shunted from France to Geneva in 1984, her marriage was over in all but name. It was also Milena's turn to be replaced in K's affections. Her nemesis was the twenty-eight-year-old Pilar Goess, who at the time was engaged to the Greek shipping heir, Spyros Niarchos.

During the high summer of 1984, K, Sally and their children island-hopped in the Aegean and Ionian, mooring their yachts in the deserted bays of the Niarchos family's private island of Spetsopoula. 'Pilar made an immediate play for K,' says a member of the Niarchos family. 'She kept appearing on board his yacht, *Shergar*, and made a great fuss of the boys. Rahim and Hussain were very flattered by her attention. She would read to them and look after them.'

By the time the anchor was upped for the return to

Sardinia, K and Pilar were on their way to becoming an item. The youngest Niarchos, Constantine, explains the situation. 'Pilar left my brother while the Aga Khan was a guest at our house. My brother was very upset about Pilar, as anybody would be about losing a girl they had been going out with for four years and hoped to marry. It was very bad-mannered of the Aga, but then he is.'

Pilar's defection continued to rankle with the Niarchos family and, that Christmas, K made the mistake of booking his family into The Chesa Guarda Ley Hotel just outside St Moritz, where Stavros owned the magnificent Villa Marguns with an indoor swimming-pool, and two other chalets.

Constantine became increasingly ill-humoured at the proximity of the man who had stolen his brother's fiancée and, in the early hours of Christmas Day, he took a taxi to the hotel. Clearly steaming, he was let in by the night porter and demanded to be taken to the Aga's suite. Sally and K were fast asleep in the same bed when Constantine burst in, according to Sally, and hurled coins and banknotes at her husband. 'He said "You love money so much – here, have some more of it", and then left,' a stunned Sally said afterwards. 'It was all very bewildering.'

Of all the Aga's relationships the one with Pilar was the most threatening to Sally. She used to say: 'What I particularly disliked about her, apart from her being with my husband, was the way my children were integrated into the affair. K and Pilar used to go for walks along the Bois de Boulogne, taking my two sons with them.'

One January at the beginning of the Nineties, Sally was on K's yacht in the Bahamas awaiting the arrival of her husband who had business to attend to in the US. The threat of Pilar had not receded and she was given a rude jolt when her peace was disturbed on board by a blonde woman with

Imran Khan, ex-sportsman and political leader.

The Hon. Sita White poses in Hollywood with daughter Tyrian after naming Imran Khan as the father of her child.

Jemima Goldsmith after her marriage to Imran Khan.

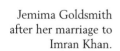

Top: Together but for how long?
Fergie and the Duke of York remain
'best friends'.

Above: Steve Wyatt and Princess
Beatrice on *that* South of France
holiday at his mother, Lynn's, house.

Right: John 'Osram' Bryan, Fergie's
'financial consultant' and lover.

Major Ronald Ferguson and polo playing Lesley Player who bedded him and his daughter Sarah's lover, Steve Wyatt.

Karim Aga Khan, spiritual leader of 4 million Ismaili Muslims, with his first wife, British beauty Sally Croker Poole, after their 1969 marriage in Paris.

Pilar Goess, the Austrian-born beauty who captured the Aga Khan's heart on a Mediterranean holiday when she was engaged to Spyros Niarchos.

Royal Ascot 1998 – the Aga Khan shows off his new wife, Princess Gabriele zu Leiningen, now the Begum Inaara.

Karim Aga Khan, 49th descendant of the Prophet Mohammed and son of
the playboy Prince Aly Khan.

The Australian Dale Harper who became Lady Tryon.

Below left: Kanga Tryon before her illness and paralysis.

Below right: Prince Charles nicknamed her 'Kanga' and she said it was love at first sight for her.

The young Luis Cosa Basualdo at home in Buenos Aires.

Below right: 'Bas' and close friend the Marquess of Blandford, later implicated together in a banking scandal.

Above: Luis 'Bounder' Basualdo at Royal Ascot.

Daphne Guinness (left), now married to Spyros Niarchos, with 'Bounder' Basualdo and her mother in August 1985.

Christina, Ari and Alexander Onnasis on his yacht *Christina* in the 1950s.

Below left: Basualdo and Christina in St Moritz in about 1971.

Below right: 'Thunderthighs' with Coca-Cola bottles, ruminating in Paris.

Down but not out – me with Johnny Kwango and First Aid girl at Stamford Bridge in aid of the Goldenballs Fund.

Jimmy Goldsmith and his wife, Lady Annabel, at the *Private Eye* court case in 1976; an ill wind reveals a well-turned thigh.

Above left: Sixties hippy look for the Earl of Lichfield.

Above: 'I haven't got Aids', says Lord Lichfield.

Atalanta de Bendern and Emma Bendern – my first wife. Photograph by Lichfield at the peak of his profession.

Kiss my ring – Imelda Marcos, First Lady of the Philippines and wife of dictator Ferdinand Marcos.

Widow Imelda Marcos runs for Government after returning from exile in Hawaii.

'Mou-Mou' Fayed and eldest son Dodi.

Cottagers – new Fulham chairman Mohamed Al Fayed at Craven Cottage football ground with spokesman Michael Cole.

Mediterranean hols for the Princess of Wales and Dodi Fayed, August 1997.

Lady Annabel Birley (later Goldsmith) relaxes with the Earl of Lucan

The Countess of Lucan with her son George and daughters Frances and Camilla.

Nanny Sandra Rivett, murdered on 7 November 1974 by the Earl of Lucan.

'Lucky' Lucan with his wife Veronica Duncan following their marriage in 1963.

a German accent and a pout. Not recognizing Sally, the mystery woman asked: 'Where is Pilar?' When Sally replied that she had not the faintest idea, the blonde asked her to give Pilar a message. She left a card which revealed she was Maya Flick, sister of Princess Gloria Thurn und Taxis and the then wife of Daimler-Benz heir, Mick Flick.

'Obviously, Pilar had put the word round that she was going to be on the boat in Nassau,' Sally told friends, recounting the bizarre episode. 'But the extraordinary thing was that this woman did not know who I was.'

Certainly K gave all the appearances of settling down with Pilar. The airstrip near her country home in Austria was extended by 1,000m to allow K's jet to land. When K's colt Kahyasi won the Derby in June 1988, Pilar and her parents – who recorded the victory on their camcorder – were in his box at Epsom.

But K was not ready to make a commitment to Pilar and was equally unwilling to give Sally a divorce. The more Pilar pressured him to do both, the less inclined he became to humour her. 'And that is why the affair ended four years ago,' says a friend.

True to form, K was not without solace for long. His new love was an old friend. K had known Ariane Zananiri since his teenage days when they were both at school in Switzerland. Of Egyptian parentage, Ariane was engaged to the Turkish Prince Tusson but she married Argentinian Francisco Soldati, whose family was involved in utilities. His uncle, Tino, was the Argentinian Ambassador to Paris.

Francisco died of a heart attack, aged fifty-two, while playing polo in Buenos Aires in 1991 and the widowed Ariane met up again with K. By the summer of 1993, Sally was more than aware of the situation, but seemed not to mind as much as in the past. 'In fact, of all K's girlfriends, she liked Ariane the best,' says a friend of Sally's. 'Or, as she put it: "I dislike her the least." Perhaps she was simply past caring.'

Trying It On

KANGA TRYON

The message from Lady Tryon (nicknamed 'Kanga' by her old friend the Prince of Wales who once said 'she is the only woman who has ever understood me') was typically mysterious. She had telephoned my office in early June 1997 and in my absence had left instructions to meet her that evening in the Royal Marsden Hospital, South Kensington, where she had been undergoing tests and treatment for cancer.

I was told to go to the Granard House entrance in Dovehouse Street, between the Fulham Road and Chelsea Square, mount the stairs to the first floor and then proceed directly to her room, No. 1. If I was asked who I was, I was to give another name. It was the usual cloak and dagger business that I had come to expect from Kanga, the former Dale Harper from Melbourne, Australia. As it so happened, when I arrived the Granard House entrance was firmly bolted so I had to go through the front door of the Mardsen (just round the corner from where I lived), up a flight of stairs and along a corridor where I found the matron in charge with the ward sister. On asking for Lady Tryon, I was motioned to a room where Kanga was waiting in a wheelchair with various ropes and pulleys above her bed. She had been carefully coiffured and in her small fridge beside her bed was a chilled bottle of champagne which she requested I opened. I poured a glass for her and declined one for myself, taking some mineral water instead. Now she was ready to talk.

'The good news is that I have been cleared of cancer after three years, isn't that wonderful,' said Kanga as I congratulated her. She was, otherwise, clearly a mess. Although voluptuous before her accident on 31 May 1996 – when she had fallen from a narrow window at Farm Place, Ockley, the Surrey clinic which treated drink and drug addiction, she was paralysed from the waist down – she had put on a lot of weight, mostly around the midriff. I guessed that she was in excess of 12 stone but did not comment, only asking about her strange fall from a first-floor window to the ground 25 feet below.

'Come here,' she commanded, and placed my hand at the back of her head where there was a massive indentation. 'That is where I was struck from behind before I was pushed out of the window. I don't know what I was doing there. One minute I was having a nice breakfast in the basement dining-room, the next I was hurtling to the ground. Someone is trying to murder me.'

Kanga, who would be fifty in January 1998 and planned to celebrate her half-centenary with a grand bash at The Ritz Hotel in Piccadilly, then named the two people she felt had the most reason to get rid of her. Ignoring this, we talked on, mainly about her abiding love for the Prince of Wales and she told me: 'We didn't meet in Australia as has been written. We met when Anthony took me to a Buckingham Palace reception when we were first engaged in 1973. It was love for me at first sight. The Prince is a wonderful person.' She then went on to describe another indiscretion about a salmon fishing holiday in Iceland, an annual pilgrimage which Prince Charles made with Kanga, her husband Anthony, Tim (later Lord) Tollemache and his wife Alexandra and a handful of other friends to the Hofsa River in Eastern Iceland, where in 1973 the Heir to the Throne had managed to catch forty-nine fish in seven days.

'Normally we flew commercial but one year Prince Charles invited me to the Queen's Flight because he had arranged a couple of official engagements. There were just the two of us and after dinner we went to sleep only to be awakened when the 'plane, an Andover, touched down in Reykjavik. No one had bothered to disturb us and when we opened the curtains we saw the welcoming party of Icelandic officials, a band and the British Ambassador outside on the tarmac. The Prince had just a minute or two to shave and get his clothes on and I made myself scarce. It was very funny,' Kanga told me, fully aware of the indiscretions she was vouchsafing me.

That Charles and Kanga had been close for many years was hardly a secret.

The daughter of Barry Harper, a Melbourne publisher whose interests included the local edition of *Vogue*, buxom Dale had set off on an odyssey with her mother Jean from Australia to seek a 'well-to-do' husband in the Old World. Dale told me she drew a blank at their first port of call, Hong Kong, but once in England in late 1972 she struck lucky when introduced to the Hon. Anthony Tryon. Born in May 1940, he was the only son of the 2nd Lord Tryon, who had been Keeper of the Privy Purse and Treasurer to the Queen from 1952 to 1971 and a permanent Lord in Waiting to HM. When his father died in 1976, Anthony, then a partner in Lazards merchant bank, succeeded as the 3rd Lord Tryon and Kanga became a peeress. Following the marriage she had a daughter, Zoë, then son and heir, Charles (born in May 1976 and with the Prince of Wales as a god-father), followed by twins, Edward and Victoria, who left Marlborough in summer 1998 after taking 'A' levels.

As Kanga was to tell me: 'Anthony never liked Zoë, because she was the first and a girl. He was desperate for a son.' This may explain why Zoë, who was in Australia last year in the middle of a massage and aromatherapy course, took up a sensual firedancing act working in such joints as the Cauldron nightclub in Sydney.

Zoë had also been in Farm Place being treated for drug addiction when her mother was admitted in May 1996 to recover from the drugs she had become dependent on for her cancer treatment; she had been diagnosed as having uterine cancer in 1994 and on top of that was told she had been suffering from childhood from the potentially crippling spina bifida. It was there (former patients had included the Mar-quess of Blandford, Countess Spencer and Lord Parkinson's daughter, Mary) that she had hurtled from the first-floor window. There was one witness to the incident, a counsellor who had been working with Sir Jocelyn Stevens' daughter, Pandora, another former Farm Place inmate. He was adam-ant, especially since he attempted to break her fall, that she had jumped and no one else was involved in the tragedy.

But at the Royal Marsden on that June evening last year, Kanga was quite clear about what had happened and said to me: 'The windows are far to narrow to take a jump out of. I was knocked unconscious and then my body was squeezed out. How could I have broken my back if I threw myself out of a window? The police say I broke my back because I fell backwards. If I'd jumped I would have landed on my feet, yet I came out head first and landed that way, breaking my spine. I can assure you I was pushed. The police are hopeful of solving the case.'

A week later Kanga left the Royal Marsden, having been given the all-clear from her cancer, and returned for further treatment for her paralysis to Salisbury District Hospital, a couple of miles from Great Durnford Manor, her 2,000 acre Queen Anne mansion which had been a girls' school until 1993. First she had joined in the twenty-first birthday celebrations for elder son, Charles, now studying at Edinburgh University, and bemoaned the lack of privacy at the hospital, telling me: 'I can't celebrate Communion next door because the place is crawling with photographers. Isn't that terrible?' Within a fortnight her stay had been extended, for on 17 June she was detained by local police under the Mental Health Act and sectioned for twenty-eight days. The story was that Kanga had been banned from Great Durnford after turning up with her friend, actress Sarah Miles, and they had gone down the drive to the Black Horse Inn for lunch. She left around 2pm and twenty minutes later the police were called to a house locally (where she says she was seeking refuge) and Inspector Geoff Hicks of the Wiltshire Constabulary said: 'Upon arrival, the police spoke to the lady and she was making spurious allegations. The allegations she was making were that she felt her life was in danger from someone else. As a result of these spurious allegations, the police officer formed the impression that the lady could be detained under the Mental Health Act. She was then detained by the police officers and brought to Salisbury Police Station, which is a place of safety under the Act.'

When Kanga – who had told me in June not to expect her to celebrate her silver wedding anniversary with Anthony in April 1998 – telephoned me on her mobile later that day, her version was somewhat different. She said she had been at Great Durnford at dinner the previous evening when Anthony returned from a fishing trip to Russia and told the children their mother was mad, demanding a divorce. 'I was shocked and distraught. Can you imagine anyone telling the mother of their children in front of them that she was mad?' Kanga said to me.

Tryon's mother Dreda (short for Etheldreda) said of the committal: 'We are broken-hearted and I am appalled for my grandchildren's sake. One is absolutely miserable. I am a very unhappy old woman tonight.'

In fact, Kanga told me she had first brought up the subject of divorce before she was admitted to Farm Place in May 1996 and, when Tryon exploded at Great Durnford in front of their children, she told him: 'Don't think I wasn't going to divorce you anyway. I have paid for everything during the marriage and I have kept very receipt of every payment I have made.'

Since leaving Lazards in 1983 after seven years, Kanga claimed that Anthony had devoted himself to 'shooting and fishing' and that the burden of the family finances had fallen on her. She told me (and anyone else who cared to listen) that she had redecorated Great Durnford and added: 'Anthony has never bought me even a pair of shoes during our marriage. The only thing he ever paid for was an airline ticket for himself to Australia when Daddy was ill. I reckon he owes me more than £600,000.'

Dreda, Lady Tryon, however, tells a different story. When Kanga left her fortune to the four children in her will and nothing to her husband, her response was: 'It is wonderful news. That's what mothers should do . . . It's not odd that Anthony is getting nothing. She took all his money anyway.'

Wearied by the continuing assaults, all Tryon would say as his estranged wife was sectioned, was: 'She has flipped before. She has said in the past I am going to murder her.'

When Kanga was released after the statutory twenty-eight days – people calling her on her mobile at Salisbury General commented on her lucidity – she dropped another bombshell. She claimed that correspondence between the Prince of Wales and her (some of it of an intimate nature) had gone missing from Great Durnford and in any case she was banned by Anthony from the family home.

She rang to tell me: 'An enormous amount of my precious things have gone missing including correspondence with a dear friend. I wanted my personal effects back so that they could be put in a safe place. What I've got left is now with my lawyers.'

Alarmed by the turn of events, the Prince made himself unavailable to Kanga and when she turned up in her wheelchair at a charity polo match in Wiltshire in which he was playing, he quickly disappeared as she hove into view. The Prince's cousin, Lady Elizabeth Anson, younger sister of the Earl of Lichfield, was in a unique position to observe matters impartially. She was a director of Kanga's eponymous fashion empire as well as being in touch with Prince Charles and told me: 'He's no longer in contact with her and her calls are not being put through to him.'

Released from Salisbury General, Kanga moved flamboyantly into a suite at The Ritz Hotel in Piccadilly and entertained friends to lunch and dinner in the hotel's ornate restaurant. She had made up her mind to fly home to Australia where her mother Jean, then seventy-nine, was hospitalized after suffering a second stroke and she paid for her new, luxurious lifestyle by selling her flat in Cadogan Square, Knightsbridge, for more than £700,000, a handsome profit. On 1 September she was divorced by Anthony on the grounds of her unreasonable behaviour. In his divorce petition Anthony had said that his former wife's behaviour caused him 'stress-related illness' and that she acted unreasonably. Kanga told me: 'I'm free at last! But the decree absolute will have to wait until all financial matters between that slob and me have been resolved.'

On hearing that Dreda had claimed that her son had been generous to Kanga – 'He paid for two expensive electric wheelchairs for her as well as massive alterations at the house so that she could go upstairs – Kanga replied: 'Phooey! The only thing he's done to the house is remove an old wooden ramp so that I can't get in. There's not one single thing that's been done to the house to help me.' Last word with Dreda, who was no longer in communication with Kanga: 'We have had twenty years of difficulty with her. I think she is now feeling vicious to us all. She loved the Tryon title and enjoyed being Lady Tryon. The whole thing is too tragic for words. My son is desperately upset by it all.'

After a month in Australia, Kanga moved on to India and ensconced herself at the five-star Oberoi Hotel in New Delhi to receive treatment from the locally based Dr Mosaref Ali who, ironically, had been introduced to her by the Prince of Wales. Her purpose was to walk again and she wanted to be mobile enough to arrive in the High Court under her own steam on 5 November to fight Anthony over the division of their estate. She telephoned me from Delhi and said: 'I'm already walking with crutches and by the time I get back to England in two weeks' time, I will be walking. I have already got some feeling back in my legs and I have treatments every day with a bag full of herbs which are dipped in hot oil and rubbed all over my back. And I have Swamaji who is the most incredible physio. I have got muscles I never had before. I'm confident of getting Great Durnford. I know it has been in his family for three generations, but I am the one who has made it into a home. It was a complete mess. I've done the garden, everything. I have spent between £600,000 and £650,000 on it.'

But when Kanga did return to Britain, it was to book herself into hospital. She was collected on Monday 3 November at Heathrow by her part-time driver, Gary Watson, who used to work for the Princess Royal and had a cottage at Durnford. He took her to the King Edward VII Hospital in Marylebone, where she found there was no bed for her and she then booked into Room 603 at the London Clinic, two streets away. In a call to me, she said: 'I'm here for good and I'm looking forward to returning full-time to Durnford. But first I have to have two operations on my spine, one on Wednesday which is not serious and one on Saturday, which is. Then I'm going home.'

Sadly it was not to be. The first reports from the London Clinic following the Saturday operation were not encouraging. Kanga had developed blood poisoning – septicaemia – after a skin graft operation and had been taken into the intensive care unit. With her were her daughter, Zoë, and her brother, Derek Harper. She died on 15 November and there was immediate speculation over the future of Great Durnford. In May her will was finally revealed: she left £1,277,739 gross (£745,231 net) to her four children to share equally as they reached the age of twenty-five.

The Ritz did not hold her booking for 3 January 1998. In any case Anthony and his mother had not been invited but the children were to have been honoured guests. Before she died, Kanga had been looking forward to the evening and was entertaining hopes that almost certainly would not be fulfilled. In her last conversation with me she said: 'I have invited Prince Charles. I am sure he will be there.'

Mint-condition Bounder

LUIS BASUALDO

I named him 'The Bounder' in my column and he called her 'Thunderthighs', nicknames which have stuck for Luis Basualdo and the late Christina Onassis who were inextricably involved over nearly two decades, first as lovers then as employee and employer, during which they featured regularly in the *Mail* Diary gossip column.

It was in the summer of 1980 when Christina invited her former lover Luis with his new girlfriend, Clare Lawman, to stay on her private Greek island, Scorpios, that he went to work for her as her *homme d'affaires*. As The Bounder tells it, the offer came towards the finish of his freebie fortnight at the end of an extremely long evening when Christina had ignored the Argentinian completely and he decided to reprimand her. He said: 'Look here, Christina, enough is enough. I won't be treated like shit. You've hardly spoken a word to Clare and me the whole time we've been here. We're leaving in the morning.' The threat was enough to concentrate her mind and she put into action a plan she had made to enable Luis to stay with her forever. She told him: 'My doctor insists I must have a regular companion. I want you. I don't expect you to stay with me out of pure friendship and I want you and Clare to stay with me and I'll pay you.'

Basualdo allowed himself slowly and with apparent great reluctance to be persuaded and said to her: 'Okay. If your doctor insists, if it will make you feel better, if it will help you, I'll take some money, I don't care. How much do you have in mind?'

Her first offer did not quite match up to his expectations and he gently explained that, as a polo professional, he could command a significant monthly fee. How much? enquired Christina. 'About $30,000 a month', replied Luis, lying through his gleaming teeth, but she accepted with alacrity. As he told me later: 'You see, I knew she wanted to own me, she wanted to possess me. For that I was to be her companion all the time, be constantly at her disposal, be her bodyguard, twenty-four hours a day I would be there, all hers. I insisted that Clare was part of the deal, with a dress allowance, and everything taken care of.'

When news of the appointment reached the Onassis head-quarters overlooking the harbour in Monte Carlo, there was disbelief and anger. $360,000 a year, all expenses paid ('the only time he had to put his hand in his pocket was to scratch his balls,' said one Olympic old-timer) and when I called the office to enquire about the arrangement, I was told: 'Mr Luis Basualdo is working for Miss Onassis as her *compagnon* as we say in French. That means a male companion. His duties are to accompany her to shows, dinners and concerts, and attend to her needs.'

It was an arrangement which was to work well for nearly four years and through various vicissitudes but doomed to come to an end when Christina fell in love, which she did a few days after her thirty-third birthday in 1983. It was in the foyer of Claridge's in London that Christina bumped into Henri Roussel, a French smoothie, whose son Thierry had had a brief affair with Christina ten years before. She had never forgotten him and his reputation was that he could 'make love to a barn door'. Henri cleverly worked on this and said to Christina: 'Thierry talks of you frequently and with great warmth. I know he would love to see you again.' Thierry was in Kenya at Ol Jogi (Swahili for Place of Many Thorns), the 60,000-acre ranch near Nanyuki on the Equator that the Roussels shared with billionaire Paris art dealer Daniel Wildenstein and his family, when Christina called over Christmas. She was at her heaviest and when she mentioned this to Thierry he came up with an irresistible offer. He suggested she book into the Buschinger Clinic in Marbella, close to another Roussel property, which top Paris models used and swore by. 'Lose 80 pounds and I'll marry you,' he said imperiously. She immediately flew to the Costa del Sol and booked into the clinic for an indefinite stay. Thierry sent her flowers every day with encouraging messages and, while the days dragged on, the weight began to fall away. She had shed almost 80 pounds when she returned to Paris and Thierry at the beginning of February, by which time she had fallen all over again for Roussel, but his first stipulation on proposing marriage was: 'Get rid of Basualdo.' Following their engagement on 23 February 1984, they wed twice on 17 March, first at a civil ceremony in the Paris XVIème arrondissement town hall, and then a romantic candlelit service in a Greek Orthodox church.

Basualdo was suddenly history, but he had plans for a comeback.

* * *

In December 1998 Christina Onassis, dubbed the world's richest woman, would have been celebrating her forty-eighth birthday. But the tragic billionheiress died almost exactly ten years ago in a rented house in the Tortugas Country Club, twenty-five miles northeast of Buenos Aires. Known as La Reina (the Queen) by her hosts, Alberto and Marina Dodero, Christina was found dead lying naked in a half-filled bath and the cause was given as acute pulmonary oedema, precisely the way her mother, Tina, had died in Paris fourteen years earlier. The body weight at the time of death was 76 kg (167 pounds), svelte for a woman of the world who had also been christened, somewhat unkindly, 'The Hippo' by Basualdo.

Christina – I had first met her at The Mirabelle in 1966 when she was dining with her father's insurance broker, David d'Ambrumenil (son of Sir Philip, a former chairman of Lloyd's) and his sidekick, Rodney Soloman – existed for gossip. She used to have my Diary page faxed to her wherever she was in the world. So much the better, she told me, if it contained an item about her or one of her friends and this is where Basualdo came in so handy.

He was a friend of her first ever lover, American Danny Marentette, and with an eye to the main chance Basualdo contrived a meeting in early 1971 with Christina at the Corviglia Club in St Moritz where he was lunching with Gianni Agnelli, her mother Tina and step-father Stavros Niarchos. That evening she invited him to her chalet, the Villa Bambi, for dinner and a movie (*From Here to Eternity*) and they soon became lovers. The son of an Argentine army officer, Lieutenant Colonel Hector Basualdo, who had married Countess Amana Theresa Bissone-Facio de Arias, a member of a notable South American family, Luis had been discovered in 1966 as a twenty-year-old polo player in Palm

Beach by John Coleman, patron of the Radiation team, who had signed him to play the summer season in England where his handicap rose to six (the highest is ten). In Europe Luis found no shortage of patrons and soon signed a deal with Alberto Darbovan, known as the Coffee King of Hamburg, for £2,500 a month, plus car and accommodation. He was also conducting an affair with New York socialite Justine Cushing (whose father owned the ski resort of Squaw Valley) and told Christina that he would shortly have to leave her in St Moritz for a tryst in the Austrian ski resort of St Anton with Justine. But overweening ambition led Basualdo to choose Christina and soon he was back in St Moritz and in her bed.

But the romance was not fated to prosper and when, in July 1971, Christina married ageing Californian Joe Bolker, Luis was preparing to wed Lucy Pearson, the younger daughter and heiress of Viscount Cowdray, whose 17,000 acre Sussex estate was the home of British polo. 'The first that John and Elizabeth Cowdray knew of Lucy's involvement with Basualdo was in the summer of 1972 when she asked them how much money she was worth. It was a significant question,' says her first cousin, Lady Beaverbrook, niece of Viscountess Cowdray. Clearly the answer – upwards of £7 million – pleased the Argentine who promptly wed Lucy at Caxton Hall, Westminster, without the presence of her parents or family. The couple moved to New York to take advantage of the tax breaks and Lucy bought a brownstone house on the upper east side of Manhattan. She was soon pregnant and their first child, Charlotte, was followed eighteen months later by Rupert (sadly he was found to be autistic and is in a special school, paid for by Lucy). Within five years Lucy had tired of The Bounder, although she had funded his high-goal polo team, the Golden Eagles, for which Prince Charles played during the English season which lasted from May until July (getting the heir to the throne was a brilliant coup for Basualdo). When they separated, Lucy told me from New York: 'It's all very sad. My husband and I parted this summer and he has moved out, leaving me with the children.'

Being rejected by one heiress only spurred the ambitions of fortune-hunter Luis to find another and she came in the shape of lofty Clare Lawman, whose father had homes in Belgravia and the South of France and had made his fortune from household fittings. Their affair was to last five years during which Basualdo kept close to Prince Charles with whom he had forged an unlikely bond, even helping him meet girls on their annual August junket to France for the Deauville polo tournament. As Luis explained to me: 'Prince Charles either met his girls at polo or took them to polo. In those days he was mixing at the Guards Polo Club and in 1974 and 1975 he played for my team, naval commitments permitting, and then played for the whole of the 1977 season and most of 1978. We won many competitions, including the Silver Jubilee Cup at Cirencester in 1977 and then Charles used to have Lady Sarah Spencer, Diana's eldest sister, with him, but there was nothing going on there.'

One of the girls Luis claims to have introduced Charles to was dark-haired Columbian beauty, Maria Eugenia Garces-Echeverria, who was in her early twenties and had been in London seeing Lloyd's insurance broker David d'Ambrumenil, an old friend. Says Luis: 'Maria Eugenia came from Columbia, her family were the best there, landowners and coffee growers and very rich. After I introduced them at the Cowdray Park Ball in July 1977, they started dancing together and it went on for hours and Sarah Spencer, who was being escorted by Charles, wasn't too pleased. Then Charles said he would drive Maria Eugenia, who had been staying with Lucy and me at Lodsworth, on the Cowdray estate in Sussex, back to London after the party and they went back to my house at three in the morning, got her clothes and Charles put his detective, Chief Inspector John Maclean, and Sarah in the back of his Aston Martin, which was very cramped, and drove off with Maria Eugenia in the front.'

A few days later Luis and Lucy, with Maria Eugenia, were at a party given by Robert de Pass at his house near Petworth when Prince Charles, again escorting Sarah Spencer, started talking to Maria Eugenia once more. 'Then he came up to me and asked if he could borrow my car. He said that Maria Eugenia was feeling a little tired and he wanted to drive her back to my house, which was about two miles away, without his detective knowing. I had a Range Rover and the brakes were not too good, but he took it anyway and did not come back for an hour and forty-five minutes. When I saw him again, I asked what had happened and what had taken him so long. He replied: 'Luis, it's all your fault, you bloody man, I might have been killed – your car has no brakes.' Then I heard from our nanny that he woken everyone up in our house because of what he and Maria Eugenia were doing. When I asked her the next morning, she was extremely frank and told me: 'As we got into bed, I said what shall I call you, Sir or Charles? And as he started making love, he replied: "Call me Arthur."''

According to Luis the romance he had helped start continued that August in Deauville where the Golden Eagles were competing with Charles in the line-up. Says Luis: 'I was staying at The Royale, the best hotel, and so was Charles and his detective and we discovered that Maria Eugenia was at another hotel, The Golf, as a guest of David d'Ambru-menil. So she moved into The Royale to be with Charles who stayed on for four days, making David very upset. I don't think Charles saw Maria Eugenia after that. She lives in New York now and is very happily married.'

Following Lucy's separation from Luis, Charles moved on to Les Diables Bleus, the team funded by art dealer Guy Wildenstein, and Basualdo remembers: 'I needed to find a patron myself after Lucy and I divorced. It was costing $100,000 a season to run a team then and Guy was very rich. Charles stayed with Les Diables Bleus for seven seasons with Wildenstein paying all his bills.'

But the Prince did not forget his old friend and when, in early October 1978, 500 embossed invitations were sent from Buckingham Palace to friends to attend Charles's thirti-eth birthday on 15 November, Luis was among the lucky recipients. Dancing was at 10.30pm with carriages at 2.30am and fifty family and friends were asked for dinner at the Palace where the Queen and Prince Philip, along with their eldest son, greeted the likes of Crown Princess Beatrix (later Queen) of the Netherlands and her husband, Prince Claus, ex-King Constantine of Greece and Queen Anne-Marie, Prince and Princess George of Hanover and Princess Eliza-beth of Yugoslavia.

Charles's favourite group, the Three Degrees (three black ladies from Philadelphia) were asked to give the cabaret. They had rehearsed the previous afternoon and were given strict instructions to entertain for no more than forty-five minutes, after which a breakfast of eggs, bacon, sausage, tomatoes and mushrooms and kedgeree would be served to all guests. Among Charles's personal invitees (all age groups were on the list) were Sarah Spencer and her two younger sisters, Jane and Diana, his old flame Lady Jane Wellesley, daughter of the Duke of Wellington, Lady Camilla Fane, who had been out with Charles a couple of times, and actress Susan George, who had shared several intimate dates with the Heir to the Throne.

When the cabaret was announced, Basualdo and the other guests moved into the Picture Gallery and he says: 'I sat next to Lady Diana Spencer with King Constantine on the other side. I introduced myself and she said she had heard of me through her sister. Diana was just about the youngest person there; she was only seventeen and looked very different from her later image – she had short, mousy hair and a lot of puppy fat. She was very shy, very naive but rather nice. Apart from saying hello, I don't think she'd ever spoken to Prince Charles.'

Despite his rather reduced circumstances following his divorce, which ended with a final £220,000 pay-off from the Cowdray family, Luis decided on a generous gift for his host that night. 'I got a bit drunk and went over the top and offered Prince Charles a polo pony for his birthday. A week later, when I was back in New York, his polo manager, Major Ronald Ferguson, called me and asked me to confirm the offer in writing, which I did, and I didn't hear any more from Charles until January when I received a handwritten letter dated New Year's Day on Sandringham writing paper. It read: Dear Luis, I am so sorry that it has taken all this time to write and thank you for your extraordinarily kind and generous offer of a polo pony, which you rather rashly made at that party in November! Needless to say, I would be delighted to accept your splendid birthday present with immense gratitude.' It ended: 'Thank you again so much for a particularly special present which is enormously appreciated. Happy New Year! Yours ever, Charles.'

Eventually Charles rejected the pony, telling Basualdo in

public at the Guards Polo Club: 'It's like a donkey,' but his split from Lucy presaged greater misfortunes on the polo field. Luis had been investing heavily on the commodity market and lost an estimated £40,000 to M. L. Doxford and Co., a St James's firm which had been paid £25,000 and planned to sue for the remainder. Around the same time rock drummer Ginger Baker, who had started a club in 1978 with Basualdo on the Northamptonshire estate of Lord Rothschild's sister, Miriam, claimed that The Bounder owed him £6,000 for 'stabling and feed' and the project had cost him his Harrow home. Then Major Ferguson had him thrown out of the Guards Polo Club, the first such expulsion in twenty-four years. The final straw came when his debts led him to the bankruptcy courts, with him owing an alleged £30,000. Boldly Basualdo told me: 'I have no money at all. It's is all in my family trust and they pay some of my bills.' He was finally saved by the Falklands War and his claim that he was unable to gain a visa to visit Britain and face his creditors. But by then he had met Christina Onassis again and his fortunes had been revived.

Christina had been married three times. After the fiasco with Joe Bolker, she wed Greek banker Alexander Andreadis on 19 July 1975 with step-mother Jackie Kennedy as a witness (that lasted fourteen months), and then Soviet shipping expert Sergei (known as Serge) Kausov, described as a one-eyed, gold-toothed KGB operative, in the summer of 1978 after meeting him in Paris the previous November when she walked into the Paris offices of Sovfracht to clarify some details in the deal for the Russians to lease five Olympic tankers on five-year charters. He was then forty, married to a Russian, Natalya, with a nine-year-old-daughter Katya who remained in Moscow, but so keen were the Soviet authorities to have Christina Onassis in their midst that they rubber-stamped a divorce with Christina paying off Natalya and making ample provisions for the Kausov daughter.

They became engaged to marry in Moscow in August but somewhat ominously she told Florence Grinda (whose ex-husband, Jean-Noël, was the uncle of Thierry Roussel) a few days before the wedding: 'I'm no longer in love with Serge, but I can't let him down. I owe that much to him. It's gone too far to stop now . . . but there certainly won't be any children!' But eleven weeks after the wedding, Christina told Kausov it was all over. She told friends: 'When we go to dinner parties, nobody talks to him, nobody finds him chic. He's a bore and can't participate in the gossip.'

Kausov exited from the marriage with a pay-off of two tankers valued at around £6 million and turned them into a fortune in excess of £100 million, subsequently marrying Ali Harkess, daughter of a South African-based judge whose wife and two daughters were called 'The Coven' by Tory MP Alan Clark in his infamous *Diaries*, which revealed that he had bedded all three.

The Kausovs had a daughter in 1992 and divorced in early summer 1997. With his fortune Serge bought, for £5 million, the Oliver Messel-designed Mustique house of Lord Glenconner, set in 20 acres beside a cove, razed it to the ground and replaced it with a Taj Mahal-style edifice costing an estimated £15 million. He also has homes in London and Switzerland.

With Basualdo out of the picture, Christina settled into married life, living in two apartments in the same building at 88 Avenue Foch in Paris, an eighteen-room Swiss house called Boislande, near Gingins, twelve miles outside Geneva, the Villa Cristal in St Moritz, an apartment in London's Grosvenor Square (which she quickly sold at a £45,000 profit and moved instead to Eaton Square) – and the island of Skorpios. She had $330 million on deposit earning interest and was banking $1 million a week. To add to her joy, she quickly became pregnant and on 29 January 1985 produced a daughter, Athina Onassis Roussel, named after her late mother, Tina (who had died in Paris, of a lung oedema, on 10 October 1974). The baby, delivered by caesarean section, weighed 6 pounds 2 ounces, and the family moved into the Avenue Foch with two nannies and a bodyguard, two chefs (François and Christian), two chauffeurs, Hélène, the chief housekeeper, headwaiter Yves Terrier, two maids, and Christina's old maid, Eleni, and her husband, George.

It was Basualdo (whose name was forbidden by Thierry to be uttered in his company) who discovered that Roussel was two-timing his wife. Roussel's longtime girlfriend, Swedish model Marianne 'Gaby' Landhage, was pregnant by him and, six months after the arrival of Athina, gave birth to a son, Erik Christoffe François in Malmo, Sweden, on 31 July, with Thierry flying in his wife's latest toy, a three-engined Falcon 50, for the baptism. Christina was 'furious' and telephoned Basualdo, offering him $60,000 to fly to Sweden to take photographs of Gaby and her child. She told The Bounder: 'I want to see what my husband's child looks like,' but he, more out of logistics than lack of greed, refused.

While $60,000 may have seemed a small fortune, Basualdo was able to refuse because he was beginning to enjoy the fruits of a larger one. Police in Switzerland and Austria were alerted when $1.2 million was transferred, in the summer of 1985, from Christina's Credit Suisse account in St Moritz, where she owned a chalet, across the border to an account in the name of Charles Spencer in the Bank of Tyrol in Lanbeck, Austria. The money was then withdrawn from that account, in cash, and disappeared.

This is what happened: Charles Spencer was a corruption of the forenames of Christina's former step-brother, the Marquess of Blandford (her mother Tina had divorced Ari Onassis and married the future Duke of Marlborough in 1961) who was christened Charles James Spencer-Churchill and known as James. He had become a good friend of Basualdo, after various bouts of heroin addiction (at one stage Christina had him kidnapped and put into a Paris clinic from which he quickly escaped), and the two men set out in August 1985 for a tour of Europe in Basualdo's Mercedes, eventually heading for Cadaques in northern Spain where The Bounder had promised to introduce James to brewery heiress Daphne Guinness, then eighteen and the daughter of Lord Moyne. First stop was St Moritz and Basualdo told his passenger that he had to 'do a little banking business'. The Bounder also had an account at Credit Suisse and proudly showed James a statement with a credit balance of almost 500,000 Swiss francs so it was not surprising that Luis demanded and got a personal appointment with the bank's senior executive in St Moritz, Mr Matisse, who also dealt with the Onassis account. After fifteen minutes, Basualdo came out of the bank and announced: 'Now we go to Austria. I have some more banking to do.' They duly arrived in the little town of Lanbeck and Basualdo asked James: 'Which bank should I bank with here, my boy?' James had no strong feelings on the matter and Basualdo decided he liked the local branch of the Bank of Tyrol and James says: 'He gave me the keys of the car and told me to come back in fifteen minutes. I was quite hungry, and went and got a sandwich.'

When James returned to the bank, Basualdo was waiting. He said: ' "Look, my boy, I've told the manager who you are and he says he's never seen a real English aristocrat before and he'd like to meet you." So I went in and Bas, as I called him, introduced us. And something I don't quite understand, he gave my passport to the manager.' Believing that the Austrian merely wished to see proof that he truly was who Basualdo claimed him to be, James did not follow the conversation between the two men, part of which was conducted in German. 'There was something about a password which you use for the banker johnnies to send you money. Bas told me about this, but wouldn't let on what the password was.'

In fact it was '*parakalo*', the Greek for 'please', but that was between Basualdo and the Bank of Tyrol, and certainly not for the ears of Christina who in the autumn on 1986 just happened to be passing through her office in Monte Carlo when she was asked how much she wished her Credit Suisse account in St Moritz to be topped up by (it was used to pay for her skiing holidays and visits to the Villa Cristal) as it was almost empty. Christina was horrified – the account usually held between $1 million and $2 million and she had not used it since that February when there was plenty of cash in it – and she immediately identified Basualdo as the mysterious 'Herr Spencer' from recordings provided her by the Bank of Tyrol.

In their separate and distinct ways, few men were closer to Christina than James and Luis Basualdo and she did not know how to deal with the situation. She was hurt, angry and frustrated and telephoned James's father, known to her as 'Sunbun', and told him what had happened. Sunbun immediately called James, who denied everything and expressed profound shock. Christina flew to London to confront James herself and invited him and his sister, Lady Henrietta, to dinner at Pier 31, a Chelsea restaurant part-owned by Princess Margaret's son, Viscount Linley, and the photographer, Earl of Lichfield. Says James: 'She had a

Greek fellow with her, a lawyer. She asked me to tell him exactly when had happened in Lanbeck. He asked me if I had signed anything, that sort of thing. Christina said: "You must have had something to do with it, James." I told her I had done some bad things in my life, but I had never ripped her off. I don't think she believed me. I was very upset.'

The meal continued awkwardly, and driving home, Henrietta said to her brother: 'Don't take it to heart, James. She is very, very unhappy. She doesn't know what she is saying.' Appearing a few days later to accept the Marquess's innocence, Christina invited him to lunch (she was staying in a suite at the Park Lane Hilton). But when he arrived at 1.30pm, Eleni told him that Christina was still asleep and did not wish to be disturbed. 'Christina later called and said she was sorry and invited me again. Half a dozen times the same thing happened. I'd turn up and she was asleep and did not want to be awakened. I gave up finally. It was sad, because I never saw her again,' says James.

Meanwhile the net was closing in on Luis Basualdo. Two summers earlier he had been stopped at 4am in a red light area off the Bayswater Road and arrested on suspicion of driving while under the influence of alcohol. He spent the night in Paddington Green police station, and in court later that morning was given unconditional bail for the case to be heard at a later date. But police had been unable to pin him down and a warrant was issued for his arrest on the matter. In November 1987, acting on a tip-off, the police apprehended him at The Ritz Hotel in Piccadilly. He again spent the night at Paddington Green and the following morning, at Marlborough Street magistrates court, he pleaded guilty to the drink-driving offence, was banned from driving in Britain for twelve months and fined £200. But as he left the court he was detained by detectives and taken to Rochester Row police station where he was informed that the Austrian police sought him in connection with the Lanbeck affair. He was asked to surrender his passport and conveniently handed over an American one (he had become a US citizen in 1979) while retaining his original Argentine document in the name of Luis Sosa Basualdo. He went back to Clare Lawman's Knightsbridge flat where he had left his clothes, took her out to dinner and, the following morning, fled the country on his Argentinian passport, heading for Madrid and a direct flight to South America. According to Basualdo, it was not until that moment that he had any idea he was a wanted man and that Christina had made a statement to the Austrian police implicating him in what appeared to be a massive fraud. He was furious, he claimed. He was sure that Christina had authorized the Lanbeck bank account herself and this was his version of events as told to me:

'My situation with Christina was that she always said she would give me ten times my salary if ever she found someone else. When she married Roussel she wanted to keep her promise, she gave me a little bit here, a little bit there. But she said: "I don't want Thierry to find out, I don't want the bank to know I give you so much money, so why don't you open a bank account in another country, a secret account, and we can use that to pay the doctor in New York (who supplied her with her 'black beauties' and other legal drugs) and Blandford and all those other bills?" She reckoned she owed more or less one million dollars.

'She wanted to help Blandford out because he was desperate, a drug addict. He used to come to see me at The Ritz Hotel at three in the morning begging me for money, crying. I just couldn't put up with this and said to Christina, "You almost locked him up in a loony bin, you help". So she said I was to get James to open an account. She suggested

Austria, so Blandford and I went to Lanbeck, the closest place to Switzerland. The account was opened by Charles James Spencer-Churchill, Marquess of Blandford. The passport on the front says Marquess of Blandford. Inside it says Charles James Spencer-Churchill. The bank settled on Charles James Spencer because they were trying to be accommodating. The account was to receive money from Christina's account. The money was transferred by cheque or by wire. They were absolutely genuine cheques. The amount was $1.2 million. Some money had to go to the doctor in New York. Blandford received about $60,000.

'Blandford opened the account in his name with his passport. It was exactly what Christina wanted. But then she tried to cover her tracks. She was afraid of Thierry, annoyed with me because I hadn't gone to Sweden to try to get pictures of Gaby and the baby; I hadn't paid the doctor in New York some money I was supposed to have paid him . . . so she denounced me.'

Safely back in Buenos Aires, and out of reach of the Interpol international arrest warrant, Basualdo says he called Christina in Paris and demanded an explanation. Remarkably she advised him to forget it. 'Forget it!' he remembers retorting angrily. 'I organized the whole thing just as you wanted it, so that I could give money to people like James and the doctor in New York, who sends you the mavro mavro pills, and now you try to have me put in prison. She said: "Luis, I am dropping all charges. I was very upset. You didn't pay the people you were meant to pay, you didn't get the pictures I wanted. I know you're not guilty. There is no more problem. You don't have to worry about a thing."'

In fact Christina was reimbursed the full amount by Credit Suisse and the Austrian authorities ignored her requests not to press charges and went ahead with their case against

Basualdo. But by then Christina had other worries – Gaby was again pregnant by Thierry and it was the last straw. She had given him, by her own estimate $57 million since their marriage. In the New Year Roussel left Europe for an extended business trip to Texas and when he returned in May 1987, he had a new daughter, Sandrine Johanna Helene Francine, born in Dallas and registered Roussel-Landhage – and an ex-wife on his hands. But the divorce was anything but final: Christina set out to have another child by Thierry and promised him the earth if she succeeded. She even made friends with Gaby, inviting her to Boislande and when she took Le Trianon, a magnificent property in St Jean-Cap Ferrat for the months of July and August, rather than go back to Skorpios, Gaby and the children were accommodated in the villa next door, also rented by Christina.

Apart from her attempts to conceive, Christina had decided on purchasing a property in Argentina, as much as for an investment as to be near her 'best friends' 'Dode' Dodero and his wife, Marina, who was having a fortieth birthday party. She flew to Buenos Aires from Paris, arriving on 9 November accompanied by her faithful maid, Eleni Syros, and her personal interior decorator and pal, Atalanta de Castellane. Just a month earlier she had made a new will, in her own writing, and it read: 'MY WILL: I, the undersigned Christina Onassis, daughter of Aristotle Onassis and Athina Livanos, being of age and enjoying my physical and mental capacities, hereby make my last will and testament and state that in the event of my death, I wish and direct that my estate (including my inheritance from my father and my mother) be distributed to the following beneficiaries, in the proportions and the amounts stated opposite the name of each one of them to the exclusion of all other relatives and any other persons.' The finished document was seven pages long and written in English. Seven beneficiaries were to share $6.6 million; Thierry Roussel was to receive a life annuity of $1.42 million a year provided the annual income produced from the estate for Athina was not less than $4.25 million. Athina's affairs were to be 'managed prudently and diligently' until her eighteenth birthday by a board of four Greek trustees and Thierry Roussel. A simple majority vote would decide all issues.

In Buenos Aires Christina was officially staying with the Doderos in their apartment but she also took a sixth floor room at The Alvear Palace Hotel nearby with a further room for Eleni next to hers. Her hotel room was her office, from which she could organize her search for a new property, and it would also enable her to telephone her friends in Europe and the United States; the hotel had direct dial, a luxury in Buenos Aires, while the Doderos had to make overseas calls through an operator.

Learning of her whereabouts, Basualdo and members of his family began to hang around the Alvear Palace hoping to see Christina, but she managed to avoid them although she talked once or twice on the telephone. As far as she was concerned the Credit Suisse matter was over and she had other fish to fry. Her escort in Buenos Aires was Marina's brother, Jorge Tchomlekdjoglou, a bachelor who looked after the family businesses, but they were not lovers. She partied, most publicly at the American Embassy, where she posed in a red dress, and the Uruguayan Embassy, at which she wore her $2 million diamond drop, and on 17 November she dined at the Cabana restaurant, famed for its giant T-bone steaks, with Jorge and the Doderos. The next day the group set out for the Tortugas for a long weekend. Within twenty-four hours Christina – La Reina – was dead.

Her remains were returned to Greece on Wednesday 23

November in preparation for her funeral in Athens and interment in Skorpios. Blandford and his father Sunbun flew to Greece and stayed at The Grand Bretagne, as did Thierry and his group. At the cathedral, with rain pouring down, there were scuffles with chairs being overturned as reporters and photographers competed to get the best views; when Thierry arrived, walking behind the coffin, the crowds shouted 'Assassin, assassin', to which he, not understanding Greek and supposing them to be words of commiseration, answered with a smile and a wave. Fewer than forty people followed the coffin to Skorpios, which Ari had bought exactly twenty-five years before, and she was buried in the tiny chapel on top of a hill next to her father and brother, Alexander, the same chapel where Ari had married Jackie Kennedy.

Thierry duly married Gaby and she produced another child, daughter Johanna, four years ago. They live en famille with Athina in Lussy sur Morges, Switzerland, with other homes in Paris, Sologne, a two-hour drive south of the French capital and Ibiza. Skorpios, left to Athina in her mother's will, remains neglected and Thierry, who is accused by Christina's Greek trustees of squandering a £60 million fortune obtained through his three-year marriage to the billionheiress, is fighting to gain control of Athina's inheritance in the Greek courts. In the event of Athina's death before her eighteenth birthday in 2003, he will get the lot.

Following Christina's demise, Basualdo managed to have the fraud case heard in Buenos Aires (which did not have an extradition treaty with Austria) and, almost exactly four years after Christina's death, was cleared by the courts of illegally obtaining the money from her bank account. He has never returned to England and sought his American passport from the police, perhaps still fearing the Interpol warrant.

His second marriage, in December 1990, to New Yorker Jan Leach ended after seven months and his last romance was with elderly heiress Martha Reid, the widow of Russian aristocrat, Prince Stanislas Kropotkin. He claimed she was in her seventies, she said she was two decades younger, but that foundered in the summer of 1993 when he told me he was dying. 'I am suffering from cirrhosis and anyone who says I won't reach fifty is betting on a certainty.'

However, in May Basualdo, the last mint condition twenty-four carat gigolo whose role model was the late Dominican playboy polo player, Porfirio Rubirosa (who married both Doris Duke and Barbara Hutton, the richest heiresses of their day), reached fifty-three and was talking of returning a New York where he remains a member of the snooty Racquet and Tennis Club on Park Avenue: 'I expect to be back there soon. There are no legal problems.'

But for a man who once said his New Year's resolution was 'To give up drugs and poor people,' he has been in and out of clinics in Argentina being treated for addiction in the last couple of years and has told friends that none of the cash he got from Christina is left. For a man who has never worked, except for parting women from their cash, the future looks rather bleak, but he retains his optimism. His last words to me this summer were: 'Do you know any heiresses that might suit me?'

Goldenballs and *the* Eye

SIR JAMES GOLDSMITH

On Monday 8 October 1973, the very first Dempster Diary lead on my return from five months in New York concerned Jimmy Goldsmith, the Eton-educated financier who had built up his Cavenham Foods concern (it included Marmite and Bovril) into a £180 million company in less than a decade. A legendary figure who had quit Eton at sixteen after winning £8,000 at Lewes races on a three-horse accumulator, Jimmy had moved to Oxford where his elder brother, Teddy, was an undergraduate and quickly beguiled his brother's circle which included gambler John Aspinall. The son of Major Frank Goldsmith, who owned The Scribe and Lotti hotels in Paris and The Carlton in Cannes, and his wife Marcelle, who came from the Auvergne, Jimmy had hit the headlines when, aged twenty, he had eloped with pregnant Bolivian tin heiress, Isabel Patino, who died shortly after giving birth to their daughter, also named Isabel. Her father, Antenor, disapproved of his daughter marrying a Jew, to which Goldsmith replied: 'And my family is worried by my association with a Red Indian.'

Goldsmith then married his secretary, Ginette Lery and lived between France, with her and their two children, son Manes, then fourteen, and daughter Alix, nine, and London where his constant companion was the Marquess of Londonderry's sister, Lady Annabel Birley, wife of clubowner Mark Birley who had named his Berkeley Square boîte after her.

I had flown to London on Thursday 4 October to begin the Diary on the orders of *Mail* editor David English. Within a few hours of arriving back in Britain I heard that Annabel, then thirty-nine, was pregnant with her fourth child, thirteen years after the birth of her last, daughter India Jane Birley. The father, I was told, was Goldsmith, so I telephoned him to get his confirmation. An old acquaintance, he chuckled and told me: 'I'm absolutely delighted that Lady Annabel is having her fourth child. But there is no question of our marrying. She is married and I am married and I live with my wife.' Off the record he added: 'Be very careful what you write.' My call to Annabel, who lived in South Kensington in half a house set in one acre and approached through Onslow Square, produced a similar quote and she said to me about Mark, who lived in two houses around the corner, on the main road close to South Kensington tube station: 'We see each other all the time. There is no question of divorce.' Three months later she produced a daughter, Jemima, who twenty years later married Pakistani sportsman turned politician Imran Khan. But within thirty months of this happy event, Goldsmith and I were at war, with him attempting to end my journalistic career.

The summer of 1976 was long and hot enough, without having to spend too much of it in the courts, courtesy of Jimmy Goldsmith, who had been knighted in the

Resignation Honours List of departing Prime Minister Harold Wilson, almost certainly because of his longstanding friendship with Baroness Falkender, Wilson's personal and political secretary. The former Marcia Williams had prepared the infamous Lavender List of individuals to be honoured, and the *Daily Express* trumpeted that Goldsmith was in line for a peerage with the headline: 'It's Lord Goldsmith.' In the event Jimmy (as everyone called him) had to settle for a knighthood and there was talk that Marcia, as a *quid pro quo*, had been offered a directorship of Cavenham on her retirement from No. 10. This Goldsmith denied to me and, in fact, it never came about although talk of a romantic relationship between him and Marcia was never denied.

I had known Jimmy for some years and, following our chat in October 1973, had little cause to contact him until June 1975, when I put in a telephone call to him at his Regent's Park HQ where his assistant was Nicholas Soames, a grandson of Sir Winston Churchill (and later a Tory MP and Minister). I was at Heathrow Airport en route to the South of France to stay with an old friend, Sir Max Aitken's wife Vi, at La Capponcina, the famous Cap d'Ail villa of the late Lord Beaverbrook and now owned by the charitable Beaverbrook Foundation. At the airport I had bumped into Dominic Elwes in the departure lounge. A social gadfly and son of Royal portrait painter Simon Elwes, he had sprung to prominence in 1957 when he had eloped with heiress Tessa Kennedy (who was a ward-of-court) to Gretna Green. They had been refused permission to marry there and flew on to Cuba where, on New Year's Day 1958, they wed, followed by another ceremony in New York. When they returned to England, he spent a fortnight in jail for contempt of court. They had three sons before 'Dommie' tired of marriage, leaving their Kensington house one evening, ostensibly to buy a packet of cigarettes in the nearby pub, the Scarsdale, and vanished for two years. They divorced in 1969 and Tessa became an interior decorator, working for King Hussein and Queen Noor of Jordan, among others, and the mistress of Hollywood film producer, Elliot Kastner.

At Heathrow, Elwes was in a clearly emotional state and asked me, as a recent friend, to help. A week or so previously *The Sunday Times* magazine had published an article, with a front page picture of Lady Annabel in Venice with Lord Lucan, and it included a drawing by Elwes, an accomplished artist and close friend of the missing peer, of a supposed scene inside the Clermont Club. The immediate effect was that Dominic was ostracized by the Lucan set – who believed he had supplied the snap as well as the drawing – and he was later to receive a letter from Mark Birley, banning him from both his clubs, Mark's in Charles Street and Annabel's. But before all this happened he was in tears at Heathrow and said to me: 'You know Jimmy, call him and say I didn't betray Annabel, Lucky or him. Of course, I drew the picture for *The Sunday Times* – it had my name on it. They paid me £200 – sorely needed.' So from a callbox in the departure lounge, I rang the Goldsmith number, which was answered by Soames and was soon put through to Jimmy. I explained to him that I was at Heathrow with a distraught Elwes and assured Goldsmith that Dominic had not been selling stories or photographs of Lucan to the newspapers. He replied that he never thought Dominic had, to give him his regards and to tell him not to worry. I passed on the message and a visibly relaxed Elwes boarded the Air France flight a couple of rows in front of me. When we were airborne, he ordered a drink and asked me to sit with him. 'I'm going to Cap Ferrat where Spenny Compton [later the Marquess of

Northampton] has lent me his apartment. None of this would have happened if Lucky was still around, it's all his fault. I know he's still alive and plead with him to contact me.'

At Nice airport I was met by Sir Max's youngest daughter Laura and son Maxwell (who became Lord Beaverbrook on the death of his father in 1985) and introduced them to Elwes. We arranged to meet for a drink at The Voile d'Or, a fancy hotel on St Jean-Cap Ferrat a few hundred yards from his borrowed apartment, a couple of days hence and it was the start of a romance between Laura and Elwes which only ended with his suicide, at the age of forty-two, that September. In between the South of France and Dominic's tragic death, he had taken Laura to Cuarton in southern Spain, which he had helped develop in 1967, and they saw each other constantly. His body was found at his South Kensington house opposite the San Frediano restaurant by his longstanding love, Melissa Wyndham, whose elder sister Jane had married the Duke of Marlborough's brother, Lord Charles Spencer-Churchill. Beside it was a suicide note, blaming 'A, M and J' for his death, a reference to Lady Annabel Birley, her ex-husband Mark Birley and Sir James Goldsmith, by then also the father of Annabel's five-month old son, Zacharias.

It was at Dominic's memorial service at the end of November at the Church of the Immaculate Conception, Farm Street, Mayfair that my path crossed again with Jimmy's, leading to the 1976 summer of discontent between us. Outside in a slight drizzle after the service, John Aspinall, who had delivered a suitable con brio address (of Dominic he said: 'He lived with topicality and for the moment. But he could never find the fame to which he knew he was entitled') to a congregation which included champion racing driver

Graham Hill, was confronted by Tremayne Rodd, the chunky former Scottish international scrum-half and heir to the barony of his uncle, Lord Rennell of Rodd. In front of me and a dozen or so people who had already left the church, he punched 'Aspers' on the jaw and ran off up the street, shouting: 'That's what I think of your bloody speech, Aspinall.' The zoo owner and Mayfair gambler riposted in typical fashion, nursing his right jaw: 'I am used to this sort of thing, dealing with wild animals. Luckily, I have a strong chin.' Later an unrepentant Tremayne, a cousin of the dead man, said: 'I am very overwrought and angry. His speech was totally inappropriate in every way. I am most upset.' The following day, Wednesday 26 November, I was having lunch with Richard Ingrams, editor of *Private Eye* where I had been the columnist Grovel for five years, when I mentioned I had been present at the amazing scene involving Rodd and Aspers. Ingrams asked me to write an account of Elwes and his feud with Goldsmith and Birley which I did, drawing on the events following the disappearance of the Earl of Lucan. I gave this to Ingrams who passed it on to my predecessor as Grovel, Downside-educated Patrick Marnham, elder son of Sir Ralph Marnham, former Sergeant-Surgeon to the Queen, and still a contributor to the *Eye*. Foolishly, he added one, hugely erroneous fact, that Goldsmith had been at the ad hoc lunch at Aspinall's London house following the murder by Lucan of nanny Sandra Rivett, and suggested in an article titled 'All's Well That Ends Elwes', and published on 12 December 1975, that Jimmy (who had, in fact, been in Ireland on business on the fateful day) had orchestrated the flight of Lucan. It resulted in the mother of all libel actions with Goldsmith attempting to have Ingrams and Marnham jailed for criminal libel and showering writs on the *Eye*, its printers, distributors and even individual shops which sold the satirical magazine around the country, some ninety-three in total. Later, much later, Goldsmith explained to me: 'Lucan was not a friend of mine, just an acquaintance. But he was a friend of Annabel's. What *Private Eye* accused me of was an illegal act. That's why I sued them and wanted to put them out of business.'

Not content with issuing libel writs, Goldsmith took out a High Court action against various *Eye* staffers, including Auberon Waugh, who penned a hilarious Diary which drew more on fantasy than fact, and me. His complaint was simple: apart from attacking Goldsmith in the *Eye*, we were able to write adversely about him in the various newspapers we worked for. He wanted to put a halt to this and I found myself being defended by Irishman James Comyn, a QC who used to roll his own Sweet Afton cigarettes (later to become Mr Justice Comyn and a knight) along with the other *Eye* journalists who were labelled 'pus' by Goldsmith and a 'canker on society'. It was all rather depressing.

On 29 July 1976 Ingrams and Marnham were appearing at Bow Street magistrates court where Goldsmith was pressing Sir Kenneth Barraclough, the chief Metropolitan magistrate, to jail the *Eye* two for criminal libel. I arrived at court with Ingrams and his wife, Mary. In anticipation of being incarcerated, he had had a haircut and bought a new yellowy corduroy jacket. When asked by a waiting journalist what he feared most about going to jail, he quipped: 'Being visited by the Earl of Longford!' Just then a taxi decanted Goldsmith and Lady Annabel, whose divided patterned frock was caught by a gust of wind, revealed a hint of under-wear. 'Disgusting woman,' railed Mary, known as Lady Gnome, as I restrained her from physically attacking Annabel.

In court, we were seated next to Jimmy Comyn and just

below the witness box into which stepped Goldsmith, who was supported also by a slumbering John Aspinall. He was like a caged tiger and at one stage Barraclough admonished him with the words: 'A little less of the theatricals, Sir James.' It was the middle of Glorious Goodwood, the end of season race meeting at the Duke of Richmond's 12,000 acre Sussex estate. Goldsmith had a horse running in the 4.05 and I went out shortly afterwards to ring a bookmaker and find out its fate. It was a winner. Back inside the court, with Jimmy still in the witness-box, I passed up a note to him which I had written. It stated: 'Congratulations, your horse has won the 4.05 at Goodwood. However, the Stewards have demanded a dope test on the owner.' Goldsmith read this as Comyn was cross-examining him and had asked him a particularly serious question. He was diverted by my note and on reading it burst out into maniacal laughter, saying: 'Very funny, very funny.' Neither Sir Kenneth nor the *Eye* QC knew what to make of this strange outburst while the rest of us chortled at the jape. In the circumstances Ingrams and Marnham escaped jail and as we all left the court, walking down a long staircase at Bow Street to ground level, Mary had again to be restrained from attacking Annabel. A Sunday paper printed the picture of Annabel and her flying skirt and commented that it was the first time she had been photographed with Goldsmith although they had been close for twenty years. The item added that, while she was divorced from Birley, Jimmy remained steadfastly married to Ginette.

The legal costs were enormous and while Goldsmith was able to finance his side from his own pocket – he was a multimillionaire – the *Eye* had begun a 'Goldenballs Fund', soliciting funds from readers who obliged with extraordinary generosity. But the magazine also staged a charity evening at Stamford Bridge Football ground, home of Chelsea, where one of the attractions was billed as a wrestling match between me and Johnny Kwango, who appeared most Saturdays on the ITV afternoon sports programme along with such favourites at Jackie Pallo, Mick McManus, Billy Two Rivers and Johnny Kincaid. All who watched realized that the wrestlers were not young but it was not until after Kwango's death that I learned he was fifty-six when I fought him. We had met at the gym at 73 Eaton Place, under the surgery of Dr Tony Greenburgh, to work out a few moves. Johnny kindly took me through my paces and we rehearsed a few throws. 'All you have to do is appear to be knocked out after a couple of rounds,' he told me.

At Stamford Bridge, a crowd of more than ten thousand gathered for the evening's entertainment, swelling the coffers of the Goldenballs Fund. Below the East Stand, I was in a dressing-room along with Johnny and we both donned leotards before being led out to the floodlit ring. Here the excitement of the evening got to me and after throwing a compliant Kwango around for six rounds, I came out confident for the seventh. 'If you don't pretend to be knocked out in this, I'll kill you,' snarled Kwango, less than pleased that I was not working to the script. I duly obliged and never saw Johnny again. I later learned that he had been born in London and his mother, Irene Best, hailed from Barbados, leaving with her sister when she was ten to join a German circus where she became a strong woman and, possibly, Europe's first woman wrestler. Kwango died, aged seventy-three, on 19 January 1994.

The battle between Goldsmith and the *Eye* made both of them famous. He became a national figure and the *Eye* circulation later rose spectacularly as sympathizers rallied to its banner, focusing hatred on Goldsmith as an overly privileged and predatory businessman who was abusing his wealth by attacking humble journalists. The war was often categorized as The Establishment (ie Goldsmith) against the naughty satirical threat of the *Eye*, but in fact it was the other way around. The *Eye* was The Establishment and the Jewish Goldsmith, whose various and nefarious business practises came under close scrutiny in the many court skirmishes, the outsider. The bruising litigation dragged on and only came to an end when Goldsmith evinced an interest in buying Beaverbrook Newspapers, publishers of the *Daily Express*, the *Sunday Express* and the London *Evening Standard*. At the beginning of 1977 he bought a 40 per cent shareholding and when I saw him at a publishing party at Thirty Pavilion Road on 27 January, I asked him what he was up to. 'It is purely for investment purposes,' he told me. 'In the last week I have made a profit of £500,000 on the shares. Tell me where else you can make half a million in a week.'

By May and after seventeen months he was tired of the libel game and settled the matter at the behest of *Evening Standard* editor Charles Wintour who told Goldsmith that if he wanted to go through with his bid for Beaverbrook Newspapers and become a Press Baron, then it would look wrong to have him attempting to close down a small, but influential, publication. It was estimated that Jimmy had costs of around £60,000 while the Goldenballs Fund had raised £40,000 and at the time of the settlement had almost run out of cash. Said Richard: 'We shall continue to write about Goldsmith, especially if he's going to be active in Fleet Street. The funny thing is that Goldsmith has become a public figure by suing *Private Eye*.' The *Eye* agreed to publish an abject full-page apology and pay Goldsmith £30,000 in instalments over ten years. In the event Beaverbrook

Newspapers were taken over by Trafalgar House, the trading group headed by Nigel Broackes who put his lieutenant, Victor Matthews, in charge of the publications. Broackes eventually received a knighthood, Matthews a Life Peerage and when the company was sold to United Newspapers, the shares had increased thirtyfold, making Lord Matthews, who retired to the tax-haven Channel Island of Jersey, an estimated £50 million fortune.

In November 1978, having divorced Ginette the previous month, Jimmy finally married Lady Annabel in Paris, physically attacking a *Daily Express* photographer and journalist who were attempting to record the event. Claiming that under French law he was allowed to do so, Jimmy wrote to *The Times* thanking the *Express* hacks for making his day. The marriage gave rise to the quip, which he always denied making, that: 'When you marry your mistress, you create a job vacancy.' Goldsmith bought Ormeley Lodge, an early 18th-century mansion on the edge of Richmond Park overlooking Ham Common from Lord Howard de Walden and in October 1980 Lady Annabel gave birth to their third child, a son named Benjamin, who followed his father to Eton.

But back in Paris he continued to live under the same roof as Ginette and soon another mistress surfaced – Laure Boulay de la Meurthe, a niece of the Comte de Paris, Pretender to the French throne. She fell for him when she went to interview M. Goldsmith (as he was known in France) for *Paris Match*. He bought her a house in Long Island and in 1984 she produced a daughter Carlotte. Later she had a son and moved between half a house in Paris (once the home of Cole Porter and the base for Ginette who lived in the other half) and an apartment in New York before Jimmy bought her a magazine of her own to edit, *Point de Vue*.

By the time he died of pancreatic cancer in July 1997 at his Costa del Sol estate outside Marbella, Jimmy had amassed a fortune estimated at £1.5 billion, bought a 17th-century chateau, Montjeu, in Burgundy, flew in his private Boeing 757, had become an MEP and had developed a 37,000 acre estate in Mexico, where he employed an army of 426 staff, to house all his extended family in separate establishments, although Annabel refused his offer of building her a hacienda on his land, Cuixmala.

His fortune had been amassed in the Eighties when he bought and sold a major chain of supermarkets, Grand Union, and took over the asset rich Diamond International and St Regis companies. Before the stockmarket collapse of October 1987, he sold out of the stockmarket, making a seven figure fortune and the front covers of *Time* and *Newsweek* for his prescience. For the last General Election in Britain, he formed the Referendum Party to contest every seat, personally costing him £22 million, and he himself fought Putney, helping to oust the incumbent Tory, David Mellor. But he knew he was dying and in June and July was at Montjeu, seeing just a handful of friends and attempting to combat the ravages of the cancer with an Indian guru who forbade him painkilling medicines and prescribed a rice diet instead. When he knew his time was up, he had himself flown to Spain where he passed away in the bed in which he had been born in Paris in February 1933. His fortune was left to a charitable foundation with instructions to look after his three families and eight children, along with the various properties. The trustees were suitably young: Damian Aspinall, thirty-eight, the son of old pal Aspers; Jamie Packer, thirty, the son of Australia's richest man, Kerry; Mark Slater, thirty-two, the son of his former partner, Jim Slater; Baron David de Rothschild, fifty-five, of the French banking family;

and Jean Louis de Gunzberg, son of Jimmy's business associate, Baron Alexis.

Typically, Jimmy decreed that they would share 10 per cent of the annual profits jointly, above a certain level of achievement. At his memorial service at St John's, Smith Square, in November, both Baroness Thatcher and Henry Kissinger spoke. The latter told the packed congregation of 800: 'My mother said he was the most intelligent and charming man she had ever known. I said to her: the most intelligent? Yes, she replied. The most.'

The service overran – it lasted an hour and a half – and ended with Chief Mangosuthu Buthelezi performing a Zulu dance down the aisle. Goldsmith and I had long made up our differences (we were brought together at a peacemaking lunch at Mr Chow's in Knightsbridge by our mutual friend Lord White of Hull, and Jimmy told me that my wife Camilla's late father had been best friends with his parents, Frank and Marcelle) and he included me in the revels for his birthday celebrations on 10 July 1993 at Laurent, his Paris restaurant, for his sixtieth birthday. As we surveyed the throng – le tout Paris and Londres were there – he said to me: 'Who would have thought that we would be here together after all that happened in 1976!'

The Shugborough Snapper

PATRICK LICHFIELD

No one in Britain in the Sixties was more swinging than the Earl of Lichfield. He had it all: bouffant hair; a hereditary title; Shugborough, a stately home set in 5,000 Staffordshire acres; the right to call the Queen Mother his aunt; and girlfriends galore, including American model Alana Hamilton (later married to Rod Stewart for five years), and Swedish actress Britt Ekland, another of Rod's paramours. Plus, for added pulling power, he was a leading London photographer who was in a position to break the heart of many of the models he worked with. But Lichfield, who was Viscount Anson and a lieutenant in the Grenadier Guards with close cropped, reddish hair when I met him at the 1959 coming-out dance of his sister, Elizabeth Anson, was destined to fall in love with someone of his own background.

Sadly she neither trusted him or returned his passion and that is where myself and the *Mail* Diary came in.

Lichfield had finished his affair with Britt (whose 1964 marriage to Peter Sellers had ended in divorce) opining 'She was no good in the country', to which she retorted, 'And he was no good in bed', but at a shooting weekend at Royal Lodge, Windsor, as a guest of the Queen Mother, he had fallen for Lady Leonora Grosvenor. She was vastly eligible – her family was London's largest landlords, with 300 acres of Belgravia and Mayfair – as well as brainy and beautiful. Her brother Gerald, then Earl Grosvenor, would one day succeed his father as the 6th Duke of Westminster and become Britain's richest man with a fortune estimated in excess of £3 billion.

Leonora, educated at Sherborne Girls' School, was the elder of two daughters of the 5th Duke (her sister, Lady Jane, married the Duke of Roxburghe) and Patrick Lichfield, who had succeeded his grandfather in 1960 (his father, Viscount Anson, had died less than two years before, aged forty-eight) told me: 'Leonora is the only girl I have ever met who understands my way of life and things that are important and valuable to me. She is wonderful.'

At Royal Lodge, early in 1974, Leonora had arrived with another man, Brian Alexander, younger son of Field Marshal Earl Alexander of Tunis. He had been at Harrow, *alma mater* of Sir Winston Churchill, with Patrick Lichfield, whom he regarded as his best friend, and had once been paired with Princess Anne but, according to her aunt Princess Margaret, 'Brian was too wet to do anything about it.' The guests were all placed in bedrooms down one corridor and while Brian, who later went to work on Mustique in charge of the exclusive Caribbean island's development, dithered, Patrick struck. By the end of the weekend, he told me, he was hopelessly in love. The only trouble was that Leonora, brought up in the old-fashioned school, felt that he was perhaps too fast, too louche and a bad bet. She rejected all his blandishments while he continued to pine.

Some years before Patrick had met a fortune-teller who said to him: 'You have two paths open to you, one formal and one less so. It is up to you which path you want to take.' Now he wanted to give up the models, actresses and bimbos and, celebrating his thirty-fifth birthday in April 1974, he had decided that marriage to the classy Leonora was all that he desired.

Patrick and I had worked together over the years, for magazines like *Queen* when owned by (Sir) Jocelyn Stevens, and for the American publication *Status*, and at one stage he photographed eligible young women, which I added a caption to and sold to Fleet Street newspapers. When I joined the *Daily Mail* in August 1971, Patrick was part of the baggage and our association continued to flourish. Three years later he sought my help over a convivial lunch at The Connaught Restaurant. The idea was simple: he would alert me to his movements and photo opportunities with beautiful women around the world, so long as I mentioned that I had heard he had fallen in love but did not know the identity of the object of his (unrequited) affections. The trail started off in June 1974 when I reported that Mme Dewi Sukarno, the widow of the Indonesian dictator, had given a party for Lichfield in Paris, where she lived opposite The Plaza Athenee Hotel. The following month the Diary followed him to Manila where he was photographing Imelda Marcos and shapely contestants in the Miss Universe competition which the Philippines was hosting. In August he was 'discovered' on the liner *France*, occupying a cabin in the name of 'Mr Anson' during a transatlantic crossing from New York and the following month I revealed that actress Alexandra Bastedo (who later married producer Patrick

Garland) had been telling friends she was in love with Lichfield.

By October he was seen lunching at San Frediano in the Fulham Road with Gayle Hunnicutt, the Texan-born actress who was estranged from her husband, David Hemmings, and was then to be found in the company of the reigning Miss Iceland, Anna Bjornsdottir. Within a couple of weeks the chase had moved to California where he was found with former actress Jill St John, who had retired from a screen career to concentrate on her property empire. He returned from America to a date with Lady Annunziata Asquith, the twenty-six-year-old daughter of the Earl of Oxford and Asquith, and one of the aristocratic models for his series of ads for the upmarket Burberrys store.

It was all too much for Leonora who capitulated in November (with the Queen Mother saying: 'What a pity, we were saving her for Charles') and the couple became engaged on the day which saw Patrick made a Fellow of the Royal Photographic Society. He told me: 'I will never give up photography, but with marriage I see myself devoting more time to family matters and the estate.'

Originally the wedding was set for St Margaret's, Westminster, in the spring of 1975 and Patrick, whose mother had married Prince Georg of Denmark in 1950, chose Brian as his best man. But the Duke of Westminster, who was ailing and using a wheelchair, decided to change the venue to Chester Cathedral followed by a reception at Eaton Hall, the ancestral 13,000 acre estate outside the city. The 1,400 guests included the Queen and Queen Mother, Princess Margaret, ex-King Constantine and Queen Anne Marie of Greece, two princes and seven princesses. The duke chartered a train from King's Cross to Chester for 220 guests and everyone was asked to a buffet lunch at The Grosvenor

Hotel in the centre of Chester, much of which was owned by the family. During the hour-long ceremony, a highly nervous Brian Alexander dropped the ring, which rolled down the aisle, and promptly fainted. When he was revived after a few minutes and the ring was recovered, he took his part in the ceremony and at the reception at Eaton Hall made a suitable speech, ending with a toast to the bridesmaids, Lady Sarah Armstrong-Jones, Lady Laura Campbell, Lady Tara Crichton, Miss Amanda Lee and Miss Selina Weld-Forrester. The couple then left by helicopter for their first night at The Connaught Hotel in London and their nineteen-day honeymoon started in Princess Margaret's villa in Mustique, continued in Jamaica and progressed to Mexico before returning to Kingston via the *QE II* which they boarded in Acapulco, before flying home at the end of March.

By chance I was holidaying in Jamaica and bumped into the honeymooners at Kingston airport when they were en route to Mexico and reported back: 'Promising his wife a slap-up lunch at the airport's famed Horizon restaurant in the middle of a tiring day's travel, he discovered that it was closed for "refurbishment" and was directed to the workers' cafeteria. There Lord and Lady Lichfield were espied toying with a curious concoction which purported to be a fried egg sandwich costing 75p. Good-naturedly the new Lady Lichfield said: "This is not what he promised before we got married!"'

Within a year, Leonora was pregnant with their firstborn, Lady Rose, who arrived in July 1976, followed by son and heir Tommy, Viscount Anson, two years later and finally Lady Eloise in 1981. Always a fitness fanatic, who performed Canadian Air Force exercises at the foot of his bed every morning, Lichfield put on 2 stone, attributing the gain to home cooking. But the marriage was not meant to last and on 12 November 1985, Patrick gave me an exclusive for the *Mail*: he and Leonora were living apart and he added, 'There is no one else involved. I suppose we suffer from incompatible lifestyles. My career is very important to me but if it means losing my wife, then it will take second place from now on. I'm afraid I've been a workaholic. I hope Leonora and I will be back together as soon as possible.'

Two days later photographs surfaced which appeared to demonstrate that he had dieted too vigorously, losing 3 stone. They gave rise to rumours of a life-threatening illness, so much so that he announced: 'I definitely haven't got Aids. If you put a picture of me next to one of Rock Hudson in his last few months, I couldn't deny it looks that way. But I haven't.'

The couple decided on a 'trial separation' with Leonora living in the family block in Eaton Square, Belgravia, and Patrick moving out to a friend's house nearby. They planned a Christmas reunion with the children but it never happened and in May 1986 I revealed that the marriage would be ending in divorce in July. Lichfield told me, bitterly: 'She never wanted to attempt a reconciliation and refused to see me. No one can understand why Leonora was so keen to press on for an early divorce. If she doesn't have anyone else, why bother? All I wanted was a second chance.'

In fact Leonora had become fed up with some of his personal habits and wanted out because she did not think he would ever change. The situation was not helped when one of the girls with whom he had worked (for eight years he had photographed a series of soft porn calendars for Unipart, the car accessory company) sold her story to a Sunday newspaper claiming a 'steamy affair' with Lichfield. Liz Hoad, then twenty-four and described as a model and TV golfer, said they had met on a working trip to the Algarve and the affair started two days later. 'He called me his Little Muffin,' she said. 'It was just his jokey way of saying I was a tasty bit of crumpet.'

After the divorce Leonora was romanced by the Earl of Shelburne, a close friend of the Prince of Wales and Camilla Parker Bowles who have met at his Wiltshire estate, Bowood, but she remains single and lives in a house rented from Viscount Cranborne, eldest son of the Marquess of Salisbury, on the family's Dorset estate near Wimborne. Meanwhile, Lichfield has been with Lady Annunziata Asquith, who was fifty in July and has never married, for the last thirty months but he says they have no plans to wed. He gave up alcohol (although he denies that drink was a cause of his father's early death) after a near fatal 12-foot fall seven years ago from the swimming-pool of his villa in Mustique on to the rocks below. 'The drugs I had to take to recover did not mix with drink, so I gave up. It's a bit of a shame as I have a marvellous cellar at Shugborough, but at least my friends are grateful,' he says.

The Iron Butterfly

IMELDA MARCOS

The Marbella Club on Spain's Costa del Sol, founded in 1954 by Austrian aristocrat Prince Alfonso Hohenlohe on his father's estate beside the Mediterranean, was an early watering-hole for adventurous Britons. Alfonso, and his manager Count Rudi Schonburg, who was also his cousin and married to Princess Marie-Louise of Prussia (a great-granddaughter of Kaiser Bill), welcomed the young at the all-in rate of £5 a day, including membership of the Beach Club; with return air fares from Heathrow under £30, it was an economic way of passing Bank Holidays and the dreary summer month of August.

Alfonso had achieved fame – or, rather, notoriety – by marrying fifteen-year-old Princess Ira von Furstenburg in Venice in 1955 when almost twice her age (they had two sons, Christoff and Hubertus, and divorced six years later), had expanded the club with a branch in the United Arab Emirate of Sharjah and, in 1979, had signed a deal with the Philippines dictator, President Ferdinand Marcos and his wife Imelda, to build a $250 million Marbella Club on Cavite, one of 7,090 islands in the republic.

To witness the opening, Alfonso had chartered a Sabena DC-10 and invited forty friends to join him. The party would fly from Paris to the Gulf for three days, and then on to Manila where they would be the personal guests of Imelda, known as 'The Iron Butterfly'. Thus it was that I joined a group which included Sean Connery (an old golfing friend of Marcos) and his wife Micheline, Princess Esra Jah, the Turkish ex-wife of the Nizam of Hyderabad, Swedish beauty Mirja Sachs, whose husband Gunther had gone ahead via Concorde to Singapore to shoot a twelve-page spread for *Vogue*, and various Spanish notables including the Duchess of Seville, whose husband was a cousin of King Juan Carlos, and Carmen, the Duchess of Cadiz, granddaughter of the late General Franco.

The English contingent was headed by the Earl of Suffolk and Berkshire and his second wife, Anita, and Alfonso's lawyer, Tom Elek, who was later to work for Sir James Goldsmith. Alfonso himself was unable to make the trip – he was in bed suffering from a bleeding ulcer – but sent along his elder son, Prince Christoff 'Kiko' Hohenlohe and sisters Beatrice, Duchess of Arion, and Princess Pimpinella Hohenlohe. In Sharjah we were able to visit the gold souk and buy bargain basement trinkets and a group of us went to neighbouring Dubai which was hosting the wedding celebrations of the ruler's third son, Sheik Mohammed, to his cousin Hissa (he is now the world's leading racehorse owner and the couple have ten children).

The flight to Manila at the end of April 1979 was long and uncomfortable (everyone was booked in the tourist section) but at the airport the group was met by a radiant

Imelda Marcos who was looking forward to having some playmates before hosting an ASEAN conference the following week. We were put up at the swish Manila Hotel, reputedly owned by the Marcos family, and each accorded a couple of police motorcyclist outriders and a personal Mercedes. 'Use them whenever you want,' said Imelda who told us that she had arranged a trip on the presidential yacht, *An Pangulo*, for the ground-breaking ceremony on the club, and a party at the Malacanang Palace to celebrate her thirty-fifth wedding anniversary.

Every day Marcos played golf with Connery and Sydney Chaplin, the Paris restaurateur son of Sir Charlie, and the morning we sailed to Cavite was no exception; while the rest of the guests were treated to cockfights and a barbecue, a helicopter ferried the President and his two golfing partners to the nearest 18-hole-course, designed by Gary Player. On the yacht journey back to Manila, Imelda, who was always accompanied by a band with singers, danced enthusiastically with her guests, starting with Connery; rather than spoil her fun, the captain kept steaming around the bay until signalled to tie up.

Although members of the group were free to roam around Manila, tabs were kept on them. For instance, Lord Suffolk was a guest at the horseraces of local millionaire Pippin Cojuanco, brother-in-law of jailed opposition leader Benigno Aquino (later to be assassinated after returning from exile in America), an act of folly which quickly came to the attention of Imelda who made a point of letting Suffolk know that she knew that he had been keeping 'unsuitable' company and was 'disloyal'.

The black tie dinner at the Palace was for 300 guests, many of whom had earlier witnessed Marcos and Imelda reaffirming their wedding vows during a Mass with their children, Oxford-graduate Ferdinand Jnr, known as Bong-Bong, twenty-one, and daughters Imee, twenty-three, and Irene, eighteen, joining the President's nonagenarian mother, Josefa, in the palace ballroom. Because Marcos suffered from an allergy to DDT, which repelled mosquitos, and the dining-room windows remained open, giant mosquitos from the adjacent Pasig River were among the best-fed at the feast, after which Imelda took a chosen few to her own discotheque on the roof of the palace. Beside it was a large helicopter – 'for a quick take off in case of trouble', Mme Marcos informed us. In true fashion she danced until dawn and during one interlude suggested a personal tour of the palace. Holding her finger to her lips to denote silence, she opened one door on the second floor and there, under a mosquito net, was a slumbering Ferdinand Marcos. Playfully cocking a finger to imitate a revolver, Imelda grinned as she mimed shooting the sixty-one-year-old President.

Sadly missing from the festivities was Jean-Nöel Grinda, the former French Davis Cup player and Nice hotel-owner, who had been admitted to hospital complaining of kidney stones. Imelda had thoughtfully sent along her personal physician and visitors to Jean-Nöel's bed were bemused to find the hapless surgeon sleeping in a cot at the end of the Frenchman's bed.

The visit ended in typical Marcos fashion. Rather than let her guests leave, Imelda suggested they stay another night although the Manila Hotel had been fully booked for representatives arriving for the ASEAN conference. While her new friends slept on in their five-star rooms, bankers from the Pacific rim were forced to slumber on airport benches until their rooms were vacated. On Friday 4 May, the party assembled in the lobby of the hotel to be ferried to the airport by coach, with Imelda and her band in attendance.

Mickey Suffolk, however, had other ideas. With two children, son and heir Viscount Andover and daughter Lady Katharine, by his 1973 marriage to former showjumper Anita Fuglesang, he had decided to visit Hong Kong with Tom Elek, rather than return direct to Europe. The only problem was that he had neglected to inform his wife but, as we were about to leave the hotel, he came over to her (she was standing talking to me) and, handing her some money, said: 'I'm going to Hong Kong for a few days with Tom. Nigel will look after you on the flight.'

The coach did not go immediately to the airport where the DC-10, which was scheduled to fly to Amsterdam, was waiting on the tarmac with other fare-paying passengers drumming their fingers. Instead Imelda had it stopped at a large aquarium on the airport road and herself gave a guided tour of the exotic tropical fish. Coming over to me at one stage, she said: 'Be kind in your report. We are a young nation.' At the airport we were still not allowed to board as Imelda insisted on an impromptu party in the departure lounge and two hours after the scheduled take off time we finally trooped aboard the plane to be met with looks of pure aggression and sarcastic applause from the other occupants who had been left in the sweltering heat of a Philippines afternoon without air-conditioning. As we took off, Imelda was still cavorting to the music of her band on the tarmac, blowing kisses at the departing flight. Already aboard was Jean-Nöel, who had a cautionary tale for the rest of us. Believing he was the personal guest of the First Lady, he had been stunned to discover that he was not allowed to leave hospital until he had settled his bill; it had taken him all morning to find the $3,800 demanded of him. At Amsterdam, we dispersed and Lady Suffolk and I headed for London. When we arrived at Heathrow, I asked her what she was going to do. 'See a solicitor,' she told me. The couple were divorced the following year.

Imelda (the 1953 Miss Manila beauty queen) did not need the helicopter on the roof in the end. As revolution stirred in 1986, she, her husband and entourage were flown out of the Philippines to Hawaii by the US, leaving behind 1,200 pairs of shoes and 500 ballgowns in her cupboards of the Malacanang (as well as 1,000 packets of unopened tights), a display of over-indulgence which quickly became a tourist attraction for the financially oppressed Filipinos, who were allowed to troop around the presidential home.

Long held to be suffering from kidney problems and on dialysis, Marcos, who had ruled by martial law for twenty-one years and had amassed a huge fortune abroad, died in Hawaii in 1989; four years later permission was finally given for his body to be laid to rest in his home town of Batac, 250 miles north of Manila. Imelda has refused the offer because she wants a hero's burial for her late husband. At the end of April 1998, Imelda withdrew from the 11 May Presidential race and still faces a twelve-year jail term imposed on her in 1993 by an anti-corruption court and which is being appealed. A $450 million fortune, traced to the Marcos family, sits in a Swiss bank and is a subject of contention between the Philippines government and Bong-Bong, now thirty-seven.

At the drop of a hat, Imelda, who once purloined one of the two Philippines Airlines DC-10s to fly forty friends to Rome for the coronation of the Pope, thereby stranding thousands of passengers around the world, will still sing for anyone who asks her. Sixty-nine in July 1998, she will probably be remembered best for that startling collection of shoes still housed in the former palace in Manila.

What Dodi Did

DODI AND MOHAMED AL FAYED

I was with the Princess of Wales when she met Dodi Fayed. It was Saturday 4 July 1987 and we were chatting on a warm summer's afternoon at the Guards Polo Club, on Smith's Lawn in Windsor Great Park, where the Harrods Polo Trophy was taking place. Some three hundred guests had been invited to lunch and tea by the Knightsbridge store and one of Diana's favoured charities was due to receive a large cheque from Mohamed Al Fayed, hence her involvement.

It was the day before the Wimbledon men's finals and Pat Cash was to face Ivan Lendl on the Centre Court at 2pm on the Sunday. A keen tennis player (and a member of the Vanderbilt Club in Shepherd's Bush), Diana asked me who I thought would win. I told her: 'Pat Cash, without a doubt. If you were a betting person, have a large wager. I can't see him losing.' Outside the marquee the polo match had finished. Dodi, a modest player with a beginner's handicap, had turned out for the Harrods team against a side including the Prince of Wales, who had a handicap of four. Diana went over to make the presentations to both teams, joked with her husband, and when introduced to Dodi showed little interest, other than he was her benefactor's son, and moved on.

Just five months earlier Diana and Charles had effectively ended their marriage. On their return from an official visit to Portugal, Charles had moved into his dressing-room at Highgrove. Diana had yet to meet James Hewitt and start her affair with him and Dodi was married to American model Suzanne Gregard; I had revealed their secret wedding ceremony which had taken place on New Year's Eve 1986 in Vail, Colorado. Neither had any interest in the other and it was to be another decade before they met again, and fell in love, with tragic consequences.

Dodi had been a friend of mine for ten years. He was the son of Mohamed by his first marriage to Adnan Khashoggi's sister, Samira, and it was through Adnan that Fayed became rich. When I met him, Dodi was twenty-two and romancing Hollywood actress, Valerie Perrine, who had starred in *Lenny* with Dustin Hoffman and fallen for Dodi after ending a seven-year affair with Lebanese Jamal Kanafoni, heir to an oil fortune.

In London to make the £15 million epic, *Superman*, Valerie, who was eleven years Dodi's senior, told me (we were all in a nightclub called Dial Nine): 'He is very polite and I enjoy being escorted around by him. We have lots of common interests and I am helping him get into film producing in Hollywood where I have introduced him to my lawyer.'

A year before, Dodi, attempting to make an impression, had invited a group of friends holidaying in the South of

France for a cruise around the Med on a yacht, *La Belle Simone*, which he said he had chartered. But when they turned up in Monte Carlo harbour, where *La Belle Simone* was berthed, no one connected with the yacht had heard of Dodi and the disappointed guests dispersed.

Before his marriage to Suzanne, Dodi had been engaged to Iranian beauty Linda Atterzaedh, whose parents lived in London. She was five years younger than Dodi, who had scored a triumph backing *Chariots of Fire* and now had a movie production company called Allied Stars, run by Jack Wiener, but the engagement fizzled out, like most of Dodi's romances. He had been briefly involved with Charlotte Soames, a granddaughter of Sir Winston Churchill and who was to become the long-term love of Andrew Parker Bowles before she married Yorkshire landowner, Earl Peel. There had been a pursuit of Koo Stark after her romance with Prince Andrew ended in early 1983, and his name had been linked with Britt Ekland and Brooke Shields. But Dodi – nicknamed Doodoo by Valerie – was still trying to become a major player in Hollywood where he lived most of the year although he was able to stay at The Paris Ritz, owned by his father, and 60 Park Lane, next to The Dorchester, where the Fayeds were based in London.

It was no secret that Mohamed and Dodi did not get on. Before the death of Samira in 1986, long after they were divorced, Mohamed had married Finnish model, Heini Wathen, in July 1985, when she was thirty. Ironically they were introduced by Dodi who had been dating her and encouraged her to move from Scandinavia, where she was runner-up in the 1977 Miss Finland beauty contest, and secured her a job at Pierre Balmain, modelling his haute couture collection for mainly Middle East clients.

But Mohamed indulged Dodi, paying his bills (which were

huge) and taking pride in his movie exploits. Following *Chariots of Fire*, Dodi was involved in *Hook*, a remake with Dustin Hoffman in the title role of the J. M. Barrie *Peter Pan* classic. After the April 1992 royal charity premiere Mohamed (who had promised Diana, who attended with William and Harry, £500,000 in royalties for the Great Ormond Street Hospital) invited 400 people to dinner at the Georgian restaurant on the fifth floor at Harrods and the lucky ones received jackets with *Hook* insignia on them.

After his ill-starred marriage to Suzanne (by then an executive with Pan-Am) collapsed – there was an estimated £1 million payout by Mohamed who complained it was poor value for the eight months the couple were together – Dodi took up with Frank Sinatra's twice married daughter, Tina, and then, to celebrate Brooke Shields' thirty-third birthday in April 1989, flew her, and her mother Terri, from America to France and a suite in The Paris Ritz, fuelling rumours of a renewal of their relationship which had begun five years previously when she was studying at Princeton University.

If Mohamed was fed up with shelling out for Dodi (Heini had produced two more sons and two daughters) he remained a munificent father. In 1990 he bought Dodi a £110,000 Ferrari Testarossa to help him with his 'courting' but there was an intriguing confrontation after Dodi came to a total halt in the Mall (some said he had mashed the gears) and the Harrods security men were sent to retrieve the flame-red sports car while Dodi returned to base where he was confronted by a furious father. Dodi claimed that he was struck by Mohamed who called him a '******* incompetent'; the incident demonstrated the fragility of their relationship.

While Mohamed was generous to his first-born, he was also busy distributing favours to people he considered important, both in politics and the world of journalism. He was particularly proud of his sponsorship, through Harrods, of the Royal Windsor Horse Show (the sponsorship was taken over by Aspreys in 1998) and employed a personal photographer to snap him surreptitiously in the company of the Queen on the final day of the show which was run from the Royal Mews at Windsor Castle. These intimate photographs were then distributed to sympathetic newspapers to show how close Mohamed was to the Monarch. Both MPs and newspaper editors were put up at The Paris Ritz and, if they attempted to settle the bill, Frank Klein, the general manager, would assure them that they were guests of Mohamed and there was no question of paying. Visits to the Windsor Villa, which Mohamed had bought on a long lease from the City of Paris and converted into a museum in honour of the late Duke and Duchess while retaining the top floor for his personal use, were also on the agenda and Harrods hampers were liberally distributed every Christmas to chosen recipients, delivered in either a Harrods van or in some style via the Harrods horse-drawn carriage.

Through his spokesman Michael Cole, Mohamed regarded the *Mail* Diary as a sympathetic tool for the advancement of his personal publicity, hence my participation in the Harrods polo day and invitations to the President's Box at the Royal Windsor Horse Show. When, four years ago, my wife was staying at The Paris Ritz as a guest of adman Frank Lowe to attend the christening of his son, Sebastian, I happened to be heading for the French capital to write a column about Europe's leading horse race, the Prix de l'Arc de Triomphe, and booked myself into The Plaza Athenee on the Avenue Montaigne. When it was pointed out to me that there was room in my wife's suite at The Ritz, I transferred and, the following morning, a Sunday, I went to the *caisse* to pay the bill. Frank Klein was waiting for me and, after the usual pleasantries, I asked if I could settle my account. Klein showed me the computer, pressed some keys and then triumphantly told me that there was no bill because the computer had no record of the stay. I later discovered that Frank Lowe had similarly not received a bill for my wife's lengthier visit and I suspect that, somewhere in the vast Fayed empire, a note of this largesse remains.

It was in Dubai that Mohamed made his first fortune, helping in the early construction of the United Arab Emirate and becoming close to the Ruler, Sheik Rashid, who spoke only Arabic. But when Rashid died, his sons, Maktoum, Hamdan, Mohammed and Ahmed, decided that Fayed had made too much out of his association with Dubai and decided to cancel his contract to run the thirty-nine storey World Trade Centre, which he had built in 1975 and was next to The Hilton Hotel. In 1995 the protracted three years' proceedings came to an end with victory for the Ruling Family of Dubai who also revoked Fayed's papers (not a passport in themselves but valid travel documents) and cancelled his licence to run his shipping company, which then comprised a couple of ocean-going tugs, from Dubai.

During the case Fayed had claimed that he was too ill to attend and was confined to a wheelchair, whereupon Mohammed Alabar, the young American-educated national who is in charge of Dubai's Ministry of Development and entrusted with pursuing businessmen who are deemed to have profited too greatly by their association with Dubai, was put on the case. In London he hired two BT vans, installed cameras inside them and took footage of Fayed bounding out of his helicopter, walking into Harrods and showing he was far from wheelchair-bound. When the court reconvened, monitors had been erected and after, Fayed's lawyers explained that he was still in no shape to attend, Alabar played the film. That was the end of Fayed's case and he told me the decision, which he is still appealing, has cost him £40 million.

After my Diary from Dubai highlighting the case appeared in March 1995, I received an invitation, via Michael Cole, to lunch at Harrods with Mohamed. In his fifth floor office, he told me: 'When I arrived in Dubai, Rashid was living in a mud hut. I had the Creek [from which dhows sailed across the Arabian Sea laden with gold] dredged, found oil for them, and made them all rich. And this is how they reward me.' To show his credentials he brought out some frayed photographs of him with the old Ruler and his sons. They were so frayed that Fayed had a fine head of hair! And when we sat down to lunch in his boardroom, with a waitress from the nearby Georgian restaurant coming in with a menu to take our order, I thought it odd how provocative Fayed was being, hoping that I would say something detrimental to the Maktoums. But I had been warned by Alabar: 'Fayed tapes everything, and if he doesn't tape it, he films it. When you enter either his office or his home, you are under constant surveillance.'

There remains a mutual antagonism between Fayed and Alabar, which is understandable. When Alabar arrived in Britain to talk to Fayed, he was treated like a tradesman. In fact Fayed told me: 'I wouldn't employ that man as a doorman in Harrods.' For his part, Alabar said to Fayed: 'You are an old man, maybe sixty-nine, maybe seventy. Why don't you enjoy your money. I am young, thirty-five, and I'll pursue you to the ends of the earth and I'll win, because I'll outlive you.'

But his problems with Dubai became a minor distraction last summer when Fayed finally achieved his ambition of hosting a holiday for the Princess of Wales and her sons, William and Harry. He had been working on her for some weeks and finally she said yes. In preparation he paid £15 million for the *Jonikal*, a 195 foot craft (Fayed liked to say it was over 200 foot) which was built in 1991 and on the market for £19 million. It came with an Italian crew of sixteen. The invitation had been proffered in May at a dinner at The Churchill Hotel after the English National Ballet, of which Diana was patron, had performed *Swan Lake* at a gala at the Royal Albert Hall, where Diana had asked Mohamed and Heini to join her in the Royal Box. He had agreed a £150,000 sponsorship of the ENB with a *Nutcracker* tie-in at Harrods over Christmas when the company opened with the Tchaikovsky classic at their new home, the Coliseum.

Diana's arrival in July in St Tropez, where Fayed had a house and guest-house, two dozen security guards and, as well as the *Jonikal*, his sailing schooner *Sakara*, which he valued at £20 million, was not well received and front page headlines criticized her choice of host, who was photographed with his arm consolingly around the Princess's shoulder. On the morning of Sunday 13 July, Michael Cole telephoned me in my office (where I was preparing to watch the British Grand Prix from Silverstone on television) and told me that Mohamed would be calling me in a few minutes from the *Sakara*. He did and we chatted and then he said: 'Diana wants to speak to you. I'm handing over to her.' Even on a mobile from St Tropez, Diana came over loud and clear. 'Nigel,' she said. 'It's absolute rubbish to suggest that I did not inform Prince Charles or Buckingham Palace of the trip. It's very difficult for me and the boys to have a private holiday. We couldn't just sit at KP [Kensington Palace] all summer. We are having a jolly nice family holiday and Mohamed and Heini and their children are being wonderful to us.'

The two families had arrived on the Friday at Nice aboard the Harrods Gulfstream IV jet and had been transported to St Tropez by the *Jonikal*, which I had never heard of. When I asked Mohamed what his new yacht was called, he laughed and said to me: 'It's the *Ali Baba*.' But within days the secret was out. But no one took much notice of the participation in the holiday of Dodi who had been summoned to St Tropez by his father with the instructions to 'make Diana happy'. Fayed seemed to have forgotten that Dodi was unofficially engaged to Kelly Fisher, who was also on the holiday, but was being neglected as Dodi danced attention on the Princess. The holiday was such a success that Diana extended it by twenty-four hours, finally returning to London on Sunday 20 July.

Back in London, Dodi was pressed by his father to continue his pursuit of Diana. Michael Cole was instructed to call favoured journalists and tell them that Dodi and Diana were two 'young people in love' and what they did was their own affair. He did not dissuade speculation that the friendship had developed into a romantic affair. They went on a five-day Mediterranean cruise on the *Jonikal* together and, twenty-four hours after they returned to London, Diana dined with Dodi, alone, on 7 August at 60 Park Lane before flying the next day to Bosnia for four days to continue her mission against landmines. Mohamed then told the world: 'She is a lovely girl and he is my son and I love him very much. They seem to enjoy each other's company a lot and it makes me happy to see them both so happy.'

On 7 August Mohamed's old sparring partner, former Lonrho boss, the late 'Tiny' Rowland, called me from his yacht, the *Hanse*, in Monte Carlo harbour. He was with

Adnan Khashoggi and, after talking to me for a couple of minutes, Tiny put me over to Adnan, introducing him as my 'old friend'. Adnan was laughing at the Mohamed-inspired romance between his nephew and Diana and said: 'Surely it should have been Mohamed pictured with Diana. He's the one in love with her, but he's married.' Tiny, who called Mohamed 'Tootsie' then added: 'This business with Diana is very good publicity for Tootsie. Adnan says it's a Jackie Kennedy situation and he hopes Diana is negotiating properly. If so, she could expect around £40 million. Dodi and Diana are perfect for each other – they are both as thick as two planks.'

Dodi happened to be in his father's office in Harrods when I called on the telephone on 8 August. He was put on the line to me. We had not met since the previous Christmas when I had seen him in the store on an up escalator when I was going down and called out. He told me: 'Wait at the bottom, I'm coming down.' We had embraced like the old friends we were and Dodi, as ever, was charm itself. After a few minutes' conversation, and promising to keep in touch, we parted. On the telephone eight months later, Dodi sounded more hesitant. 'What's going on between you and Diana?' I asked him. 'We're just friends,' he replied. 'And in any case, there was another woman on board with us.' When I asked Dodi the name of the other woman and his relationship with her, he clammed up. 'Goodbye,' he said. 'We'll speak again soon.' Of course, we never did.

On 20 August, Diana returned from a Greek holiday with her closest friend, Rosa Monckton, wife of the *Sunday Telegraph* editor Dominic Lawson and daughter of Major-General Viscount Monckton of Brenchley. They had once again been flown to Greece on the Fayed Harrods Gulfstream IV (which Diana deemed to have 'common' decor) for a five-day cruise around the islands and then ferried back to Stansted where a Harrods helicopter took them on to Battersea heliport. On the holiday, Rosa reported that Diana had started her period (thus scotching any rumours that the Princess was pregnant on her death at the end of the month) and stated later: 'I know it would have been biologically impossible for her to have been pregnant at the time of the crash. As for marriage [to Dodi], there was no question of it. While we were in Greece, she said of Dodi Fayed to me: "He's given me a bracelet. He's given me a watch. I know the next thing will be a ring. Rosa, that's going firmly on the fourth finger of my right hand."'

When Rosa spoke to her last, on the Wednesday before her death on the night of Saturday 31 August, Diana showed no indication or desire to marry Dodi, whom she had known for just six weeks. Even Lady Annabel Goldsmith, who spoke to Diana on Friday 30 August, was told by the Princess: 'Don't worry. I'm having a wonderful time but the last thing I need is a new marriage. I need it like a bad rash on my face.' Earlier that month I had reported that Diana had told her friend Taki Theodoracopulos: 'I haven't got out of one bad marriage to get into another one.'

By all accounts Diana's last cruise on the *Jonikal*, to Sardinian waters from Nice, with Dodi was truly magical. They flew back on Saturday 30 August, again in the Gulfstream, from Sardinia to Paris with Diana excited that on the following day, the Sunday, she was going to be reunited with her 'boys' who had spent August with their father and other members of the Royal Family at Balmoral. The rest is history but Mohamed Fayed's attempts to rewrite events should be viewed with suspicion. Certainly he lost a son, and the opportunity, perhaps, to become step-grandfather to a future King of England. But his urge to force events into a channel which suits him should be queried. On 23 March 1998 Mohamed invited me to lunch at Harrods. We had corresponded over the death of Dodi and he had replied sorrowfully to my letter of condolence. I arrived at his office on the fifth floor promptly at 1.30pm and was kept waiting, although a butler brought me a glass of white wine. After a quarter of an hour or so, Mohamed appeared and ushered me into the Georgian restaurant to a table with our backs to the wall while two security officers sat a few yards away balefully keeping an eye on us; the rest of the restaurant was busy with Harrods customers. We were offered sirloin of beef on the trolley and the waiter told me that 'the chairman' liked his well done. I replied that I liked it underdone. We were presented with two plates, swimming in gravy, with a Yorkshire pudding each and vegetables and a fine bottle of Bordeaux claret was served to us.

In the middle of lunch, Mohamed, seated on my right, put his left hand on my thigh and said: 'Nigel, I know 1,000 per cent that MI5 and MI6 killed Diana and Dodi. I also know from Repossi (the Paris jeweller near The Ritz) that the ring he was going to give her was an engagement ring and they planned to marry.' When I told Mohamed that I was aware of the workings of MI5 and MI6 – where my elder sister had worked for forty years – and couldn't imagine either being implicated (why, for instance, had they allowed bodyguard Trevor Rees-Jones to live?) I saw I was treading on private grief. After a cup of coffee each he called over the bodyguards and took me on a tour of Harrods, principally to show me the shrine to Diana and Dodi in the basement. With a bodyguard to front and rear, Mohamed swaggered through Harrods, pretending not to be recognized. After we inspected the shrine, we proceeded to the ground floor west side exit of the store with the bodyguards pushing unfortunates out of their boss's way. At the door on Hans Road, Mohamed shook my hand and reiterated: 'Remember, I know 1,000 per cent that MI5 and MI6 killed Diana and Dodi. They didn't like her marrying a wog.'

Somewhere Out There?

LORD LUCAN

On the morning of Friday 8 November 1974, I was telephoned at home (it was my day off) by the News Desk of the *Daily Mail*. What did I know about the Earl of Lucan? I was informed that he had disappeared after the murder the previous night of Sandra Rivett, nanny to his three children, and the attempted murder of his estranged wife, Veronica. I was unable to help although the *Mail* Diary had written of the Lucans' problems on 31 May that year. With a picture of Veronica and a headline 'Hard Times for the Countess . . .' the article revealed:

'These are harsh times for the stalwart Countess of Lucan. Deserted a year ago by her husband, she now finds he has peremptorily cut off her Harrods account. While this may seem a loss that most of us could bear, Lady Lucan has been using her credit at the Knightsbridge store to feed her three children. The dashing Earl of Lucan, thirty-eight, was once considered for the James Bond role, and may be found much of the time hunched over a backgammon board at places like the Clermont Club in Berkeley Square. Divorce proceedings are contemplated and the children – heir Lord Bingham, seven, and daughters Lady Frances, ten, and four-year-old Lady Camilla are wards of court. Lady Lucan, thirty-five, and a major's daughter, has been obliged to support herself, offspring and nanny on £40 a week, all in. The couple were married ten years ago.'

Lucan himself I knew slightly but he was not of my generation and was a man of curious habits. For instance, he ate every day at the Mirabelle restaurant in Curzon Street and his order of cold lamb cutlets never varied; at night he ate hot lamb cutlets. I had last seen this eccentric aristocrat a few months before at Sunningdale, the Berkshire golf club, when I had played that summer in a four ball behind Lucan and three of his cronies.

The idea that he could have been involved in any murder seemed alien to me but, with the twenty-fourth anniversary of the last sighting of the lofty earl falling in November 1998, there have been many foolish stories about the events of that fateful night and the following hours when he was last seen alive.

It is obvious to all his pals that Lucan killed himself because of the terrible mistake he made, although Veronica's brother-in-law, Bill Shand Kydd (himself paralysed in a riding accident in October 1995), is confident that Lucan is both alive and innocent. One former Scotland Yard detective, who has written a book on the subject, admits privately that Lucan is dead while maintaining he is alive to reporters, explaining: 'The book will sell more that way.'

Veronica calls herself the Dowager, Countess of Lucan, in her certainty that her husband is dead, while their son John, Lord Bingham, a merchant banker with Kleinwort,

Benson, is taking steps to have his father declared officially dead so that he can inherit the earldom which dates back to 1795.

Before the main protagonists grew too old or died (five have subsequently passed on – Jimmy Goldsmith, Gordy White, Steve Raphael, Ian Maxwell Scott and Dominic Elwes are all dead, and Lucky's greatest supporter, John Aspinall, is fading from leukaemia and melanomas) – I decided to investigate everyone (except Lady Lucan) who had been involved in Lucan's life. They all had a firm opinion about what happened on the night of 7 November, and my findings ten years later, in November 1984, remain, I like to think, the definitive account of that fateful night.

Lord 'Lucky' Lucan disappeared after murdering his children's nanny, in mistake for his wife. In this special dossier, I have penetrated the closed world of the Lucan circle to talk to those friends who immediately rallied round to protect his reputation and maintain the myth of the cavalier earl.

On the tenth anniversary of the last sighting of the Earl of Lucan, I can reveal dramatic new evidence which is unknown to the Scotland Yard Murder Squad and to almost all of his tight-knit circle.

In the year leading up to the violent murder of nanny Sandra Rivett, killed in mistake for the Countess of Lucan, 'Lucky', a competent power-boat driver who had raced in the Cowes–Torquay classic, bought a 20 foot speedboat. He kept the craft at a discreet mooring on the South Coast; and as he formulated his plans to dispose of his wife of eleven years, it became an integral part of his scheme to commit the perfect murder – and get away with it.

Twice during the summer Lucan made dummy runs from the starting-point of his rented flat off Eaton Square. After killing the 'target' and stuffing the body into a sturdy bag, he drove from London to the South Coast. Rather than his own flashy Mercedes – which he was buying on hire purchase – he used ordinary cars belonging to friends, the sort which would not receive a second glance along any of Britain's roads.

Transferring the sack containing his wife's body – he took one of similar weight to the 8 stone Lady Lucan on the dummy runs – he put out into the Channel and headed for the deepest part.

Lucan had worked out tides and currents and had ascertained that there were certain parts of the English Channel where bodies, should they rise from the seabed, would float parallel to the shore and not towards it. Having weighted down his victim and dumped the body overboard, he planned to retrace his route and be back at one of his London haunts around midnight. When the mysterious 'disappearance' of Lady Lucan was eventually reported, he would have what he thought would be a foolproof alibi.

In the event Lucan did have a body to dispose of – his own. Friends are now certain he executed the rehearsed plan on the morning of 8 November 1974, taking the boat out to sea and scuttling it after he had weighted himself down. Whether he killed himself first, or drowned, is the last unsolved mystery. Nothing of Lucan's premeditated, murderous scheme to rid himself of an irksome wife has ever been uncovered in the costly police investigation, still in progress.

It was revealed by writer Taki Theodoracopulos who met Lucan at the start of the 1962 Cowes–Torquay powerboat race and became a firm friend. Taki, who played Davis Cup tennis for his country and captained the Greek karate team, told me yesterday:

'Lucan borrowed £5,000 from me and another Greek friend just before the murder; and I knew something was up when I found him training in Hyde Park; totally unconcerned with his health previously, he suddenly stated getting himself into shape.'

Taki continued: 'The information about the boat and the dummy runs was given to me in the greatest confidentiality but after ten years, I feel it should be known. There is no doubt in my mind that Lucky is dead.'

'Following the murder, the police made no attempt to question me, although I was at home in Greece. Even though the Murder Squad knew I was a very close friend they have never attempted to contact me.'

Known as John, or 'Lucky' after a gaming win, Richard John Bingham, 7th Earl of Lucan, Baron Bingham of Castlebar, Baron Bingham of Melcombe Bingham in the United Kingdom, and a baronet of Nova Scotia, was last seen in the early hours of Friday 8 November 1974, six weeks before his fortieth birthday. He had arrived before midnight, looking dishevelled and wearing bloodstained trousers, at the Uckfield, Sussex, home of his very close friends, Ian and Susan Maxwell Scott.

A barrister, Susan, fifty-one, was alone and Lucan told her that he had been passing his London house that evening and seen a man attacking his wife. He described the evening as 'an unbelievable nightmare experience'. Mrs Maxwell Scott waited thirty-six hours before informing the police of the visit.

Lucan then sat down and wrote three letters, asking Susan to post them for him. One was to Bill Shand Kydd. Then, saying he had to get back to clear things up, he drove off into the night. It was 1.15am. Shortly after dawn, the car Lucan had been driving, a borrowed Ford Corsair, was discovered parked in Norman Street, Newhaven, on the Sussex coast. Residents agree that it had not been there at 6am, but it was certainly there, empty, two hours later.

The previous night Lucan had invited some friends to dine with him at 11pm at the Clermont, the Berkeley Square gaming-club founded by John Aspinall in 1963. Possibly to establish an alibi, he drove his Mercedes past at 8.15pm and asked the doorman, Billy (later jailed for being lookout for a gang of robbers), if any of his friends were inside. The answer was 'No' and he drove on.

He returned to his basement flat in Eaton Square, close to the house his estranged wife Veronica lived in with their three children, and, changing his clothes and car, went to 46 Lower Belgrave Street and let himself in with his own key. Because he saw his three children all the time – despite losing a bitter High Court custody case which cost him £40,000 in legal fees – he knew that Thursday was nanny Sandra Rivett's night off. Upstairs, Lady Lucan and the ten-year-old Frances were watching television. Unfortunately for Sandra, who was separated from her security guard husband, Roger, and dating a barman called John from the Plumber's Arms pub opposite the Lucan house, she had taken the Wednesday night off instead.

Lucan, firm in the belief that the only woman in the house was his wife, removed a lightbulb and waited in the darkened basement; when a female figure came down the stairs he launched into a frenzied attack.

In fact, Sandra had been sent down stairs to make some tea. When she did not return, Veronica Lucan went down herself calling: 'Sandra? Sandra?' Lucan climbed three steps to meet her and struck her a fearsome blow on her head. When she screamed he told her to 'shut up' and managed three more blows to her forehead before she twisted and grabbed his genitals. Then he went for her throat and when she spluttered out 'How dare you touch my pearls?' a chord was struck and his fury abated.

Veronica was able to coax her husband upstairs to the bathroom to clean up and to get some towels. As soon as she heard the water running, she fled downstairs and out into the road to the Plumber's Arms which she burst into at 9.50pm, screaming: 'Help me, help me, I've just escaped from a murderer . . . my children, my children . . . he's in the house . . . he's murdered the nanny,' she screamed and then collapsed. The police were called and Lady Lucan was taken to nearby St George's Hospital, then at Hyde Park Corner.

Collecting his wits, Lucan rang his mother Kaitlin, Dowager Countess of Lucan, who had been a widow for ten years. He told her that there had been 'a terrible catastrophe' at his house and asked her to go round there. When she arrived at No. 46, he telephoned her again from somewhere in London and then set off for Sussex. In sworn testimony at the inquest into the death of Sandra Rivett, Lady Lucan positively identified her attacker as her husband. After thirty-one minutes' deliberation, the jury returned a verdict of murder by Lord Lucan and he was duly committed for trial at the Old Bailey.

Of course, Lucan has yet to be arrested and to stand trial for his alleged crime and many believe that, should he be alive, he would never have a fair hearing. In the letter to Shand Kydd he wrote: 'The circumstantial evidence against me is strong, in that V [Veronica] will say it was all my doing and I will lie doggo for a while . . .'

At lunchtime on Friday 8 November 1974, as news of Sandra Rivett's murder filtered through, five close friends of 'Lucky' Lucan made their way to the £1 million Belgravia house of zoo owner John Aspinall, who used to employ the earl at the Clermont.

The group comprised racing figure Charles Benson, forty-nine, who had been at Eton with Lucan and played golf every Friday with him; gambler Dan Meinertzhagen, forty-one; stockbroker Steve Raphael, seventy-two; amateur rider and racehorse trainer Bill Shand Kydd, forty-seven; and Dominic Elwes, a social gadfly.

'We met because we were expecting "Lucky" to get in touch with one or more of us and wanted to work out what we should do,' Benson said. 'We all felt then we would see him turn up in the next day or so. None of us believed he had committed the murder.'

The group raided Aspinall's fridge and found some smoked salmon and various cold meats which they shared with a couple of bottles of wine. 'It could not have been described as a feast and, anyway, food was furthest from our minds', I am told.

His friends were, by and large, a generous bunch. Absent from the group, but also a close friend, was financier Gordon White, who was knighted five years before and who then built up the American side of the £1,679 million Hanson Trust conglomerate. After Lucan's disappearance, he gave £2,000 a year for the education of Frances and Camilla Bingham, and, when the Lucan family silver was auctioned to pay off around £70,000 of debts in November 1976 at Christie's, Sir Gordon (late Lord White) paid £10,000 for a silver service with the Lucan crest, which he used at his Tite Street, Chelsea house.

Fellow financier James Goldsmith, who was knighted in 1976, was quick to come to the financial aid of Lady Lucan and the three young children, and gave her an undisclosed sum as well as paying £5,000 to settle one of Lucan's debts.

From New York, where he had made an estimated £500 million fortune in the last two years, Sir James, fifty-one, told me: 'I liked dear old Lucan a lot but he was never a close friend. The whole thing was a ghastly tragedy. I was a creditor of his having guaranteed a loan and never expected to be repaid, so I gave the money for the children's education.'

City stockbroker, Stephen Raphael, who had once shared a Los Angeles home with Errol Flynn, was owed £15,000 by his old friend but waived the matter and did not press his claim with the trustees in bankruptcy, and others conveniently forgot monies owed to them by 'Lucky'.

The main financial burden fell on Bill Shand Kydd who inherited a wallpaper fortune. With his wife, Christina, Lady Lucan's younger sister, he looked after the three children as they grew up.

But what of Lady Lucan? After six months in a national health mental ward at Banstead Hospital, Surrey, the Countess returned to her Belgravia home, a virtual recluse shunned by family and former friends. At the age of forty-five her life appeared over, although she continued to exist, haunted by bad dreams and daemons and largely unaware of the progress of her son and two daughters.

The eldest girl was Lady Frances Bingham, then twenty and reading law at Bristol University, while the youngest, Lady Camilla, fourteen, had in 1984 started her O-level course at St Swithin's, the Winchester boarding-school which her mother had also attended. Son George, who officially holds the courtesy title of Lord Bingham, was at Eton, his £4,500 a year fees paid out of a family trust fund. Described as bright, personable and hard working, he was studying for his A-levels. George celebrated his seventeenth birthday in September 1984 and Bill Shand Kydd said: 'He's very like his father, certainly in build. He is very slight.'

The family have so far refused to petition to have the Earl of Lucan declared officially dead, a process which may take place any time after seven years have elapsed. 'George shows no inclination to become the 8th Earl of Lucan but, of course, he may change his mind when he gets older,' says Bill.

If Lucan had reappeared in 1984, when he would have been almost fifty, he would have been worth between £200,000 and £300,000 in addition to his Irish estates at Castlebar, County Mayo. That was the considered estimate of Stephen Raphael, who remains convinced of his innocence. He believes that 'Lucky' is in South America and presumes him alive until he is found dead. 'Coutts, the Queen's bankers, look after his Marriage Settlement Trust which, I believe, will go to George on his twenty-first birthday,' said Raphael, another Old Etonian. 'The bankruptcy was paid off in full, and there is an accumulating sum.'

The Lucan family trust owns 'considerable' land in Laleham, Middlesex, and, across the river, about 100 acres in Surrey which are leased by the Laleham Golf Club with 550 members paying £200 a year. Secretary Robert Emms told me: 'Lord Lucan was President of the Club until last year, when the general committee met and submitted the name of Mr Joe Mitchell to succeed him. We didn't feel Lord Lucan would be coming back.' The trust is sitting on a potential goldmine which is thwarted by planning permission; there are gravel deposits up to 28 metres deep under the Laleham acres, and in 1977 the trust gave a lease to a company called Marco to mine Ten Acre Meadow, which was used as the Club's practice ground.

'That is about to revert to us, and further applications in the area were blocked a year ago at a gravel extraction inquiry in Chertsey,' said Mr Emms. Ten Acre Meadow is believed to have yielded more than £1 million of gravel. In 1984 Lord Bingham had an £80,000 trust fund for himself as well as owning the Belgravia house – valued at around £150,000 – where his mother resides in seclusion. At the time, it was said that Lady Lucan made quite a substantial sum from selling her story to the newspapers.

'The two girls are skint,' says a family adviser. 'I know Bill Shand Kydd, their uncle, is hoping that Lucan's old friends will rally around one last time, but ten years on it is more difficult.'

A curious situation existed in Ireland where ancestor Captain John Bingham bought a castle in the 16th century in Castlebar, and the Lucan trust owns a considerable part of the town, which had a population of 8,700 at the last census. However, Lucan's Irish tenants have mostly refused to pay rent since the events of 1974 and local solicitor, Rory O'Connor, told me: 'The agent, Michael Joe Egan, refuses to reveal anything, but we estimate that the trust could own 600–700 houses. But the ground rents are from £8 to £15 per annum and, even if everyone paid, I doubt the trust would collect £10,000 a year.' There was no doubt in the mind of financier Sir Gordon White that his 'old pal' Lucky was dead and he told me 'Quite simply he gambled and lost. No one could step up to Lucan and say he didn't pay his gambling debts – and having lost the major gamble of his life he paid the bill like a gentleman.

'He couldn't have survived outside his world, and although he could have survived in prison, he wouldn't have wanted to. During the course of the tremendous hassle he underwent over the custody of the children, I watched him disintegrate.'

Every Friday morning Lord Lucan would drive with his

Dobermann dog Otto to play golf at Sunningdale, Wentworth or the Berkshire with Charles Benson and Ian Maxwell Scott, a cousin of the late Duke of Norfolk. Benson is convinced he is dead and said: 'He had a contingency plan and Plan Two was self-destruction in case Plan One went wrong. He had become incredibly bitter about the administration of the law, during his fruitless custody case. He felt he had been completely let down by solicitors, barristers and psychiatrists and so he decided to take matters into his own hands. I miss him terribly. He was a bloody marvellous man. If he were to come back today, I doubt that he would have changed at all. He was very conservative in dress and outlook. He was also a very generous man. It was never mentioned, but people actually owed him money at the time of his disappearance.'

Mayfair gaming club owner John Aspinall said: 'There's absolutely nothing new to report on Lucky – he's dead and I assume he did himself in.'

Old Etonian Dan Meinertzhagen recalled: 'I knew that his marriage couldn't go on. I could see Veronica steaming and insulting Lucky's friends while she sat night after night at the Clermont at what we called the Widows' Table. I also knew he was depressed – and people like Lucky do not lose their children to an unstable woman and take it lying down.'

The Earl of Suffolk and Berkshire's cousin, Greville Howard, who had waited in vain with his then wife Zoë to dine with Lucan on the night of the murder, is sure his old friend is dead. 'What I suspect is that Lucky – if guilty – took the noble way out. By disappearing, he made sure his children had a mystery as a father, rather than a murderer.'

Before he himself died, Ian Maxwell Scott was 90 per cent sure Lucan is dead and told me: 'If he's really alive, then he must be a Franciscan monk – that is, he changed his habits completely. He did care about Veronica, who had an acute nervous condition. He would wake up in my house at Uckfield with a monumental hangover and drive to London before his game of golf, to get her the pills which she needed to stay calm – and forgot to bring with her time and time again.'

Following the final break-down of his marriage in January 1973, Lord Lucan did not become a womanizer. In fact, friends say he was never completely at ease with the opposite sex. However, he did have a girlfriend in the weeks leading up to the tragic night of 7 November and that morning telephoned former debutante Andrina Colquhoun, 32 (now married to Sunningdale member, Bob Waddington) to arrange dinner at 11pm at the Clermont. Andy, a sometime photographer, who later worked for Sir Terence Conran, founder of Habitat and became close of novelist Jeffrey Archer, who gave her a BMW with the personalized number plate ANY 1, had known Lucan for about two years, and she told me:

'We had met one night at Annabel's, and he used to confide in me about his wife, although I have never met her. I had already seen him that week and when he rang I found his plans for dinner rather muddled.' Lucan suggested that Andy make her own way to the Clermont which is situated above Annabel's at 44 Berkeley Square. There she would be joined by Old Etonian Greville Howard, forty-three, and his wife. At that time Howard lived in the mews house owned by Lucan, which was directly behind his family house at 46 Lower Belgrave Street. The two houses were connected and a body could easily have been spirited away from No. 46 through the mews. As it happened, the small dinner-party at the Clermont convened around 11pm, but one chair remained empty . . .

Scotland Yard's Murder Squad have always perversely held out 'strong' hopes of arresting the fugitive Earl of Lucan. In charge of the continuing inquiry in 1984, Det. Chief Supt Ronald Hardy, fifty-two, said: 'After a long, thorough and exhaustive investigation into the murder of his children's nanny and Lord Lucan's subsequent disappearance, there is still not one scrap of evidence to support the suggestion he is dead. My experience teaches me it is perfectly possible for a man of his background to "lose" himself for ten years and avoid recognition.'

Det. Chief Supt Hardy held the still valid warrant for the arrest of the errant earl. On the notice board of his Murder Squad office he displayed the police photograph of Lord Lucan together with the Interpol circular distributed world-wide requesting his apprehension. At that time, the Yard believed that the Seychelles, Mozambique or South Africa were the most likely hiding-places for Lucan. Yet Det. Chief Supt Hardy declined to state positively that his quarry is alive. His Murder Squad detectives drew heavily on the final letters written by Lord Lucan which simply state he must 'lie doggo for a while'. The letters also produced a plausible alibi that he stumbled by chance on the murder scene while passing by his estranged wife's house.

Every year that passes serves to diminish the Crown case against the vanished earl. But if Lucan is found, the Yard are adamant that a full trial by jury will go ahead.

As the Lucan saga enters its twenty-fifth year, there have been positive moves by his family to end the sorry saga. In April 1998 Lady Lucan, fifty-nine, announced she was also taking steps to have him declared dead. Convinced that her husband had committed suicide she admitted: 'I still get frightened, especially at night, that my attacker will come back and try again to kill me. He should have killed me. But I am very strong up here [tapping her forehead] and I did not go down. The police are merely doing their duty saying they are keeping the murder file open but they know as well as the rest of us that my husband died twenty-four years ago. I would stake my life on the fact that he is now dead. That is why I call myself Dowager, because I am a widow.'

Naturally Scotland Yard, which enjoyed pursuing fruitless searches for Lucan in hot climates during winter months (Africa has been a particular favourite) refused to confirm his death. 'The matter is never closed until we have a conviction,' they said, uncompromisingly. But they would, wouldn't they?

How did he die? Added Veronica: 'It was a terrible storm on the night his car was found and I believe he jumped from a boat. I would stake my life on the fact that he is now dead. We are proceeding with the legal process to have my husband formally declared dead. An affidavit is being sworn by an executor of the will.'

In 1997, George began preparations to have his father declared dead and inherit the 200-year-old title, but then put his plan on 'hold'. He said it would be a struggle to prove his missing father was deceased, although in 1995 Lucan was sworn dead through a court-order obtained by his family, enabling trustees to deal with his financial affairs.

In April 1998 Lucky's younger daughter, Lady Camilla, twenty-seven, became engaged to fellow barrister Michael Bloch, QC. They had met eighteen months previously and Michael, forty-six, a divorced father of two, proposed during an Easter skiing holiday in Courcheval. Lady Camilla's quaintly worded betrothal announcement declares she is the daughter of 'the 7th Earl of Lucan, wheresoever.' She does not expect to see him at the ceremony, however.

Index

Index

Index

Index